"Milestones To God"

Healing Mind And Emotions

Dr. Lori M. Poe

HEALING BOOKS

The Place Of Light Publisher Cincinnati, Ohio

First edition, 1990

Milestones To God
Healing Mind and Emotions

Published by The Place Of Light

Library of Congress Catalog Card Number: 89-92799

Library of Congress Cataloging in Publication Data available.
Poe, Lori M.
1. Esoteric—Spiritual Life, 2. Self-Identity—Self-Help, I Title.

ISBN 0-9624804-0-1

Printed by BookMasters, Inc., Ashland, OH 44805

Manufactured in the United States of America.

ACKNOWLEDGEMENT

With very special thanks and sincere appreciation to the Theosophical University Press, of Pasadena, Califonia, who kindly provided the quotes pertinent from Madame Helena Petrovna Blavatsky.

DEDICATION

To all who seek God

and

To those who reached their

Destination

INTRODUCTION

Milestones to God is a compelling, impactful book. The message depicts mental healing, physical freedom and spiritual liberation. It impels the seeker to self-honesty, self-reliance and to meet the issues of life and God head-on. You will learn how to transmute fear through *Love* and how to lose the fear of death *permanently*.

This book brings into focus the strength, power and immortality of the soul and proves no other intercessor can bring you into Supreme Union with God—but His Spirit, since it is an *Act of God* that takes place within *You*.

You will find, man's first duty is to himself, that he become God-taught and self-commanded—and to uncover God within to save himself. No other saviour will do it for him and nothing less can lead him through the Gate of the Soul. The journey to the Kingdom is a personal one. It is won step by step, mile by mile, and freedom is lost the same way.

All you need is within you—here and now. There is nowhere to run to, nowhere to go, for every moment of your life you are already there. When you become "still and know that *I am God*", you will find yourself at the foot of the *True* Master, who will replace broken dreams with Supreme Happiness and will fulfill every deep longing in the soul—and appease the hunger.

It will be shown, that in the predestined cycles of evolution and involution man is his own source of sorrow and pain, which he may eliminate through Divine Understanding. You are what you think. What your thoughts create manifests the life you must live. The Law of Consequence works swift and slow, is precise, enduring and pitiless, for it is the energy man himself set forth—rebounding. No other evil can befall him.

When the human being learns to abide by the Law that governs him, obey Its Commanding Spirit and *Omniwill*, he will find God as himself, and indeed, that he is his God incarnated.

Once duality of mind is layed to rest and you come to God with clean hands and clean heart, naked, unabashed and serene, the path of good and evil will have ended, and the mind will be free of haunting shadows and healed.

Your inner and outer world is ablaze with Love and Light, but soul must open its mind and heart to let it enter. In the epicenter of each soul love assembles, and from the heart its joy deploy.

–The Author–

BOOKS BY DR. LORI M. POE

Wake Up And Walk With God
Mystic Wisdom For Richer Living
Teach Me The Way
Journeys To Worlds Beyond
Dynamic Keys To Self-Healing
Milestones To God
Healing Mind And Emotions

TABLE OF CONTENTS:

1.

The Nature of God

Imagine you were just born. You awaken to a world most beautiful. Sunshine, blue skies, a soft warm breeze is embracing your being. Where did you come from? Where are you going? What lies ahead? Right now you are unconcerned. You are happy, content, carefree, and feel protected — somehow.

Time moves on, cuddling you, watching you blossom through early youth, and slowly the door to inner worlds is closing. The realization of your responsibility to yourself and your world begins to impress itself on your conscious mind. The sweet solicitude of playful happiness and youthful attitude step aside to the curiousness, stress and pressure of young adulthood. You must try your wings. Will you succeed? Whence your help?

Since you perceive the problems of those near and dear, and others all around, you begin to consider the possibility of a Higher Power. And, in a moment of deep questioning, a Light begins to dawn. A subtle truth unrealized before wells up from deep within and incites an unknown longing. But for just now you only know: I am — a human being with an unsure destiny that spans ahead. And you do not know where or how it will end.

As shadows slowly lengthen over the path of life, you realize you need more than comforting words from others. And as you question: 'Who am I? Where, why and what is God?' — the answer casts a beam of warming Light across your heart that awakens you to deep joy, to equanimity, by a subtle assurance of an unseen, All-Abiding Presence. There are many milestones on your way to God — one by one you will conquer them all! And every step you take towards the Kingdom, you must prove to yourself before it can be real to you.

RECOGNIZING YOUR DIVINITY

But what, as some say, if there is no God? Then you yourself give proof of God by your human and superhuman powers. *Born* through the action and interaction of Sound and Light, you are the Word made flesh and crowned with divinity — a being fully conscious.

The inner man is the manifestation of God and God is the Essence of subliminal man. Your form is the vehicle of Trinity. You attest to God by your ability to think and speak, by your clear cognition of right and wrong; by the way you can love so grandly and hate as much, by your ability to use the subtle energy that moves the body into action and withdraws it into sluggishness and sleep. By your deep motivations to be honest or to deceive, by all of these and more — you prove God *is*. And whatever God *is* you are. From whence did your life and energy derive if not from a Higher Source?

God within you living and active is expressing as You. But most men do not recognize Omnipotence until they come face to face with their own limitations, for insensitivity holds no interest in God.

When the Nameless Lord is approached in trust, honesty, humility and strength — He will be met. God is an irresistible attraction you must experience to know. Anyone who truly awakened to God and encountered the Presence no longer hankers after wayward beliefs nor after the passing pleasures of life, for he knows all riches are found within himself here and now — so is God. To realize the Radiant Lord is just the beginning of the Infinite Voyage of the soul, even though it searched for Him life after life, death after death.

Now, if you were to look into a mirror and detached yourself by relaxing your vision, you would see a wondrous emanation of light surrounding your form. This divine radiance is the reflection of the Indwelling Presence that mirrors back your divinity. In this you will realize that only the best holds true for you, for the best is all you hold inside. As long as the Nature of God does not prove Itself in your everyday reality the gap is yet to be spanned.

The Radiant Power pervades all life, *is* life. You live because Its breath and Holy Energy pulsate through you, you walk because the Supernal Force that permeates every cell and atom of your body empowers the motor nerves to move and act. And since you are sustained from *within*, the more you attune yourself to Its Flow, the healthier you will be.

Your body is not a separate creation as believed. Born of the Womb of Matter it is God Substance, even as your inner bodies are of spiritual material nature, ionic compositions of enlivened, sparkling atoms through which the nourishing Life Force perpetually flows.

Now what is matter? Since all things are born *and* created of the Celestial Principle and Protoplasm, matter is therefore a vibration set into motion by various electrical frequencies, even as cognizance and spiritual power operate on dissimilar vibrational levels. If matter — fine or dense,were not a vibration and pulsation, things could neither grow nor heal, for they would have no interrelatedness nor interconnection with *Spirit*. It is then not unusual for an unfolded individual to appear and disappear before you and simply means he/she has become adept to move within the subliminal ratio of higher frequencies and vibrations. This is natural to every soul and does *not* imply nor attest to true spirituality, much less to sainthood. It's no phenomenon nor the magic feat of which some boast, especially since the acquisition of spiritual power is *not* learned, but *earned* over the course of many lifetimes. Quite clearly then, God is the quality and movement of all things that goes unnoticed except to him who felt the charging of the Force.

ALL THINGS IN GOD

All things exist in God, without God life would cease. Every *enli*vened ensoulment in all of Cosmos, no matter how minute, feels joy and pain. God is the Lifegiver of all manifestations, but to say God is One is still expressing limited understanding; for the Eternal Lord is limitless, boundless, without beginning or end.

As long as you think of the Presence as mysterious, magical, and as something outside of yourself it remains foreign to you and you will fear It, because the mind makes it fearful and hypnotic. But when you recognize the Nature of God is your very breath, life and energy, and that God *is I*, you will then utilize it consciously, subconsciously and with appreciation.

There is no genuine happiness, no deep joy, no true abiding peace, until the Sun Rays of God's Most Sovereign Light fall upon the soul and Its Holy Sound begins to chime and sing through our being and reawakens us. Concerning the Nature of God, the Invisible Master said to me:

> "The human being is such that the Nature of God manifests to him without his knowledge. A sudden, profound uplifting, an unknown impulse and fierce determination to do right take over. Then he begins to love and love truly, not knowing why this should be nor whence it came. Often the heart cries out in longing and sings with joy so great it feels one moment more and it would cease to be. Such is the Way, the Nature of God, yea, of Redemption."

The Illumined Teacher Epictetus exclaimed in his 'Golden

Sayings' LIX and LX: "God is beneficient. But the Good is also beneficient. . . where the real nature of God is, there is to be found the real nature of the good. What then is the real nature of God? — Intelligence, Knowledge, Right and Reason. Here then without more ado seek the real nature of the Good. . . Thou art thyself a fragment torn from God: thou hast a portion of Himself within thyself. How is it then that thou doest not know thy high descent — doest thou not know whence thou comest?

"When thou eatest, will thou not remember who thou art that eatest and whom thou feedest? In intercourse, in exercise, in discussion knowest thou not that it is God whom thou feedest, a God whom thou exercisest, a God whom thou bearest about with thee, O miserable! and thou perceivest it not. Thinkest thou I speak of a God with silver and gold that is without thee? Nay, thou bearest Him within thee! all unconscious of polluting Him with thoughts impure and unclean deeds. Were an image of God present, thou woudst not dare to act as thou dost, yet, when God Himself is present within thee, beholding and hearing all, thou dost not blush to think such thoughts and do such deeds. O, thou art insensible of thine own nature and liest under the wrath of God."

THE MEANING OF LOVE

Knowing God means to feel His Love and to pour It forth. Mere acquisition of knowledge does not suffice. Until you have been touched by the Living Current of Impersonal Love, the heart remains a deep, dry well. God is realized beyond feeling and emotions. The Love of God is the energy and power of life. When you feel the intensity of Divine Bliss, God is telling you how much He loves you. Then you know Supreme Happiness. And other times the Presence is so enveloping, penetrating and profound, you can't help but weep by Its Touch.

Unless you discover *Love* within yourself, you shall not find it anywhere else; and you cannot give out what you have not experienced and therefore cannot feel. Divine

Love is not begotten through another person, nor through those who claim to provide His Grace.

The Nature of God is the Essence of all things, but in paradox God is *not* all things but is manifested as *Life Force* through His Emanating Spirit. Therefore God does not live in us wholly, nor can anyone contain God in any measure greater than the divine spark within, since the body would disintegrate by the high voltage of His Power. And though God is man's innermost spirit and the Life of Creation, none can incorporate or possess It. Thus, the *Spirit* is the Emanating Principle of the Supercelestial Lord, His Will within us.

God is the divine nature of man, of every creature and living thing. As soul became embodied as man, it manifested the incarnation of God. But even if you stood in the very Presence of God, He could be no greater than your realization of Him. Now, the more you *consciously* dwell in the Radiant Light, the more real God will become to you. There is no personal God! Every tree, bush and flower emanates His Breath and whispers His Name. In every cloud, in every raindrop, in every ray of sunshine — there is God. God here, God there, God everywhere! God is *Love, Light and Life* manifested. Consciousness.

GOD IS NO MYSTERY TO THOSE WHO CAN SEE

God is a *realization.* When we let go of psychic illusions we are ready to experience *Truth.* God is the Force of the Dynamic Path, that is not only recognized in ecstasy and bliss, but more importantly in the crucibles of daily living; in the dregs and drain of pain, in sorrowfulness, sacrifice, happiness and overflowing joy. For there the Energy of God is at work to reawaken the soul.

God is the Chief Source — the *Father* of Life, Love, Power and Wisdom. The Absolute. The Mother is the negative, feminine aspect. In lower worlds she is the builder of form and its destroyer. Creation is the visible Work of God. Uncreated and manifested, the *Spirit* of God is the *Only Begotten Son,* the Divine Word — and sustaining Energy of

Life.

In man, the *seed* or Word is sanctified, for man *is* of the Spirit and of the body in which he dwells as *Soul*. Consequently, the soul is nothing that he owns, but what he *is*. Though the *seed* or energy can exist independently of the body, the body cannot exist without the Seed. Thus the scriptures admonish: "It is better for man to cast his seed into the belly of a whore than cast it on the ground." The living fluid in man holds the Essence of the Holy Word, the Cocreative Force of Creation.

The Nature of God cannot be grasped by intellect since it is beyond its borders, beyond thought and imagination. Anything based on reasoning, books, texts and belief is not true knowledge of God, since the Radiant Presence must be *entered consciously* before God can become your reality and Truth in fact. Now, there is a difference between intelligence and knowledge — or being well-learned. Intelligence is of the Spirit, knowledge is of the trained mind. While an unlearned person may pour forth the Radiance of his Maker, one who knows every scripture by heart will only radiate the shades of his mortality. The Realization of God provides knowledge and understanding *beyond* intellect and reasoning.

Once God has become your realization, you find religious edicts have nothing to do with the Life and Teachings of Jesus, Whose Instructions were Sound, Light, Karma and Rebirth. The Flame of Original Truth died out with the Ascension of Jesus. What followed were mere reflections of what He was supposed to have taught, and the teachings of men who were themselves looking for God created the formidable ambrosia of diverse beliefs that followed.

God is met within, perceived through inner perception and realized beyond the senses. Since divine sentience belongs to the nature of soul, everyone is intuitive and perceptive. When the prophets communed with God, the only way they received the answer was through spiritual sensing. God never speaks to *anyone* directly. The Holy Sound conveys to each soul what it needs to know. Its Music speaks to the heart. What the prophets conceived holds no importance. Only what *you* yourself realize within and qualify has true value. We cannot remain so involved in exoteric philosophies and the edicts of radical annihilators that we forget to listen to Inner Counsel.

When you think of God, you should envision the Brilliant Sea of Light, Love and Mercy and attune to Its Sound. Nothing can grant you more energy, stability and deep joy. His Holy Spirit moves today as it did in the days of Pentecost. Its supernal bliss and quiet assurance are available to every sincere seeker. But you must become receptive before it can enter your heart and infill the mind with grace, courage, sound reason and Presence.

It's not difficult. When you close your eyes and turn your thoughts to God, His Spirit is already there; either appearing as Light, Form, a noticeable vibration, or as a feeling of profound peace. Then, take heart. Step into the Radiance, or into the Sacred Quietude, live *It*, be *It*, and don't get off the Current until you step into the sunfilled Country of the Father. Best beloved of God, there is no other God but God, and only *One* God for all people.

GOD AND OTHER GODS

Of long ago, man believed there was a good and a bad force at work. One to bless him and the other to do him in. But mostly he needed someone to listen to his woes and troubles. Instead of looking for the cause of his grief within himself, he began to please the gods of his imagination through primitive ceremonies and living sacrifices, that not only satisfied his senses but made him feel closer to God. This was the beginning of ritualistic religion, which is on the opposite pole of the Divine Spectrum — and opposed to the true religion of the soul.

Since then, even as today, man needed a devil, and a redeemer for his wretchedness, he created them as easy as anything else in his world. Through persistent visualization he brought his wicked and benevolent gods into being. The more he endowed them with his will, his breath, and his own attributes of wrath and contempt, the more powerful they became. These are the gods of every religion! Wherever you find ceremony, ritual, statues, threadbare relics and idol worship, the energy of man made gods is attached to them.

Once manifested, these pagan gods will do man's bidding, help him out of trouble and carry out his vendettas, because they are his own inventions, born of his fantasies, will and imagination. But they will readily dissolve when he withdraws from them his energy and attention. But while in effect, these entities demand man's perpetual devotion — else they cannot exist. What he did not count on was *and is,* that the gods he created wind up running his mind and life. And when they too begin to take their vengeance out on him, he calls it the Wrath of God — but persists worshipping his idols! Everything bears its price.

However, there are also the Wise and Strong of Cosmos, the True Servants of the Lord, that aid the man who petitions them in earnest. They are Noble, Selfless Souls that aid every ascending lifewave. You will meet these Shining Ones on your journey inward. The deeper you ascend into Heavenly Kingdoms, the more majestic and effulgent will be the Beings you encounter; from Emissaries and Ruling Lords of Pure Esteem, to Divine Energies robed in Refulgent Light, that relay their commands and gentler inflections from their Silent Center. All are God *personified*, an expression of the Ultimate Source.

CHRIST AND OTHER CHRISTS

This is not a gentle subject. Truth can be unsparing, but it sets free. The world has never been without illumined teachers to show souls the way back home to God. But while one *claims* to be christ, the other *is* the Christ.

No matter how much the teacher bears out to be the stand-in for God for souls on earth, and to *be* the *Holy Spirit* in human form, believe him not. The physical condition of such a *master* does not attest to spiritual health, Truth, or heavenly perfection, nor does his lifestyle; for a True Master is wedded to *God* and has laid his passions at the Foot of the Lord.

To worship such individuals as the embodiment of the Holy Spirit and cower to them, is to be snagged on the psychic hook from which you will struggle to get free. Especially when you are bound by the *master's* fear tactics and favorite threats (I heard them all): that "You are going to lose what you got and lose the protection of the Master!" unquote. This is not the Heavenly Lord speaking to you, but the power-hunger of unredeemed man, and their surrogates finally get the *master* confused with their Lord.

Earth-bound 'liberators' who peddle their softwear and *sacred* discourses for a fuller brush, stalk their subjects like greedy predators and are no more evolved than the weak-witted who believe in them. W. H. Alden said it so well: "We are on earth to help others, what on earth others are for I don't know!"

You easily recognize the pseudo master by the way he demeans the Lord Christ, though he will *paraphrase* His Teachings to make his leadership appear authentic. Cults get away with their deceitful facade because they pick any one of the recorded names of God that becomes their 'copyright' and Logo, after which they enshroud their evil doctrines with power-play, secrecy, and *mystery* that become the honey on the flycatcher, by which they rope in curious seekers and deceive the public at large.

Many individuals who are tired of dogma, church and ecclesiastic wrangling, fall prey to them. A True Master has no need to teach from books of his predecessors or to refer to them, for his message issues out of the Spirit of Eternal Light and Wisdom. A small mind reiterates, a great mind *knows*! In reference to the materialistic enterprises of epicurean teachers, the Ancient Masters of the Far East admonished: ". . . he who lives off the offerings of his disciples is *not* a guru or master, but a beggar. . . the *Guru* is always the *Giver*."

No human elected by mortals becomes God-empowered, though he will slyly insist it was an inner process! Believe him not! Jesus Himself was not imbued with Spiritual Greatness until after His Empowerment by the Holy Spirit during His baptism.

On your way to God you will stumble upon many traps. Cults and religions evolve out of their own nature and ideas, God never made them.

Jesus was the Great Exemplar of morality, virtue and spiritual greatness. He showed man the Way to the Kingdom and to Ultimate Freedom. Christ is no man and no man is Christ. Nor is Christ the image of the Man. The non-christian, True Christ is the Emanating, Flaming Spiritual Fire of the Holy Ghost. Which you realize when you are touched by Its Enmantling Force that has *no* Name since It issues out of the Nameless.

This Holy Christ Spirit, called by many names, is the dearest Presence of unspeakable Love man can experience while on earth. It is the sweet Spirit in your fervent prayer that clearly speaks: "Lo, *I Am* with you always. . . *I Am* the Light of the world, he that followest *Me* shall not walk in darkness but shall have the light of life." Until we receive the manifestation of Its Holy Light and clearance in Its Spirit, we fall prey to every hoax, deceit and delusion.

Jesus made clear who the *True* Master is and left this Truth for all generations to come: "I leave with you a comforter, *which is the Holy Ghost*. . . who will teach you all things." He did not say I leave with you a living master. Only the weak-witted would balk at trading their monotheistic misery for the boundless freedom and happiness found in the Holy Spirit of God. Those who seek social clubs look to man. The seeker of God finds Him through the Perfect One *within*.

Without followers would be no cults. However, the seeker has the Guidance of the Grand Christ Who spoke through Jesus the man: "My sheep hear my voice (Sound), and I know them, and they follow *Me*. . . and they shall never perish, neither shall any man pluck them out of my hand. . . and *no man* is able to pluck them out of my Father's Hand. . . *I Am* the Good Shepherd (Spirit), and know my sheep and am known of mine."

And of the *other christs* he said: "But he that is an hireling and *not* the shepherd, whose own sheep are not, seeth the wolf coming and leaveth the sheep and fleeth; and the wolf catches them and scattereth the sheep." St. John 10 -

THE GREAT SACRIFICE

The qualities of Buddha, Kristna, Zoroaster and other saviours were the qualities of Jesus. The contents and meaning of their teachings were the same. The Lord Jesus did not only die for His Cause, but also to Himself.

Only because the Spirit of God gave Itself *through* Jesus did it depict the Great Sacrifice. And this same Spirit gives Itself daily through all human suffering and pain. Though all saviours endured the tortures of the ignorant and died a terrible death, no Enlightener before Jesus was as radiant and powerful. But we tend to overly deify and glorify and should rather look at what makes of man a God. Jesus was a Kabalist, endowed with every power available to a God-Man; which was not given Him freely, but that He had to *earn* to receive. In lieu of this, of the many that followed Him, only a few were initiated into the Mysteries.

Individuals whose favorite sanctimony is "pleading the blood", should know: the Blood of Christ is the Vital Essence of Cosmic Power and only because it permeated Him with great intensity, was Jesus powerful. In this sense alone was the Blood, the *Divine Power* of Christ shed for the people of *His time*. And since the Power was *in* the blood, the earth did not tremble and quake until the first drop fell and touched the ground.

Moreover, Jesus was not conceived through the Holy Ghost but the natural way through His parents, and, Mary was no virgin. His name was Joseph and He was not named *Jesus* until His initiation into Saviourship. Jesus never claimed to be Christ, which men appointed to Him long after His ascension; ignorant of the fact that Christ is the innate quality of every human being. If we freed Jesus from the ecclesiastic robes and rubbish man placed around Him, we would find the Light He came to convey, that shines brighter today than ever, and we would be touched by uncontainable *Joy*! In this Light we can face each day with new resolve, with geniune optimism and unparalleled generosity of spirit.

Moreover, Jesus did not come to earth a Perfect Master, but was well prepared for His Mission over the course of many lifetimes. Now, since the Spirit of God only takes up a body of a being made *perfect* on every physical, spiritual and causal level for Saviourship, it is the only way It will ever manifest on earth as Emancipator. So we can readily see that any self-anointed christ is no more than a deceitful human being.

The very Nature of the Divine Spirit enabled Jesus to bridge the gap between man and God, by which He brought mankind into a new awakening. In time to come there will be other saviours, but to date no human since Jesus has reached this exalted estate.

INSTANT FORGIVENESS

Ecclesiastic statements that all sins are forgiven just as long as you believe in Christ, are as absurd as their infernal rampage of eternal damnation. That Jesus died in advance for the sins we shall yet commit defies all logic; and is as sad as the case of a mother's detrimental faith, who refused her child medical treatment, because she claimed Jesus healed her child 2,000 years ago at the crucifixion. . . and the child died. This is not faith, but pure ignorance.

If such forgiveness held true, there would be no reason for living on earth; and the hell bound would transport to heaven since there would be liberty *without* justice for all. A pat on the back from the preacher: "It's alright, Jesus loves you, He forgives you, yea!" or the priests: "Go my child and sin no more!" will do nothing when the Finger of Karma knocks on your door to collect its dues.

That Christ takes the burden is another myth. The Spirit of God is an *Impersonal* Force, indifferent to what we brought upon ourselves and came down to earth to rectify.

When you take a good look around, you will readily observe the heavy loads the 'faithful' still carry, even though they claim to have been *"saved"* for years! Your burden only becomes *light* when you begin to live in the Consciousness where emotional turmoil and pain do not exist, and abide by Its Rules without regressing to lower states of mind. Burdens drop off when you dwell on that which is lovely and enduring, since then you advance beyond all heaviness of heart, for it was in the heart you felt the burden.

However we wish to believe, the Spirit of God will direct us to Rightness. The road sign points to Spiritual Truth. The left-hand path shows a road sign less illumined, where all have the choice to change their mind. God never says No. A little further down are no more turning points in sight, only a few small sparks of fleeting lights among the shadows, after which the road turns dark; where you see entities that once were man fiercely struggling, stumbling, groping in oblivion. Who thought it was the proper route to take, that instead led to re-embodiment and repeated death.

This darkness is by no means allegorical, but reminds me of the penumbral atmosphere and dark tunnel one travels through, before the awesome hell planes come into view.- Our God knows neither anger nor wrath. Burden and relief are within *You*.

THE SPIRIT WITHIN

No mortal can save you, Dearest Friend, in time he will have enough to do to save himself. Those who sell you their saints, pernicious doctrines and 'masters', are in need of awakening to God. The Principle Source of the Living Spirit is the True Father, the Lord of all men, of all nations, and Cosmos. Since you are Its very own, you may go to God *directly* without the interference of carnal man or woman. This is no myth. The moment you close your eyes and think of God you are already in touch with His Presence. By and by, you will find that the blitz and thunderbolts of Karma reel down from Above on all alike, even on the unredeemed *master*. Whether you are flawed or perfect makes no difference.

Now, you might ask: "Why Karma and Reincarnation, if indeed Christ saves? But *no*, it is through karmic pain we come to the Spirit within, else we would frolic in merry-making and forget to evolve. The Spirit within lifts us into Its Wondrous Light and Sound Current that makes whole. Its symphonic inflections are the Divine Voice and Force that pull us into the Golden Stream of Supreme Life and re-connect the seeking soul to the Master Power of the Holy Spirit.

Many times Christ has come to you but remained unrecognized, through a vision of heaven, as a Light, or a comforting nearness. The Great Mystic Angelus Silesius wrote: "Though Christ a thousand times in Bethlehem be born; and not within thyself, thy soul shall be forlorn. The cross of galgotha thou lookest to in vain, unless within thyself it be set up again." -

2.

Sound and Light — The Key to God

> "In the beginning was the Word and the Word was with God, all things were made by Him; and without Him was nothing made. . . The wind bloweth where it listeth and thou hearest the sound thereof; but canst not tell whence it cometh and whither it goeth; so is everyone that is born of the Spirit." St. John.

Since the Dawn of Time, those awakened to Sound and Light attested to Its Wondrous Reality. God is Energy. Energy is God. The Aspects of this Energy are Sound and Light, therefore the two are One and referred to as *One*. Sound is the Power and Emanation of God, the Lifegiver and Redeemer. Being the Principle Source of all life, It stands alone. In the Bible the Sound is the Word. The Greeks call it Logos. The Hindus: Shabd. To the Sikhs it is the Bani, *Nam*, or Name of God. And so, the Radiant Sound or Lord is called by different names throughout the world. Since *Nam* is nameless, every religion christened it to their own understanding that more often takes on a personal note.

In Arabic God is known as *Hu*, which means *the Nameless*. Therefore *Hu* is the *Sound*, and original Name of God. Though the Holy Sound or *Word* is everywhere, its Current cannot be contacted outside of us, since it is already within us as Life. *Hu* is the Spirit of every sound, the Life and Power of every living thing. Any name other than *Hu* are limited expressions. In the Om or Aum-expression, your lips are closed; therefore the *m* becomes the limiting factor and will carry you no further than the Mental World to which it belongs.

Hu is the unlimited flow of the Sound. It carries the soul as far and deep into Spiritual Kingdoms as it may determine, and as its progress warrants. *Hu* means God. *Man* means mind. Therefore only through mind can the *hu-man* understand God and only through and beyond the senses of soul can God become your true reality. Thusly, God can only be realized while *you*, the *Soul* dwell in form.

This alone sets man apart from lower creatures, but he is equal to them, in that he shares their grains and unbridled passions, and lower than they as he kills them and eats their meat. *Hu* is the Power Current, the nurturing Lifestream that flows down from the Heart of God through all creation. *Hu* is heard in every voice and sound. Unfolding in *Its* Brilliant Light, you become a God-conscious being, meaning: a being fully conscious on every level of Divine Life. Light is the Enlightener, Sound is the Glorious Body of God of which you were born. But though Sound and Light are within everyone, not all desire to realize *It consciously*.

GETTING ON GOD'S WAVE LENGTH

When restful, take a few cleansing breaths. Breathe from the *soul*. Now close your eyes and lift your attention to the Third Eye center, about an inch above the bridge of your nose. Relax your energy towards the brain. Then mentally or audibly, softly begin to chant the HU-u-u-u- and you will find yourself on the wondrous wave length of Sound and Light, in touch with the Presence. You will feel profound peace and relaxation and at times a great flow of vibrant energy running through you. Never use force, never overdo, but remain steadfast and God-centered. Softly chanting Hu means calling out the Name of God. The call begets the answer. I'm not a chanter and would not recommend anything else but the Sound of *Hu*. It is the Peace and the Light.

The energy of *Hu* creates a shield of unfailing protection *within* and around you. Problems sleeping? Silently humming the Name of God will move you into deep, restful sleep within seconds, for it is the Energy of your Father, the Holy Sound.

After being accustomed to contacting God and having adjusted to higher vibrations, you will hear the Sacred Sound reverberate. I've heard it come back in two syllables — *H* and *U*. The glory can mean nothing to anyone unless he has experienced It. To hear the Sound is hearing the Voice of God that will bring you into the fullness of His Holy Spirit. No other Voice is real.

The Sound is the Great Emancipator and only Saviour. Through It all things come into being. Without It nothing can exist, since it is the Primordial Energy and Power of Creation. To enter the living stream of Sound and Light should be our main objective, for it is the Key and the Way to God and Eternal Life.

The Holy Sound makes you come alive, infills you with boundless energy; enlightens and illumines you to attain Its Highest Ideal and Supreme Happiness. Soul is enhulled by mind, matter and illusion. Until the Flame of Immortal Love laps away the dross and the soul is suffused with Its Light, the individual remains restless, happy today and depressed tomorrow. For such souls, life is sheer misery and often seems a total waste. Fear of the Unknown creates panic and anxiety, Light and Sound lay fear to rest.

Well-meaning individuals who knock on other people's doors to bring them their woeful message of hellfire and salvation should knock on the door of their heart instead to receive enlightenment. Some suffer an insatiable lust to reform. But since reform takes place within, no human can reform another. While crusaders avow their deep love for God, without the experience in Sound and Light they do not know Him, nor He them. But while man struggles against the Truth that would set him free, the Sovereign Lord gently enfolds him with the Love that holds the Secret of Eternity that will reawaken him on the brightest day of his life.

Without the personal contact with God through the Sound Current or Son, you cannot get out of the spiritual darkness of lower worlds. Once you glimpse the rolling vastness and immense luminosity of the Cosmic Ocean of Love and Mercy, your life will never remain the same.

Sound and Light Energy is the Nature of God and because you were born of Its Fabric you will feel the manifesting Current to various degrees. The first experience is *total* Bliss. As you unfold deeper into the Audible Lifestream, the energy will gradually increase to which you become accustomed.

In the beginning you may feel trembly and sometimes shake violently for a few fleeting moments. But it will pass and you will not panic, since you know the Holy Spirit of the Father is replenishing and rebuilding your whole system. The results are rejuvenation on every level, wonderful calmness. Your mind will feel fresh and bright, cleared of all clutter, inharmony and cares. However, the shaking effects of the Sound must not be confused with physical conditions that may warrant medical attention. Those on the Way know the difference. To be born again — or reborn, means new life. Only when you experience the process can your new birth become real to you.

GLORIOUS SOUND

The pains, fears, joys, tensions and agonies man endures serve to sharpen, preattune and prepare him for the "Coming" of the Light, or *Lord*, and high frequencies of His Great Sound. Since the Sound is your lifeline, you should not think of it as something foreign or outside of yourself, but as the wellspring of your life that makes you whole and well-adjusted in every way. No doctrine or religious theorizing or master can do this for you, though it is what they promise. The journey to God is a personal one, each must take alone.

The Brilliant Sound is the Emanating Presence of the Lord. You may accept its shining invitation, enter It, live in It and receive Its every blessing. Once touched by the Light, when you walk out of doors and look to the ground, you will readily see Its Golden Rays encircling the shadow of your form.

The Sound is realized through inner hearing. Though it exists in all things, it is not associated with anything in your physical world. The Sound is the Holy Word, the Divine I-ness of the Force in which the personal I-ness or ego gradually disappear until there is only — God. Nescience follows beliefs and creeds. Wisdom moves the soul to follow the Presence and to become wedded to It. The Word is the Holy Ghost, Light, Sound, Dominance and Love, the Formless within form and Radiant Presence that is the True Mate of every soul and the love it yearns for and seeks, life after life.

The Heavenly Lord comes quietly and when least expected to awaken the soul out of its lethargy and sleep. Though the Sound is soundless, you can hear it drone through inner chambers. Even as the tide comes in and its waves lap against the shore and nourish the ground, so the electronic lifewaves of the Sound Current roll in and kiss the shoreless life of the soul into awakening.

Then God becomes the True Beloved, a Love Song, Love Story and Romance unspeakable. And at times when He falls silent and the Light recedes from view, He leaves a yawning emptiness and dreadful longing in the soul to draw it ever closer.

To denounce worldliness, vanity, any other vice or to pray, does not bring you into the Lifestream of Spirit, nor into the Realization of God. Only the Holy Spirit can do this. Without Its Grace, Love and Mercy, the Gate of God cannot be entered.

LET GOD COME IN

No need to worry, God will awaken you. No need to look for Him, but to believe He Is and to become receptive to His Presence will establish the connection. Soul and God reside in the same body, but so long as the veil exists in the mind, there is no communication. As during meditation the Light slowly dawns on the screen of the mind, the veil begins to dissipate and you will meet the Master Face to face.

THE COMPLETED CIRCLE

When you give yourself to God, He will give Himself to you. The Love between soul and God is an inseparable, endless bond, though when your efforts slack and you attempt to yield to worldly enticement, the Presence will not hesitate to make you feel utterly abandoned.

Attached to Love, your thoughts are continually on God. It's a natural part of the Love He instilled to your heart, that remains active, exciting and alive. You always anticipate the time set aside when you can close your eyes and ears to the noise of the world and meet with the Father.

Those who say: "I would like to meditate more, but I'm too busy!" — have yet to meet God. Now, when you love someone very much your thoughts are always with him/her and you are ever so happy to meet your beloved again. Loving God is no different, except the magnetic attraction is far greater and the Love more powerful. Concerning God, it does take something mightier and grander to pull the mind away from its wonderful loves and dreamy infatuations that keep it bound to earth.

IN THE ARMS OF LOVE

The Voice of God speaks every language, it is the mother tongue of the soul. Its Melody is the Divine Magnet that pulls you back to inner worlds and to the Father's House.

The Holy Spirit is the Light of every other light, when you reach for It you will find emotional darkness swept away. Of course, the esoterist will quickly retort that the Holy Spirit is but a lesser degree of manifested God Power, because he does not acknowledge the One Power in all existence. The more he *claims* to be God, the more he needs Him. But by and by, we will reach the perfection in which we can stand unwavering in the Presence of Divine Love without disintegrating from our insurrections.

I sought, searched, pondered the lives of saints, saw the Light, entered the Melody and high charging of Its Voltage, moved through heaven worlds and hell planes; and experienced life in worlds where Light, Peace, and Joy reigned uttermost. What else? Something was missing.

To find the answer, I threw my questions directly into the Radiant Light. Immediately a deep peace fell over me and I felt a heat unspeakable, nearly frightening, that was followed by sensations of boundless joy running through my being and the profundity of a wordless Voice that manifested a deep knowing, and revelation words cannot interpret.

I found the Holy Sound was utter stillness. A Sound in soundlessness that moved within a Sea of calm and Shining Light that blithely vibrated by Its Breath. It could only be approached in full serenity, free of want and desire, free of searching and *absolutely* free of questioning. And within this motionless state that in paradox lay in the vibrancy of constant undulation, the Light grew so bright that the inner eye could barely endure. It oscillated and swayed by a psalmody and pastorale of Music that swooned the soul with holy ecstasy and nearly feigned my senses.

And then I stood in midst of my own being — that was God, and God was I. All around great calm prevailed in the stillness of this center, that was a center within another center from which the Rhapsody of God welled up and diffused the boundless Sea of Heaven. And as the Melody danced and sang through every atom It created, it left behind Its quiet comfort, peace and strength.

At long last, I never again knew the gnawing longing and unquenchable thirst for Truth. God was no longer apart from me, but a radiant Presence alive within, here, now, and in every second of every present moment. The search had finally ended. When you still the mind and listen deep, life is just beginning.

The sound is utter Peace. It is the antidote for all that ails mankind. It heightens your inner perception and makes you immune to the evils at large. It enables you to understand yourself, your life, and to become the master of your fate. The Sound of God will reach into the depth of memory and heal the hurt no matter how deeply rooted it may be. Once soul pulls the mind through the Gate of God, it finds the Master to Whom all others must retreat.

THE BRILLIANT LIGHT

As Sound and Light pour down from the Heart of God into worlds below, it shines upon the sleeper and lifts the veil that the blind may see the Glory of the Self in God.

Individuals who believe the adoration of Divine Light is pagan, devil or sun worship will find even more Light in the words of St. John 1:5, 5:35, 12:36, and Psalms 36:9

The manifested Light is the Seal of God in your forehead. Revelation 9:4 points out: "And it was commanded them, that they should not hurt the grass of the earth, nor any green thing, nor any tree, but only those men *which have not the seal of God* in their foreheads."

Light is the consciousness of life and shines forth from the center of all things. Light is the Enlightener. Until it manifests itself to you, can be no true understanding.

The manifestation of Light became the First Adam, the first manifested positive energy and *Law* in lower worlds. Thus the Unmanifested Principle of God manifested is the quenchless Light and Presence of All Good. Ever flaming, creating, withdrawing, remanifesting Itself and vibrantly alive, it is the masculine energy of *Adam* that in double aspect holds within itself the feminine principle of *Eve,* which opposes the fairy tale of Adam and Eve.

When the Radiant Light of the Father covered the earth and removed the darkness "from the face of the deep", Its Force manifested matter through Spirit and all that came thereafter. The Ancient Egyptians taught: "The principle of Light is *not* the Light itself. Its masculine part is the creative

Force, the feminine part is the nurturing Light and Wisdom, and from the two that are Intelligence, Power and Freedom, emanates the Holy Ghost." -Ibid.-

PROTECTION OF THE LIGHT

The Clear White Light is more powerful than all the atmospheric forces you encounter. Divine Light is Force, Power, Dominance and Action, which you are using to lesser degrees in every conscious and unconscious way. The Light is nothing imaginary. Traced back to Its Central Source you find it is Pure, Brilliant Energy, that bursts forth from Its Boundless Core into all creation, where It dissipates Itself, correlates again, and returns to Its Center —a Blinding Presence. Since you are constantly suffused and surrounded by Its Radiance and Protection, It requires you to consciously attune yourself to It and to live by Its Rules.

Though Light ensouls all things, some individuals are soulless personifications of evil, but as good is good and evil — evil, malignant energy can only affect you when you are off guard.

When confronted, evil individuals become overly protective of themselves to hide their corrosions. Labeling the children of Light demons and devils, they wonder why God does not heal them and Divine Light remains out of reach. Suffering from deep-seated paranoic disturbances, these become their conscious and subconscious forms of projections, of compulsions, abnormalities and anilities they infuse to others.

Since the Master Light perpetually protects you, the consequences to the evil-minded can be disastrous. The Force refracts the energy to the sender with a thrust that would boggle your mind. And it will do so whether you are aware of evil being projected to you or not. Distance does not matter, since in Spirit is no distance. Such is the Grace of God to every True Soul. Save it be your own returning, no other harm can come to you, for nothing can penetrate the Protective Shield around you.

Lesser lifewaves that know nothing of God or belief are

protected by the same Light, which you can see surrounding the outer edge of their auras, as a fine, razor sharp brilliance. Some of their little countenances shine brighter than that of human beings.

THE GUIDING LIGHT

Since the Light belongs to every one of us, we should learn to use it. When conscious of Its Force, you begin to utilize It with your higher senses. Light is the energy within you. Thus you are not employing a strange force outside of yourself, but your innate ability and spiritual power. You are the manifestation of the Great Light, the Resplendent Word made flesh and the Power of God in action. When *you* act, *God* acts. In example:

> "The Power of light is within me. Its protection and healing pour forth freely and boundless into every avenue I direct it. And so let it be."

When you act indiscriminately, you are expressing the negative aspect of the same power and reap the consequences. Pronounce a name or power word, and you set energy into motion. This also pertains to answered prayer, which is not something God granted but the result of soul-energy moved into proper action. Congregated, it becomes a force for good or evil. There is more black magic going on in ritualistic religion and in the minds of the *pious*, than realized.

ACCEPTING DIVINE LIGHT

The Light within you is the *Reflection* of God. To see the Light and merge into the flow is a minute realization of the God-Self. Its magnitude is incomprehensible and it is well we do not always think of it in this way, since apprehension would block the way.

Become quiet, sit still awhile. Envision the Radiant Light surrounding you. See it gently descending, rising up from deep within. Do not will It, acknowledge It and allow it to be.

Begin to breathe from the soul. Allow the Light to infill your body and spiritual centers. Feel Its warmth surging through you, and expand into a twelve foot radius around you, below as above. Envision — and it is already established. Then bring your attention back from the center of peace, to waking awareness, and go about your daily activities.

At another time envision a trillion sparkling, dancing atoms of light surrounding you. See them correlate into a soft cloud or veil before you. Mentally step into the Light. . . energy follows thought. . . now it is real. . . see? What do you feel? The word joy, exhilaration or Love do not quite cover it. God hears within. All good comes to you from the Light.

Now, to say: "Lord, surround me with Light!" will do no more than stir up a little psychic energy. You must accept the Light manifesting here and now. Your breath and the power of your will set energy into swirling motion. Light-energy provides the balance between good and evil and will guide you safely along the road of life.

People who tell you, you don't need the protection of Light because the very thought of protection will remind you of danger, are world-wise, ignorant of God and will lead you into pitfalls of every sort.

YOUR THIRD EYE

The Moslems and Orientals call the Third Eye the Tisra Til or Tenth Door. During contemplation the energy of the body draws up to the Third Eye, where the Light becomes visible and reveals the Radiant Form of the Invisible Master Who guides you into the experience of God. It is here that you gain Self-Awareness, and the beginning of your release from lower worlds.

Meditation leads to contemplation. At the point when the soul becomes oblivious to its external world, the Light pulls it into Itself. As you enter Inner Worlds, you hear their Sounds and see more clearly, for the senses of the soul are keener and perceive more distinctly than the physical senses.

Your spiritual bodies have a brain, eyes, nose and mouth as your physical form, otherwise you could not sense and experience on Higher Levels, and you would not be the *Soul*. When during contemplation you reach the Third Eye of the third brain (and there are more), you have arrived at the Tenth Door — I call the Gate of God. While it is the Tenth Door, the other nine are the body apertures.

Now, where you can see a picture or a vision clearly from the first and second spiritual eye, you may see nothing at all from the Third Eye level, but in paradox perceive it more distinctly and clear-cut. For the Third Eye is for stepping *through* and joining the scenery. In any case, you never sense or think that you see — *but you see*, and in the next moment you become part of the activity of the Sunny Country you entered. Saint Anthony described:

> "I entered into my inward self, Thou being my guide. And able I was, for thou wert my helper. And I entered and beheld with the eye of my soul, such as it was, above the same eye of my soul above my mind, the light unchangeable. Not with ordinary light which all flesh may look upon. . . Not such was the light, but other, yea. . . He that knows Truth knows what that light is, and he that knows it, knows Eternity."

From Marina de Escobar:

> "When in deep ecstasy, God unites the soul suddenly to his essence, and when he fills her with his light, he shows her in a moment the sublimest mysteries. And the soul sees a certain immensity and an infinite majesty — the soul is then plunged, as it were, into a vast ocean which is God and again God. It can neither find a foothold, nor touch the bottom. The divine attributes appear as summed up in one whole, so that no

one of them can be distinguished separately."

FIND YOURSELF, REVEL IN THE SEARCH

It is not enough to dream, to think and read about spiritual being. We should make it our reality. Spiritual freedom need not be sought, it is already within you and belongs to those who do, dare and live it. With every advancing step your longing for God will intensify and the bond grow stronger. Inner stillness brings mind and soul under the control of Spirit, and lifts you across the borderlands of illusion into the Life of God.

Some individuals cannot bear solitude. To them the music must rock, roll, blast, and everything else must remain in constant motion. Running here and there, what are we running to or from?

One intensity follows another. It is not that there is no time for God, we lack the interest to take it. How can sound directions be found when we do not pause and listen within?

We say: where love is there is home. But the Love of God is different, it does not turn on and off as do human emotions, though Its Volume can intensify considerably to unclog our ears!

On the other hand, people will say: "I and the Father are one!" which are meaningless words until conscious union with God occurs. Only then can it be said that you and the Father have *united*. Only then will you know what it means to have an innate capacity to love. Moreover, no soul can contain the immensity of its Supreme Parent, it rather becomes reassimilated into His Light.

Infinite Oneness means unconditional surrender to Unconditional Love. This then depicts the finishing point of lesser inquiries, of uncertainty, doubt and blind faith, and is the beginning of true enlightenment and the ingress to eternal life for the individual soul.

In his interpretation of the Dead Sea Scrolls, Dr. Edmond Bordeaux Szekely quotes Jesus:

> "He who expounds to you the scriptures speaks to you in a dead tongue of dead men, through his diseased and mortal body. Him, therefore, can all men understand, for all men are diseased and all are in death. No one sees the light of life."
>
> — *The Essene Gospel of Peace*, Page 24 —

The remedy for human troubles is Spiritual Light. When the Light has not been realized, it is because the attention of the mind is fastened to the material world.

Even as the Light grew ever brighter as the three Wise Men approached their destination, so the star of this very Light will turn to intense brilliance as you approach the Presence of your Lord. It will guide you safely through life's many nights into the Radiance of Eternal Morning.

The wilderness of drifting and searching ends at the illumined Portal of the Soul. Each day make time to contemplate the Presence, and whatever image you cast on the reflecting ethers, may it be God. Then, when the fine rays of the Light form into a brilliant Star, and you allow your spirit to flow with the vision, you will be in God.

RADIANT EMANATION OF LIGHT

While some persons are initiated during contemplation and out-of-body consciousness, a fearful soul will receive the Light while in dreamstate; while another may experience it outwardly, but at the same time receive it within, since the Light always appears on inner planes. The *way* it manifests depends on the inward preparation, receptivity and temperament of each soul.

The Great Awakener comes to everyone, mostly when least expected. It was on a winter evening in December. The person who came to be healed had just left. A subliminal scent of jasmine and rose was slowly fading away. The hour was late when I laid down my pen, but decided to go to the other room to jot down a few more thoughts. A day well spent, God's Peace seemed well in order, when a visiting friend called out: "Hurry, come quickly, see the light!"

I ran back to the living room where he stood ashen-faced, shivering from head to toe. I looked but saw nothing, only a fading mist that might have been anything. My friend turned to me with quivering jaws, as trying to fan his last spark of strength, and muttered: "A bright light, big and round shone through the window and threw a wide beam across your desk. In a matter of half a second it moved to the right, then to the left and illumined the door, even the big tree next to it. The tree was bathed in light, I could see every inch of it, even its smallest twigs, its branches were brighter than daylight."

When I looked outside, all was so very still, seemed like the stars went out it was so dark. There were no cars going down the residential lane, no radar turning signals, only the dimly lit street light at the corner casting its soft beam across the snow-covered ground and into the night. Somehow I knew his experience was real.

My friend didn't look as though it was the end of the world, but almost as he could see it happening from where he stood — trembling like an aspen. I felt the Light appeared to remind him of the Greater Life, that every heart should seek if it would ever be truly happy and content.

LIGHT AND DARKNESS

Light is the Brightness of Spiritual Fire, a Light without form that shapes the formless into matter. It is the Intelligence that illumines thought, without it thoughts would be uncreative, fleeting shadows; and through It man receives his vitality, talent and genius. But what of darkness?

Darkness cannot exist without light, both are of one energy. Thusly we measure darkness and light according to our understanding, and as we perceive them by degrees. Now, daylight is darkness to the bat and other creatures of the night, even as some people think of bad happenings as being beneficial, while another may find them a curse. In a similar way material man thinks of God as his punisher and tyrant, while another may perceive Him as Love and Benevolent Light. Without light can be no darkness, no darkness without light and no good without evil. In his present evolutionary state man is conditioned to both. So long as he does not seek the Light he continues to follow his shadow. We are all blind in some way, some to daylight, some to dark, some to God.

MYTH OF SALVATION

The myth of salvation has created a combat zone of diverse opinions. It is not up to man to reform his fellows into his chosen dogma, nor to bring him to God. It's astonishing to hear the fallen preacher stake his claim on having saved uncountable numbers of souls. Never in history has salvation been gained by force or subjugation. Since redemption is distinctly an Act of God, vicarious atonement and instant salvation are ideas of the fearful, who will be fearful past their bitter end. Equally ludicrous is the belief that the *'saved'* will vacate the planet and rise into glory, while the rest will suffer in corruption. One could surmise it would be in what they, the 'saved' would leave behind.

Opinion makers insist that once you *accept* Christ, all is *saved* and forgiven. And given that this were so, why do the *born again* struggle so fiercely to get out of their emotional and physical hell? Because they feel the reverberating energy of their pastlife actions. Now, when we learn the Laws of God we begin to understand our suffering. The Law of Retribution is prescribed to everyone, what man believes or disbelieves does not change it.

IT IS UP TO YOU

Only God can bring to life the extraordinary qualities of soul. This depends on: salvation through the Sound-Current or *Word,* surrender of the lesser self to the Force and *conscious* attunement to the Holy Spirit. One is contingent upon the other. Man must save himself. The Law of Cause and Effect (sowing and reaping) makes it possible.

Whether saint, saviour or average man, all die to themselves. The Lord Jesus did not die for anyone. As the saviours before Him he was murdered by fanatics, who, if given another chance would crucify Him today just the same. The story of Calvary has been quite distorted.

The Divine Spirit or *Sound* is the Saviour, that gave Itself *through* Jesus the God-Man. Jesus was not Christ, he bore Him within. When at physical death It withdrew Itself from His body, Its Light beamed forth in Celestial Glory that flooded and diffused the whole planet with the blinding intensity of Its Brilliant Emanations. Thus the planet was cleansed from the dominating, sinister Spirit under which man regressed into degeneration. But the world was not saved. It is worse than ever. When we look at planetary conditions today, will it take another Supreme Sacrifice to save man from self-annihilation? Or is it too late?

The Supreme Act of God balanced the Forces and redeemed the helpless from adverse conditions, which are no different today. It purified the lifewave *of that day* of all contamination. A new dispensation began. The christian dogma became gradually established and adopted Jesus as their risen saviour. But for all the pagan worship of idols, imaginary and concrete, they failed to perceive the True Saviour. There was never a time when the world was without the Saving Christ.

The birth and death of every saviour was paramount. None of them ever came to reform the world, but to take souls back home to God. The transfiguration saviours demonstrated will in time be accomplished by all. The advancing soul absorbs more and more Light, until its ultimate reabsorption into the Radiance of God. Then the soul shall again resemble its Divine Parent, the Formless. In the measureless realm of time, how momentous and endless are the vital issues of the soul!

The true meaning of salvation is Spiritual Liberation, not a religion or doctrine, but the way of the immortal soul and the Way back to God. And it will come to pass that a decision beyond mortal understanding will be made by everyone. When God shall ask each individual soul for its last surrender. Then it will be free.

Spiritual Liberation is the emancipation from repeated re-embodiments into lower worlds, to regain your divinity. To experience God has nothing to do with faith, hope or religious convictions. It manifests by Grace and merit. Only then will the heat of life lose its sting. Salvation is the New Dawn of the immortal soul, but you must ask for transformation to be transformed. Then, with each advancing step you give up a little more of your old ways.

No power can break your innate bond with God. Love is the cause! Once you enter the Portal of Liberation, it shall close behind you. To turn back would mean great suffering. For the heart would find no resting place in your old world, and the gap you created to Worlds of Love difficult to span.

The affection of faithful souls is such, that every thought and deed is interlaced with spiritual honesty, loftiness and quiet happiness; heavenly radiance shines from their faces. Such souls were not transformed by ritual, church or sermon, but by the Radiant Lord within. *Acceptance* does not bring salvation. And salvation holds no promise of the outcome, which is left to your discretion, since progression, retrogression and fate are in *your* hands. Otherwise why would the preacher lament over the *backslider*?

THE CONTINUUM OF SALVATION

Your way to redemption has been a gradual one, for it takes place on every level of consciousness. Atom by atom, molecule by molecule, cell by cell, the *inner* man evolves into Godhood and into the Kingdom of his Heritage. The cycles of re-embodiment make it possible.

Each time you master a new plateau and *maintain* that sanction, the lesser, purified light is absorbed into the Supreme Light of God. It is therefore the lesser, unfinished self that seeks re-embodiment and tenders to evolve and reunite with the Empyreal Self.

In lieu of this, we move from sphere to Sphere, from world to World, until we regain divinity. Then and only then can it be said: we are saved! It is Grace and Mercy that enables us *to save ourselves*. Clearly, salvation is a continuing process which does not end until the Journey of the Soul culminates in its Supercelestial Source — to go out no more.

You are endowed with cognitive power, with sentience, foresight and reason, to spare you from needless harm. God loves you to the core. Without daily introspection soul finds no comfort in its world, nor peace. The fact remains: you can't thumb your way to the Kingdom, you must get there by yourself.

WHEN TIME IS RIPE

To come to God we must go through the cleansing Fire of the Holy Spirit. If there were any other way, we would be sure to take it. When persons infilled with religious sadness come to *It*, they grow satisfied, content and joyful. Your inner longing is moved into action by God. To surrender is an act of free will, rendered in love and trust.

However, the God-directed life brings you to realize that not all you dreamt of equals your expectations. Birth means new life, and *change*! Your reactions to changing conditions will be to the degree of your yielding. You may either be mortified when without notice all you loved and cherished literally disappear from your life, and loved ones and friends walk into other directions; or you may just accept it without second thought. Really, as with anything else, it's just the way you look at it!

As far as God is concerned, what your worldly affairs, wears, lack or plenty consist of neither matter nor count worthwhile, but what you *are*, think and do! Spirit has no interest in the pleasures nor wants of the body, but in the progression of *Soul*. You also realize God can be completely relied on, but not *leaned* on, as salvation means self-mastery and self-reliance in every way. And since it means Self-Reform, *it forbids your reforming of others*.

And soon, Dear Friend, the whole world will seem to you as one great, enormous Temple where the Living God dwells. Everywhere you go you recognize Love manifest and clearly perceive the Holy Presence that now walks beside you. The more you allow yourself to unfold, the clearer the mystery of your existence will unveil.

We should get into the flow of Vibrant Life and stay there. God is *One*, not many. When others ask you to follow their god, ask them if there is a different God in their belief. Perhaps so. Believe in God with your whole heart, and in nothing you cannot prove to yourself. There is no blind devotion in knowing God.

WITHOUT PRESSURE OR FORCE

Redemption occurs when the soul is ready. God is always mindful of your needs. Once He draws you into His Brilliant Light, He will stand squarely behind you with every support and protection.

At first the Love you feel, or rather your interpretation of it, invokes deep emotions, but as you mature in God it becomes a very calm, serene, almost reserved feeling of belonging. Though fervency belongs to the astral plane of emotions, until we become fully unfolded we must feel to understand. Soul is sentient always.

Now, the problem is, when some individuals experience the wondrous Touch of God's Love, they become power-hungry and greedy. The gluttony for cash and false sense of omnipotence to rule others opens them to a diverse flow of electrons they are sorely unprepared to handle. This energy has a razor sharp effect on the fanatic's nervous system. He often suffers from shakiness, hallucinations, depression, sleeplessness, paranoia, loss of appetite, change in body temperature, hysteria and worse.

It is of utmost importance that he/she who received the Light should remain ever so humble, forebearing, loving, tolerant and kind. That he/she takes the Grace received seriously, and, overcome with Love as he/she will be, reciprocates in kind through service, dedication and compassion; which permits the energy to flow freely through him. Congested energy can make the body very ill. Nothing can be forced or hoarded. Nothing at all.

No harm can come to you when you remain receptive to

the Spirit of God and allow It to manifest and work through you on Its Own Terms. Then It will enmantle you with Gentleness, grant you Its Strength and guide you in every way.

In comparison, think of electricity, the coarser manifestation of spiritual power. When you stick your finger into a live socket, chances are it will kill you. For even though endowed with subtle intelligence it is a blind force. But if you use it correctly and with respect, it will sustain you, make you feel well, homy, warm and secure. So it is with the Power of God.

BOUNDLESS PRAYER

The prayer of the True Soul is endless *Love.* To pray without ceasing does not mean to pray with words, but to *dwell in the Word,* the Radiant Lord. Ritualistic prayer as perpetual demands bring no result and do no more than appease the bedlam of emotions.

God hears in silence. For prayer energy to reach the Source it must be *un*conditional and a clear-cut, direct statement; free of forming thoughts (or desires). True Prayer issues out from the heart of the soul. It is directed *inward,* never to an outer deity, saint, statue or symbol and may *not* express the desire to change anyone's life.

Boundless prayer is free of beggary. It fully trusts. As your prayerful affections reach the Radiant Life, sadness gives way to joy, and to a special closeness, a sense of genuine belonging to God, that will linger in your life. In this *wordless* prayer, there is only Presence. Your whole being becomes so absorbed with *It,* you begin to live, think and breathe God *consciously* and your life bears Its Fruit in witness. This is the Joy of Prayer.

To pray without being inwardly attuned to His Presence, is wasting time to no purpose. Genuine prayer does not stare into blank space, but is attentive. God should not be sought for earthly things, since He provides them through you. To love God because He *is God,* — and for no other reason — moves prayer power into action. Desiring His Presence above all things manifests the Ultimate

Blessing of Prayer.

ETHICS OF PRAYER

To pray for people without their permission is interfering in their life and accumulates new Karma. To send energy to others when you just happen to think of them breaks divine Law. Most do-gooders obsessed with meddling in other people's affairs are unable to say *no* to their hang-ups. Soul is born free, *is* free. People have the right to live as they choose and many do *not want* to conform to *your* belief or lifestyle. Often one left to himself will emerge stronger and more courageous than those who attempt to pray him back to health or wealth.

If infernal meddlers recorded their prayers, they would find how much pleading, bargaining and domineering they contain. Such individuals would trade their very soul, yea, themselves, to gain desires and revenge. In any event, who would want the prayer of those who beg for themselves?

I never had need for man's blessings and I'm repulsed by those who pray for/and to me! — and refract their energy! What can they do for me who hang on the wailing wall of beggary and deceit? They have great need for spiritual inwardness and have yet to recognize their True Source of help.

I've received letters from petitioning christians who lament "Dr. Lori, Jesus loves you!" — whose lives are full of woes and dissension; because the Jesus they declare loves *me*, does nothing at all for them, else they wouldn't petition and solicit my help.

The great Mystic, William Blake, who lived from 1757 to 1887, well summed it up when he wrote:

> "The vision of Christ that thou doest see — is my vision's greatest enemy. . . Thine is the friend of all mankind, mine speaks in parables to the blind. Thine loves the same world that mine hates, thy heaven doors are my Hell Gates. . . both read the Bible day and night, but thou read'st black where

I read white. . . Seeing the false Christ in fury and passion — I made my voice heard all over the nation."

Constructive prayer receives the answer. It saddens me when persons ask me to pray for them more than once for the same. God hears the first time. If not, the burden remains. Constant petitioning attests to lack of trust in God. Emphasis should be on *trust*, not on futile reiterations.

Life is for learning and not for someone else to work out the problem and predict what's going to happen next. Learning comes through experiencing and *doing*, and by attuning to Inner Worlds. The disciplines Spirit imposes only become painful when we rattle and strain against Its barriers. Therefore we should pray: *Lord of Light, Infill Me With Your Presence* — "If the only prayer you ever say is Thank You, that would suffice." Meister Eckhart-

Instead of praying: "Please help me!" — it is better to entreat: *"Thank You Father For Seeing Me Through!" "Thank You Father, I Am Now Strong and Joyful!* — removes all doubt. When solutions do not readily appear, we should consider what good we set forth to warrant the answer. There are no *free* blessings here or Beyond. Every blessing is well earned.

The prayer of the heart needs no intercession, since it is an *intimate* conversation between soul and God. It bears a feeling of genuine appreciation — of love projected to the Giver, that in response invokes the warmth of Divine Love.

Never planned, radiant prayer is spontaneous: "O, Father, Thank You!" — totally overjoyed, you see. Now, you can only pray *effectively* when you are happy and content. No need to pray when you are sad, sick, or downhearted, for then you have nothing to be thankful for. And since God will not remove what you came down to earth to meet and conquer, you may again be thankful after the misery has passed. Content prayer manifests the energy of healing. Like attracts like on every plane.

THE QUINTESSENCE OF PRAYER

God is the energy and answer of your prayer. When the Will of God becomes *your* will and you first and foremost pray for the needs of all other creatures to be filled — and name them as you can; when you cease badgering the Father for trifles, cease haranguing Him with complaints and stop telling Him how to run the lives of other people — and His Universe — your prayer will find *prompt* acceptance and realize results.

Answered prayer is the return and result of positive energy you set into motion and commanded to achieve. Every thought and act, good or evil, is a prayer that molds your condition. When your prayer is loving and happy, the uprising energy grows into the powerful stream of the *one* prayer that is *always* heard. For it moves the atoms and molecules of visible *and* invisible matter into substance, and manifests the health, vitality, happiness and abundance you seek.

God is the living Word *in you*. Its Law is *Oneness*. Realizing this Oneness you manifest substance and have no further need to entreat God with anxious words that magnify your grief. Because all you negatively decree must manifest to you again — by the same law.

LIMITATIONS OF PRAYER AND PENANCE

Though nothing else may be ever more desired, prayer, remorse and penitence do not weave the seamless robe of redemption. It is better to desire peace and light, for then Love will spur you on, trust will sustain you. Without Love and trust the soul wends its way from life to life, searching, and keeps putting things into its pockets instead of in its heart.

The internal process of spiritual emancipation is awe inspiring to the mind, but natural to the soul since it has never been without God at any time and constantly realizes Him on deeper levels. Therefore the *mind* must reawaken to Spirit, but not everyone has the humility and patience to wait upon the Lord. The heart must come to God in love and abiding trust, it has nothing else to give. There are no sins to offer up, man does not sin in the Eyes of God! Sin is not of the soul, but a performance of man's mind and will. A necessary function. Would he reach for God otherwise than through the suffering his errors allow him? When God permits us to understand — we will.

TAKE HEART, TAKE THE PLUNGE

We travel far; are baptized and rebaptized in holy rivers, cry at Gethsemane — and denounce the world. But it has not cleansed the mind from its evils nor brought the individual one step closer to God. Unsparing tongues wag just the same and perpetuate gossip as ever before. Pleasures are pursued with the same vengeance, meanness of thought and spirit prevail. But to immerse yourself in the Sound Current takes courage. For here you take no thought whether you will live or die, because more than anything you desire God.

Man fears this weightless, disembodied state, because he loves the world, fears death and does not know God. But the Current of Sound and Light will set him free. No other Power can take him out of the clutches of the Negative Force and carry him across the boundaries of lower worlds. By and by, this Great Challenge will confront every soul. And yielding, it will know it touched the Face of God and entered His Kingdom in full awareness. To enter Divine Worlds while in human form, is the way to lasting peace, superior happiness and deep satisfaction. Mind by itself cannot realize you may be born into Eternal Life while still on earth. But a mind free of carnal want will aspire after nothing else but *being*. So many milestones to God —and you will conquer them all!

SIT STILL AWHILE

Let your world be at peace. To survive within is all you need. When you close your eyes, envision a sparkling mass of shining light surrounding you and close the circuit. Then contemplate Divine Light. Seen or unseen, it is always there. Listen deep to hear Its Sound — be patient with yourself. Desire to know only God. Allow the Presence to enter the stillness of your heart, until you are fully filled with God. And then be not afraid to soar, for His Holy Breath will carry you into His Boundless Silence, where all is Joy and Love and prayers are answered. His Hand will shield you uttermost, now and forever more. -

Ah, yes, His Spirit will weigh you down with a Love so irresistible and intense your longing for *It* shall be greater than your joy. It will gently pry you loose from all the nothings that mean so much to you now, you regard reality. But caught up into the boundless flood of Love It will move you into Its Own Great Light; then you will be *truly* alive, rich beyond measure, happy and content. Then you will know God.

God did not create man because He was *lonely*, as the saga goes, nor does He desire anyone's adoration and prayer, as would lesser gods. Only man without God is lonely, so he thinks God must be lonely too! Knowing God provides the realization of constant Presence, you will never want for more ideal Company. The beloved of God never feels alone, for the power of prayer enables him to bridge the gap.

Rather than praying in sadness, look to goodness, trust with joy! Let the past recede, your wonderful memories and the sad, allow the future to move out of sight. Then you have only the present moment — and God.

3.

Exploring the Nature of Mind

So many traumas beset the human being during a lifetime. We grow wise too slow and old too fast. All misery and ailments that affect the nature-bound body begin in the mind, which can be restored to health and balance. But to understand the healing process, it is necessary to examine the nature of mind and search out its primal origin.

The universe of mind and matter is ruled by Divine Mind, which is the Governing Lord of lower worlds to which mind belongs. Under this influence, all things live, die, act and react, and the effects of their actions, negative *and* positive become the principle cause of Rebirth.

Soul is as much a prisoner of its lower part, the mind, as mind is slave to its senses. But when soul comes under the control of Spirit it is then no longer the slave but the master. Mind dwells in the body, soul dwells in the Higher Mind, but the awakened, God-realized soul exists on every plane, in every universe and world while still in physical embodiment. As long as lower energies tie mind and soul together, both remain bound to earth.

Divine Mind controls all life through mind action. Its creative energy flows through every world, through all creation and through the mind of man; lowering and adjusting its frequencies as It vibrates downward. In coarse manifestation, energy becomes electricity and accelerated — the highest of all powers. That God is *Energy* is well realized by those who felt *It* surge through their bodies and awakened to Its Power.

Whatever you think and do, good or otherwise, is the manifested energy of the One, Universal Mind, which by necessity is dualistic. Without Supreme Intelligence expressing through Divine Mind would be no thought, for thought is the manifested Vibration of God and only Spirit can think.

CONTROL YOUR ENERGY AND BECOME FREE

To say you are free and *being* free are not the same. To control your inner forces and keep them in check is the key to well-being, inner growth and spiritual freedom. To control your inner worlds and the forces you encounter every day, it is necessary to bring the mind into submission to Spirit that will teach you how to harness them. Not a simple feat, since the negative power will spare nothing to deceive the soul to keep it bound, that it would learn to evolve. How does it work? Through your own thoughts and — people!

MIND CONTROL

Looking at solutions does not pamper the ego, nor provide what we want to hear. But how otherwise can the mind be healed than through self-honesty?

Mind control means *self*-control, the control of your psychic energy. Once you realize the benefits peace of mind brings, it is easy to say *no* to unwholesome impulses and to the energy of vulgar individuals. As lesser energies come under *your* authority, the mind will shut off inharmonious vibrations at the onset, from within and without. Then, as you develop a strong sense of *Self*, you can stand in the middle of the havoc and remain unaffected.

To be removed from emotionalism is the key to mental health, self-mastery — and to cosmic power. Self-control forbids the controlling of others, physically and psychically. You will find, individuals who wield the emotional axe have no control over their own energy. Even their walls exude domineering emanations. People with self-respect have no need to demand it from others, nor will they impose their unwanted concerns on them. You are *Energy*. What you project is what you are. Personalities of low esteem are often overly apologetic and trip over themselves always censoring what they say or do, but at the same time looking for praise. Such characters love to manipulate other people — and *You*. While quick to befriend, resent and betray, they are very lonely and unhappy beneath the surface. Self-honesty and inner control restore the mind. To live from the soul is the remedy for mental illness.

THE LIGHT OF MIND

To be able to sense, see and live from the soul are results of unfoldment and soul action. Only in the Light of mind can conditions be seen for what they are and truth be known. For what good is Truth to one who does not understand it? In the Light of mind the lower mind cannot judge, anatomize, ridicule and reject what it refuses to learn. When man's attention has been brought into focus with Spiritual Light and at moments he becomes the Light Itself, he will know true power. After sick thought and violence are uprooted from the mind, mental and physical regeneration take place.

In the Light of Spirit lower inflections lose their hold. Then the luminous emanations of the heart pour out to all life, for it now carries the Light that illumines dark places, heals up wounds and comforts the weeping.

THE LOWER MIND

When trained rightly, the mind is a magnificent tool. Now, the average mind loves indoctrination, repetitious thinking and following the mapped out path, since it does not have to think for itself. For example, wherever people congregate, let someone say: "This way!" — and all make a mindless turn about and follow.

Now, if you look at a situation from the mind it appears one way. From the higher viewpoint of soul it is another. Because the soul lives by the Reality Principle, sees things realistically and not as they appear. The lower mind does not see it this way, mainly since it misconceives and blocks out what it does not wish to accept. While manipulating others, it manipulates itself. Whereas the soul is unconcerned with tangible manifestations and personal feelings, the lower mind frets: I possess — or I might lose, — or I am loved — perhaps loved no longer! Mind declares: 'this is mine, and what's left thine!' Whereas the soul says: 'Take all and be happy!'

The train of negative thought rolls along its systematic track of happy feelings, fear, hope, hopelessness, and from joy to condensed depression and despair. Bitterness and insatiable want are soul's worst enemies!

The lower mind is deceptive and never satisfied. Whatever it has, it wants more. It will grease the palm and use its charm or the death rattle to get it. Mostly, people tell the truth when it is convenient. The dualistic mind will evade, smooth over, avoid, lie, and do anything to protect its interest, business and sagging reputation. Paid talkers well trained in manipulating facts tow the line of guile, else they must reconsider their position. But in the end get stung, as does the scorpion by its own tail. Behind what or whom will man hide when he stands naked before God? Unless the milestone of double-dealing and perfidy is eliminated, Divine Truth will strip the debaucher of his profanities and reduce him to size. People think God is an illusion. No, Dear Friend, God is *Real* and met soon enough. No deceiver can endure the Light — nor withstand It!

You cannot realize the High Self unless you can come to face with personal shortcomings. Some find self-acknowledgement utterly distasteful. Unable to get past their personality and lower ego, they fall short on realizing God; and will lace into anyone who even slightly suggests they should take a better look at themselves. The dual-minded readily turns vicious and defensive.

While untruthful persons abuse their vocal cords and end up suffering from diseases of the mouth, eyes, ears and throat; other oppressors suffer from respiratory ailments that affect the whole body. No one can squelch the life out of another without Life retrieving it back out of him. Mind and soul belong together. Since man's thought energy stands written on the soul record, he cannot deny his actions after final repose and remains caught up in his duplicity even there.

The deceitful mind cannot be changed by intimidations, psychotherapy or reprogramming, but by Spirit alone. When the body finally weakens through negative mind actions and the individual loses his strength all at once, Spirit calls for introspection and accurate self-honesty. Since man is what he thinks, who is to blame for his troubles? Mind is not the problem, you see, but man's willfulness that moves energy into negative actions and trouble producing results.

But no matter how pure the mind may become, it cannot enter eternal heights, no more than purifying the body can infill it with the Immortal Essence. Only God can do that. The constructive power of the mind heightens with *Truthfulness* and *Love*. Clean, honest living and God-oriented thought are as necessary to the mind as cleanliness is to the physical form.

LOOKING AT FACTS

Thrill seeking individuals never look within. Their eyes are pinned on the fateful glitter of the material world, while their hands already grip the spokes of the Wheel of Sorrow and Reincarnation.

The more a person worries, the clearer the picture images of unpleasantries and grief impose on the screen of his mind. And since soul is the embodiment of creativity, it creates its own conditions. When the mind is trained and disciplined to daily contemplation and centered on the Light, its convulsive surface is soothed to harmony, balance and peace.

A negative mind is the tool of sinister forces. Yielding to them it breeds weariness, listlessness, boredom and discontent and sprays negative thought-*entities* into every direction. These energies then roost in the thinker's mental/emotional force field, bring him to grief and whatever he touches becomes tinged with woe. He calls his dilemmas the Wrath of God or the hex of the witch of Endor, that is in fact his own returning. Persons who suffer from delusions, general distrust and self-induced confusion learn many needful lessons.

A mind that moves toward destruction is more powerful than a cyclone. But since by its very nature mind power is unstable and only momentary, a sudden rush of rebounding negative energies bring the thinker to undoing.

To the illumined individual every trick of the mind stands clearly revealed. If you don't hear the deceit in the undercurrent of a person's voice, you see it in their changing thought forms and auric emanations. Whether you talk to them in person or long distance does not matter. The revelation takes less than a second.

RESTING THE MIND

The restless mind seeks satisfaction. The way to get out of the rut is to adapt wholesome, rhythmic habits and establish clear, deliberate thought patterns. Adding the zeal (not zealousness) of Spiritual Love and a genuine appreciation for Life and God, the mind becomes a brilliant tool and faithful servant of soul and Spirit.

Seek moments of quietude, repose and relaxation. Relinquish reasoning and shift your thoughts to the calm beauty of Inner Worlds. Let the mind rest. Let it be!

At times persons have difficulty to stay their racing thoughts. Running here, running there — to what? Often not until disaster strikes will they align to Everpresent Peace, that will lift them out of the negative stream into the soothing vibrations of Harmonious Life.

When you rest the mind daily, the Light of Soul begins to guide you safely through the thickets of life and reveals every snag. With less to contend with, you will feel free, dynamic, in control, and totally *You*! An individual who has muddled through vicious entanglements and ran the gamut of the emotional race, will readily give up and turn to Peace. And though mind itself feels no pain, it often shuts off the memory after the damage is done.

A mind opened to God will willingly close all doors to guile, craftiness and evil. In the Presence of Light all things are made new. Let your mind be flooded with the Light of Peace, Love and Joy!

WHAT IS MIND?

Mind is the filament, faculty and instrument of the soul. Automatic in action, it cannot work by itself, nor does it have power to produce thought. The mind acts under the direction of inner and outer energies and influences. It is moved into action by the Energy of Divine Mind, which provides the force of the will. A weak mind is easily dominated by a stronger personality, will readily submit to programming and carry out autosuggestions. Such persons usually join cults and any master who tells them he is God.

Whether the mind is activated by impulse or circumstances, agitated by anger or excited by joy, it creates thought forms that become mindless entities and follow directions. When we speak of individuals dispossessed of reason, it means the mind has run off its track, is out of control and devoid of Divine Guidance.

As the nature of the mind is not altogether intangible, its ethereal filaments are still matter in part. Thus the entities it can produce are as compact as any other creation and when misuse is employed, bring the thinker to grief. But a mind infused with Spiritual Light, will wield more power than the forces of nature and even they will obey its command.

MIND ACTION

Your mental health depends greatly on your alignment to the Divine Force. Unless due to karmic causes, senility is unlikely to be encountered by God-oriented individuals.

All physical and mental expressions are the tool of Spirit. Thoughts, high and low, represent the Thought of God. Though over the centuries scholars have extensively analyzed the nature of mind, no psychiatrist or psychologist (unless an initiate) can evaluate the deeper Self and spirit in man; since it is only known through higher cognition and to those who have the ability to *consciously* live in the Lifestream of the Audible Sound Current. And we know it takes an *exact* evaluation to help the mind to recuperate.

When soul is well-rooted in God, the mind becomes its precision tool, powerful and perfect. The more attuned and flexible man's thinking, the more Spiritual Love and Power flow through him into his world. Then, when decisions are to be made, he no longer consults his feelings, emotions or will, but uses his cognizant powers. For his will has become the Will of God in action that directs his way.

The lower mind adores routine. Conditioned to anger it remains angry, conditioned to alcohol and drugs it keeps indulging; conditioned to inertia and irresponsibility it remains in that state and so on. Until the Light of soul breaks up the pattern and sets it free.

An individual may ardently wish to remove himself from his emotional pain and dilemmas and prays things would improve. But his hope lies in the balancing Power of God. Man can only do so much for his fellows.

Negative persons tire quickly, or hyperactively run on nervous energy until the 'burn out'. Physical work is rarely the cause of undue exhaustion, the energy drain of negative attitudes and restless greed are the cause.

At times persons become so infuriated the mad run ends in the safe port of a straitjacket to avert self-destruction. When such an individual is on the rampage you no longer speak to someone you know, but to a strange, foreign tenant that now occupies the body.

The consciousness has been temporarily pushed out until the person regains his sanity through medical help. Locked into the domain of their own thoughts, such persons are captives of the mind. And as much as the prisoner clanks his tin cup along steel bars, such individuals clang their thoughts against the invisible bars *they* created — and no one hears.

Mind is neither good nor evil. It is what it is: mind, the fabric and faculty of the soul. The thinker himself infills it with evil and being evil thinks he is good. When soul lacks the strength to control the mind, individuals destroy themselves against their own will, by alcohol, drugs and other poisons. Whatever affects your emotional body injures the mental body. Staying out of the company of quarrelsome, angry and possessive persons is to your great benefit.

Remember then: disintegration, regeneration and healing take place within. Controlling your emotions, remaining alert, aloof, detached and God-centered; to radiate kindness, compassion and tolerance, cultivate and produce mental health. Every mind grows healthy when it forgives the hurt and remembers the kindness. When unforgiveness meets Divine Light, it dissolves into forgetfulness, therefore forgiveness.

A DAILY AGENDA FOR PEACE OF MIND

Each day make time, sit still awhile. Close your eyes and look to the Light within. It will appear as a light-blue mist, or as a soft-white radiance that reflects on the mirror of your mind. At such moments, permit yourself to gravitate towards It and to stay with the flow. And the Light will turn into a Blaze of Heavenly Brightness and heal you in body mind and soul. Daily communication with God is essential to your total well-being. Persons who enter the Spiritual Life find their thinking faculty wonderfully sharpened, refreshed, and clear.

Mind becomes spiritualized and healthy when it lifts through the Door of the Soul. The illumined mind is the tool of God through which His Wonders find expression and creativity flows. The energy of the pure in heart can dart out to the remotest parts of the world; cure the disabled and comfort the desolate. One small stream of pure energy directed into the ethers with purpose, can avert disaster and save lives. For here The Divine Spirit directs the flow of energy into Its Own Cause. This is true, silent service. It differs from the practice of those who inflict their energy on the unaware. Such energy sent forth is tinged with the aberrations of the dispenser and harmful to the recipient.

When man removes himself from the vice-laden treadmill, he then becomes a qualified servant of the Radiant Lord. To profess a thing, differs from living it. Permeated by Divine Light, the thinker becomes the Knower and the pray-er becomes the Do-er. All things suffused by Light leave a purifying effect on the whole.

Mind craves pleasures, soul desires peace. There is no compromise until the Sound Current liberates them. To be whole we should rise above the pleasure syndrome of the senses and turn to the Greater Power within us. Until then, the lower mind will find its way back into the repetitious trench of self-satisfaction and old problems will arise in a new guise. Sound and Light can end the misery.

We should neither be negative *nor* positive, as both aspects belong to the lower Universe of Mind. The activities of the mind should be interchanged with actions of soul and Spirit to keep balance. Mainly, because when you live from the soul, karmic causes and consequences will diminish. The karma*less* life begins when every thought and action are rendered in the Name of God — thus neutralized. Now, you might think this could drive you over the edge, but it is easy; your very thought of God gets it done and needs no verbal enforcement.

HEALING MIND AND EMOTIONS

Mental health clinics are frequently overcrowded with persons who are charged with emotional instability, anxiety and related syndromes. But whether a person is stable or unstable, the emotional body is constantly changing. By its very nature it is in continual flux and undulation, pouring thought impressions and feelings into new molds and readjusting accordingly. Therefore emotional instability can be easily misdiagnosed. Only when mind energies drift out of control and the mind pursues its own conditions, do psychological disorders occur.

BE ORIGINAL

Be unique! Maintain your sense of self, *Self* is what you are. At times you will encounter individuals who claim to see everything through your eyes. No one can live their life through you. No one can feel what you feel, because your experience is unique as *You*. You should politely remind them to find their own inner values. Moreover, you are not the image of another's distorted perception and have no cause to live up to it. You can heal your life and nerves by disassociating yourself from those who ferment in their own personality. You are not being unsociable, you are merely living up to the responsibility you have to yourself.

Now, you find people tend to judge you by the yardstick of their own character. People mockers suffer from self-delusion and lack of self-honesty. Instead of being naturally warm, honest and caring, they can be overly compensating and woeful sacrificers. Dishonest with themselves and others, such individuals seldom find deep relaxation and feel friendless and unloved. Francis Thompson's poem expressed: ". . . and the Voice beat more instant than his feet, all things betray thee, who betrayest Me."

MIND OUT OF BALANCE

Mental disorders as physical illnesses are karmic and point to lack of God-awareness. We shrink from turning to God in fear it might deprive us of earthly joys. When indeed it enables us to live life more fully and happier. It brings us to realize we *can* make love and prosperity happen and create our own happiness. Be happy in your own way, for yourself — and not for others. Then others will feel the happiness and will want to be with you.

When the High Self takes dominion it brings the mind back into balance. The Bridge to Higher Consciousness must be spanned to counteract the shadowy ills of the personality. When the shadow falls on the Light, the Light absorbs it. No matter how dark the night, Divine Love steadily strengthens you. If we are not grounded in Its Powerful Light, darkness will obscure the Brightness, uproot us and leave us at loose ends.

HEALING STRESS AND DEPRESSION

Persons who lack control over their mood swings become easily depressed, anger quickly, and seldom have anything inviting to say. Depression is a useless, forlorn and unlovely feeling. Instead of wallowing in self-pity and remaining disconnected, professional counsel should be sought. Nothing can be healed on superficial levels. Depression is inaction. Even though it can be counteracted with creativity, nature walks and by developing new interests, these do not always solve the problem. When depression becomes debilitating, it is time to employ help. The shame is not in falling apart, but in ignoring the problem. Some things in life are neither good nor bad; they are opportunities to make new choices.

Unhappiness is not a condition of the soul, but of the emotionally disturbed mind. The senses of the depressed are clouded by memories, hurts of the past and pent up emotions. Now, if the process of re-embodiment would be understood, the past and all tensions would lose their hold. Depression prevails when you look to what might have been, instead of what is here and now. Stress, depression and anxiety can be healthy, in that we do not pretend with our feelings, and more, they can help us to tap our spiritual resources, seize inner strength and move us to take positive actions.

Happiness is within you. You can bring it out. You *can* make happiness happen! Joy as unhappiness are formed by your attitude, that colors your life with all you deeply feel inside, and draws more of the same to you. Can you find a bit of humor in your condition? Take time out — laugh awhile! Sadness can wait! Let depression roll away. Be happy — one day, one hour at a time. Forget tomorrow.

Live *Now*! Depression has no part in God. When you are down, you're down. Tell me, Dear Friend, who cares? But with a glimmer of hope that is *always* there, you can straighten up and start anew. Say *No* to destructive attitudes, what good are they? You *are* the Radiance of God; the shining center of your life and actions. With this thought in mind you can turn the tide with ease and heal your conditions.

To heal the mind does not mean to infill it with new ideas, but to empty it from its clutter that the Idea God has for you may manifest. To constantly overload the mind with emotional frenzies strains the electrical circuits of the nervous system, that, when overburdened, will break down as any other machinery and you have a classic nervous breakdown.

A mind at peace is a mind permeated by the *Ease* of God. A deeply healing encounter. Now, to be cured of depression does not say you will not be depressed at one time or another. Life itself can be that way! There are no miracle potions to healing, but when we have done our part we recover by Grace.

To heal mental illness, spirit voices and strange thought-inflections must be silenced; if the steaming mists enveloping the soul would again be clear and shining. This might call for a change in associations, since the angry, gloomy projections of others draw degenerate entities to you. When you cease entertaining whispering voices and strange feelings, you short circuit them. Let your mind become empty, God-contained and free. Allow it to bathe in the Stillness of Divine Love and be healed. Divine Light absorbs the shadow.

Man has free will, but not entirely. Whether for right or wrong, a subtle power moves him to think and act — to evolve. Living in a beautiful, but fatalistically geared world, man should begin to use his reasoning power, instead of running on impulses. As we are pressured into action by natural law, it is left up to us to grow or regress. Our actions and reactions influence our mental health and physical well-being. So, we either learn to handle stress, or become *dis*tressed. It is unimportant whether you scream out in anger, or withdraw into a slump, but to realize *Why* and to do something about it. To cater to others and suffer in silence is self-punishment. To heal depression requires self-honesty and your all absorbing thought of *good*.

DO NOT SHIFT THE BLAME

To see conditions as hopeless and despairing and blame everyone else, marks a weak character. If errors were great did we learn by them? How did we crush and tear up our life? Too much listening to others? Perhaps the trouble is not in your circumstance but within you? True solutions are never complex, since they come from within. We ask God to help us. When He does, we turn around and do our own thing because we did not like the solution! But at times we must evolve *through* the lesson before we are permitted to move on.

To cling to pride, to bitterness and to refuse to let go of uncompromising situations is calling forth the thief that robs you of every happiness, because *Love* is absent. When you focus your attention on what is true and abiding, you will have all the happiness you dreamt of. God never says no. He only says *No* when you do.

A rational person cannot stay depressed for long, too many worthwhile ambitions engage his attention. Instead of withdrawing from your world, ask yourself: 'How can I make things better?' To look at things objectively and with detachment means to see clearly. Then, in whatever guise the lesson may appear, we will see it as forming, molding us to let the Light shine through. To sin is our condition — we have no other means to grow by — until we meet the Radiant Light.

To attain Self-Mastery is the purpose for living. You are a winner for all your life, and a winner if you failed — because you tried! Remember then, you cannot be blitzed and disconnected from happiness or success unless *you allow* it. And so it is said: 'A free man is a brother of the Light, a brother of the shadow is a man in bondage by his own choice.'

REACHING THE TOP

Take time to rest, time to play, live for this day. Unhappiness is unreal. Only joy, peace, laughter and happiness are real, for they are of the soul. Keep goals in mind. You *can* create them! Nothing happens on its own accord. Never think how you are going to feel along the way, whether great or small, concentrate on the accomplished goal. Happy activities swallow up depression and sadness and heal the mind. And along the way do not concern yourself with changing others to your way of thinking. To change *Self* scores the triumph. Never employ half-idealism. Concentrate on *your* success instead of on the failures of others and your creative energies will soar. Why perpetuate futility?

As you reorganize your life and extend your creative interests, make it a point to meet persons with vitality and inner strength. Stay away from naggers, sad sacks, complainers and long-winded ranters. They do no more than steal your strength. Incessant talkers have no inner peace. Know what you want and set clear aims. Learn to keep silent. Let no one sabotage your dreams! Accept yourself. Wonderful *You*! And you will express the Greatness of a True Soul. Let it be *your* fight, *your* dream — and not what everyone else wants. It is the Way you reach the top!

TALK IT OVER

Suppressed emotions cause mental disorders and physical pain, that take on one form after another. They are called psychosomatic illnesses. When the medical doctor's final diagnosis is: "It's all in your mind!" — he is quite correct, since the pain stems from the individual's mental conflicts with himself and others, that began in the mind. To become bitter and dwell on repaying in kind, injures the mental/emotional body even more and intensifies physical pain.

To talk it over is the way to uncover deep-seated complexes and to heal the cause. It enables you to understand yourself, to take charge of your emotions and to get your life back together again. To pray about it brings no relief. Instead of fretting and traumatizing, we need to be up, doing, and *changing* to create a positive environment. For what can God heal when we are bent on taking the same poisons and keep spattering our emotional venom?

Neuroses is not always the result of contents of character, but also the effect of past life traumas — energies carried along on subconscious levels. To eliminate the effect, one must search out and heal the cause. More often neuroses is traced back to lifelong inharmonies and relationships the individual was karmically forced to endure; he could not cope with in a positive way or lacked the emotional stamina to sever. Though by and large all things are curable, some destinies do not allow them to be healed.

Angry? Yell it to the walls! This is far healthier than unloading unstable emotions on others and allow resentment to fester. Anger takes your energy and tears apart the fabric of the mind. Nippy attitudes, prickly moods and carrying grudges harm body and mind. You stabilize your emotional roots by acknowledging your feelings, by tuning into them to understand *Why* you feel — what you feel. And not by plugging into another person's energy and draining them. Why not draw from the energy that dwells abundantly within *you*?

Face your hidden secrets and begin to release them. Self-honesty and openness are important to wholesome relationships, private, public and to your mental health. This does not say your private life should be exploited. To brood creates ill will, deception and inharmony. Now, force never affected a cure. Nothing *pushed* out of the mind will heal it, for the mind will pull it back into repetitious thinking.

In example: when an alcoholic has gained sobriety the addiction still exists, because it has been set aside through mind over matter (force), instead of being cured by Spirit *diffusing* matter. Would a cure have been affected, circumstances involving alcohol (or drugs) could no longer be a threat to the individual. Until the Spirit of God takes over, lower entities will continue to entice, tempt and harrass the overcomer. Moreover, through the power of the spoken word you *are* what you decree. To decree 'I am an alcoholic may be emotional comfort and show courage, but binds man to his condition through identification. However, persons who have mastered abstinence deserve every respect for their self-evident discipline the majority lacks.

To be set free the mind must learn to rest in the Eye-Center, the space between your eyebrows. For when the mind ascends through the Gate of God and enters Worlds of Spiritual Light, it becomes free of attachments. Emotion means what the word implies: e-motion — *energy in motion*. And when this energy becomes well directed, loving, patient, tolerant and kind, there will be emotional stability and mental health.

STEPS TO MENTAL HEALING

Your thoughts influence your well-being. To be whole in body you must be sound in mind. When healthy, the mental body sparkles with an undulating radiance of colorful, delicate hues that are of great beauty. A perfected astral vehicle is wondrous to behold, but also signifies a forthcoming departure into Higher Life.

The thought energy you project colors or discolors the vaporous fabric of the mental/emotional body and astral vehicle as a whole, and leaves a tint of the nature and quality of thought on the fabric of the soul. Since thought is energy, your thoughts are immortal and live on from life to life until the energy is either transmuted or liberated. Purified energy reverts back to the Source, pours back into Creation and becomes the lifeline of other species to evolve. Life is *One,* and much remains caught up in between the Veils!

Supercynical and hostile individuals are mostly possessed by their own thought forms and by thought-*entities* of others that gravitate to their own likeness. Such persons become irrational and psychotic because their auric vehicle and mental body suffered the infestations and abuse of their own creations. These do not only look like worms and warts of diverse colors, but will also penetrate the aura of other persons who will experience harrassing anxiety and temporary mental maladjustment. Whether through personal contact or via phone conversation makes no difference.

Every thinker is influenced by his thoughts and unless in full control by the energy of others. Your thoughts and feelings comprise your attitude. The way you live is an expression of them. Born of Divine Peace, you can resurrect its stabilizing force and manifest it in your world. Then your life will grow harmonious and healthy on its own accord.

LEARN TO SAY NO

We tend to blame others for our troubling conditions, when simply saying *No* would have spared us months and years of grief. To be caught up in an unhappy situation is not always due to karma, but due to our incorrect choice. Except for karmic consequences you cannot escape, you *permit* everything else that enters your life. Some individuals spend a lifetime extricating themselves from one predicament after another. Controlling conditions before they *command you*, and learning to say *No* — is to your great benefit.

People will treat you exactly as you allow them. Say *No* to endless talkers and whiners that drape themselves around your neck each time the phone rings and take up your day. To learn to say *No* will make an end to your constant fatigue and you will have energy to spare. Perhaps you recall how during a phone conversation you suddenly felt all 'hyped up'? And another time when you had no energy left? This is how other person's thought-entities suffer you! Your solicitor does not care how much negativity he unloads on you. He/she have only one problem: themselves! When you feel the sympathy hook or outright demands tugging on your heartstrings, say *No*!

Constant talkers cover up their yawning inner emptiness they seek to fill with *You*! Learn to turn off the intrusion at the core. When persons endeavor to draw you into their problems change the conversation and walk away. If this is not possible you can get off the emotional leash by refocusing your attention to your awareness of God. When you withdraw your attention the aggravation loses life, because it no longer exists for you. The whiner forgets his woeful tale and the perpetual talker suddenly runs out of conversation. It works every time.

The effects of speaking to a balanced, spiritual person are very soothing, uplifting and healing. You should sift through your relationships, retain the pearls and give your truest best to them. Let go of the rest. Once you draw the line, set up rules and *abide* by them, you will have peace and energy to spare. Who is in charge? *You*!

GIFTS AND FAVORS — THE GREEK NEMESIS

Gifts and monies cannot purchase what each must find within himself. Gifts of the world are anchored to heavy chains and subtly attach themselves to your life. The greater the bequest, the more outstanding will be your sacrifice. And since it mainly affects your nerves and personal freedom you will ask in the end — how you could have paid so much for so little! Carnal nature is selfish. Everything bears its price, only *you* can wager its worth. There is nothing free. You pay for what you get and not always in money. The giving of meddling deriders can in time crowd out the personality, as they patiently try to inject their debased character into you — to *be* you. Tragic givers! How can those devoured by greed and those who demand your constant reassurance of how well they treated you extend a token from the heart? You might recall the stress and obligation accepting gifts have wrought.

Some endowments demand more than they are worth, namely: *You*. There are no shackles attached to a gift from the heart, nor to your privacy nor life. Your lack is the usurper's advantage; your acceptance of gratuities the trap to further exploitations. Some givers properly apologize for imposing on your time, yet will continue to inflict themselves on you. To them Corinthians 13 -clearly speaks: "though I speak with tongues of men and angels and have no charity I am as sounding brass and tinkling cymbal. . . and though I bestow all my goods to feed the poor and have no charity I am nothing.

Once you felt the menacing abuse, subtle bribery and rebuttal of gifts given for the 'Love of God' — when each coin turns into a lash and the spirit of human compassion shows its other face called: opportunism — you will learn no longer to accept them and cease tap dancing on demand. There is only *one true* coin and that is Love.

As long as your palm is open you remain the willing victim of usurpers. The coin of the world has two faces. Both are ugly and exacting. Unconditional giving is a virtue found in few. Did you ever listen to a sorry giver? On the other hand, some individuals will always have an eagle eye of how to get something for nothing; and most receivers have yet to learn that large bequests are *Karmic Money* to be used *to benefit* the whole, and not to satisfy their greed, lusts, personal interests and extravaganzas! The words of Henry W. Longfellow well apply: "Honesty looks the whole world in the face, for he owes no man."

Gifts of any sort demand your energy and attention, your obliging smiles at grubby little stories, your enduring appreciation and your time on demand. You might decline with a warm *No*! For all the goodness some attempt to prove — *It* never knew *them*.

MASTERING YOUR EMOTIONS

You master unwanted circumstances by withdrawing your energy and attention. The more involved you are, the more the controlling entities of others will wield their power over you. By controlling *yourself* you inadvertently control the energy of others and anything unwanted that moves in and out of your life, simply because intruding energies have nothing to hook onto and find no port to roost. This is how you manipulate matter through *nonaction*. Should you encounter the shrill and rude, withdrawing your attention will silence them. So we see, it is not controlling others as such that works, but controlling *self*.

Bless the mean-hearted! Take the competitive edge out of your voice and permit your gentleness of spirit to calm the storm. People often jump to conclusions and start an argument without knowing the facts. Now, have you ever observed when one person gets angry how the whole family follows suit? Such individuals are quick to profess their love for God, but treat those ugly in whom He dwells. Emotional power-wielders and pious moralists are unhappy, lonely and fearful inside. When the chilling Breath of Spirit refracts to them their own, they fold up with a whimper.

LET GO OF OPINIONS

Let go of likes, dislikes, gossip, prejudging and opinionatedness, for these leave a trail of unhappy consequences. The warring elements within us mellow, when we realize we are karmically indebted to all that comes to us. Truthfulness, benevolence, calmness and impersonality are signs of inner strength and builders of a healthy, radiant mental body. Thought energy creates patterns that extend into many future experiences. Well-directed, harmonious thoughts energize and heal conditions. To increase your awareness of what goes on in your world of vibrations, can completely reduce stress.

ELIMINATING ANGER

Persons will tell me they are plagued by sudden qualms of anger they find difficult to control. These inflections have various causes. It can be the energy of others, one's own returning, or an accumulation of base energy resurfacing to be rectified, from a lifetime when emotions and wildness ran their course without the individual's effort to control the flow. Here the momentum of energy comes into full focus. With each new burst the hateful force reawakens and is painfully overcome. This often happens to persons well on their way to God-Realization, when the Inner Light excites lesser, dormant energies into action, to bring them into transmutation.

To feel these *seemingly* foreign energies is part of inner growth. Nothing can be done except to remain unafraid and let the happening pass. Since negative and positive energies are of the same Force, neither can be effaced. But you *can* bring them into balance by remaining detached from whatever goes on for the moment. This will stabilize the energy and restore you to peace.

REBOUNDING NEGATIVE ENERGY

Since the personality belongs to lower worlds it is demonic. Evil exists because the lesser nature of man brought it forth. As evil evolves out of itself it must also terminate within itself. Evil thoughts and actions call forth reactions out of which other evils grow. By itself, real or imagined, evil does not exist. Nevertheless, its manifestations serve evolution, in that deceptions and hurts remove our personal evils in the end. Now, if the mind would cease perpetuating wickedness, there would be no evil and nothing left to be redeemed.

Where you find the *appearance* of evil, there is also the Force of Good. To control the evils of the mind through ritual and magic is futile. The practice differs from the spiritual control that comes from deep within, exerts no pressure and does not manipulate. It sets free through nonresistance. Thus permits the energy to return to the point of cause — or sender, which evil doers are woefully unprepared to meet. When your thoughts and activities include God, the negative flow goes into reverse, becomes neutralized and positive. A positive outlook changes the flow of vibrations all around.

As your inner being absorbs the higher vibratory rate of the Force, It will much like a lightning rod refract assailing energies. No self-respecting devil will attempt to oppose It! But the Force will not interfere with your karmas and permit you to work out the intensity of misdirected energies.

TRAPS ALONG THE WAY

Anger is ugly and has no room in the spiritual life. People who goad others into arguments need protection from themselves. At which point anger turns into violence, who is to say. The energy of anger is attached to an ugly, ferocious entity, a living mass of red and grey blubber. Anyone who has seen it, shuns anger at all cost. Its horrid emanations lead to psychopathy. Mental muggers and rogues can victimize you psychically, as any other manic abuser would physically.

Though of one energy, the vibrations of peace and anger do not mix, but interblend in such a way the *inner* becomes the outer for all the world to see. Some hide their anger under the facade of kindness, while the inward churning of hate is subtly killing them.

Energy is the Patrolling Force of God. It literally assaults the aggressor by rebounding his energetic compulsions — and aversions, to bring him to peace, sometimes permanently! Angry individuals love to manipulate people and goad them into a *mental* brawl to release their dammed up vulgarities and frustrations. Usually their faces look pale and drained, hard lines around their mouth run to the chin bone. Gentle smiles may wish to cover up the callous core, but reveal hidden bitterness and the pain of hate. Mental abusers harbor a strong sense of self-importance and of being maltreated. As much as some solicit physical abuse, other paranoiacs crave emotional pain as means of self-persecution and outlet of mental/sexual energies — or stimulation, after which there is always a *reward*. The psychotic heckler sustains deep guilt and accuses others for starting the argument. Ever notice how quiet and attentive the mental abuser becomes after he/she succeeded to rile you up? With some humans, viciousness is like a birthmark they carry from life to life.

Milder hostilities issue out of a person's need to be heard and understood. Then be a good listener, remain impartial and anger will mellow and fade out. Other times a little tactful untanglement provides the answer. Life is a game, Dear Friend, we should learn how to play it — to keep the peace.

The road of life is studded with traps that cannot snag you when you keep out of harm's way. What does it mean to keep all things harmless? Clearly, and to mention a few: not to take pleasure in the misfortune of others, never wishing anyone loss, pain or want. Never to criticize, instigate inharmony, gossip or slander. Following that, the majority would have little left to talk about. Possessiveness, pragmatism, domineering and sadism are the mark of deeply troubled souls.

Harm has many ugly faces. Cruelty to animals, willful destruction of wildlife, looting, polluting and many other mischiefs, all belong to harm. If nothing else, animal abusers should realize it is the Energy of *God* they are harassing, that some day, somewhere, shall exact its full dues. Angry individuals who inflict their insanities on God's Little Ones, should study *and digest* the following Creed from the American Humane Society:

> "Hear our humble prayer, O God, for our friends, the Animals, especially for animals over-worked, underfed and cruelly treated; for all the wistful creatures in captivity that beat their wings against bars; for all that must be put to death. We entreat for all of them Thy mercy and pity, and for those who deal with them we ask a heart of compassion and gentle hands and kindly words. Make us, ourselves, to be true friends to animals and to share the blessings of the merciful."

And to *all* oppressors, religious, political and common, I direct the words of Horace Greely: "I am inferior to any man whose right I trample under foot." To keep things harmless covers a wide spectrum and includes self-abuse, the death wish, the desire for rebirth into lower worlds and every other sort of purging.

ANGRY CONSEQUENCES

Now, if you kick a dog, it might just have the awareness to spin around and maul your hand or leg. To harm anyone or anything in thought or deed is highly impractical, since the energy will find you again. Consequences to past actions can appear at inopportune moments. On my way through Tennessee, a young man told me he never in his life abused an animal. But while he bent over to rearrange the things in the trunk of his car, a dog came racing after him out of nowhere, and took a hefty bite. . . well, the karma was paid.

MAINTAINING PEACE OF MIND

Never yield your tranquility to those who spin their psychic net and would snatch it away. But you see, many anger-ridden individuals do not want to be the way they are. The inner struggle to be free is always there. Few succeed without professional help. But who is expert in depression, anger and sorrow? Certainly not one who never felt it and has not overcome the hurdle within himself.

Though at times mild conflict clears the air, it must never lead to unloveliness and outrage. But silently enduring you will become so enmeshed in the other person's resentment you begin to feel you deserve the abuse and become as mentally ill as your partner. While in midst of things you cannot see things objectively, from a detached viewpoint nothing appears as tragic as it seems. Maintain peace of mind. Allow nothing to bother you too greatly, for our conditions on earth are transitory and illusive. When you think you cannot cope, say to yourself: "This is the world I live in, but it is not my True Reality. Whatever I do and experience — God shares. God in me is *present* here and now." Above all, I would desire you to bear in mind and *perceive*: you are *not* weak. Your spirit is indomitable, powerful, stable and daring, all else are negative projections of the mind.

To maintain inner peace you should face all things in truth and acknowledge *facts*. You listen to people, but do you hear what they are saying? While upset, people express what they *truly* feel, which is the reason for their anger. Your silence is more powerful than verbal crossfire. Who can argue with silence? This is not to say you should be a yes-person. To compromise and be obedient out of love or fear, including to the scripts and edicts of theologians, denies self-expression and originality out of which the mind evolves into Selfhood. This sort of obedience emerged out of traditionalism, was instituted by man and not by the Authority of God. But we may be compassionate, understanding and loving. In so being, you begin to recognize the Formless Glory that dwells in your own heart — and everywhere.

EFFECTS OF HOSTILITY

Mean-spirited individuals are in need of learning humility, selflessness, self-understanding and patience. Mostly they need love. But a person must *want* to change in order to benefit.

The blitz of momentary anger leaves many unanticipated reactions in its wake. Like pebbles thrown into a pond, the expanding, outrunning ripples of emotions, good and bad, become repercussions. Whatever falls into the Sea of Consciousness beautifies or disturbs the rhythm of the whole. Anger destroys all that is kind and good dissolves. Smouldering resentment poisons body and mind. On subtle levels the low undercurrent creates a negative polarization that attracts a host of other negative influences. Aggressions and constant upset affect the blood pressure, impede the natural lifeflow and suffer your circulation. The fevery pitch of rampant energy blurs your eyesight. You've heard the expression: "blind with rage." Karmic effects of mental cruelty extend into many lifetimes. If we knew today were all we had, we would be kind and loving to all.

Individuals who inflict mental injury on others often remark they cannot stand violence. This is not because they are spiritual, but their own vicious energy has sensitized them to such a degree, where every ray of discord is felt as a lash. People argue to demand respect, to get attention, to work off their sexual frustrations, and for whatever sets them off to go on a tangent to prove their point. Remain unresponsive to individuals who would inject their anger into you. Else you will soak it up like a sponge and suffer. When you associate with liars and brutes you become of like mind, since their mental patterns, lifestyle and the fury of their nature begin to interblend with yours.

Anger and depression go hand in hand, can lead to manic depression and at times to suicide. To pamper the depressive does not improve their condition but worsens it. To allow them qualified counsel is loving them far better. Though we think ourselves compassionate, the sad laments of melancholic gripers fall on deaf ears, because everybody loves a winner and nobody wants a glum pal. Be happy, be joyful, let go of anger and resentment, let go of it all!

CONQUERING THE MILESTONE OF ANGER

Instead of magnifying the destructive force, you can control, refine and utilize it to noble ends. When reacting to angry personalities you deny them to work off their karma and create more for yourself. Besides, you can only end up on the other side of their psychosis. Why tiptoe through other people's emotional mine field when you can be at peace?

Now, think of two persons in a fight. While one wins, the loser learned a sore lesson and gives up. This is how it should be: give up enmity, give up the emotional fight. Arguments have no winners, both parties suffer abuse. When you can do this, you will find yourself well grounded in God's Love. The Governing Force brings us many trying tests, we must pass to gain liberation. But until then, we return to earth to laugh, to play, to cry and die; in search of the One Love we most yearn for.

USING DISCERNMENT

Persons should not be evaluated by their speech or dress, but by the quality of their *energy*. Discerning this way, you will find the overly kind more often crude and perfidious. Because their projections issue from the sex center instead of from the heart center. Radiating vulgar energy is not what they deliberately do. Their energy simply attests to what they truly are and leaves no margin for error. Whereas the energy emanations of an awakened, humble individual feels lovely, refined and warming at any hour. Energy emanations do not belie the true character of a person, but prove what he is. Energy *Is* the *True* Reflector.

Many spiritual workers, as self-advancing messiahs who claim to have conquered the top of the mountain, have in fact never left the astral slums. While parroting *unconditional* love to *all*, they throw out their crude energy like lightning bolts never realizing that those more advanced see through them. Attempting to *save* souls and the planet, they run humanity deeper into the ground. Ever short on specifics but long on embroidered philosophies, these advocates of *truth* are always on the collision course with something and someone. And most of them uncertain! When in doubt about persons inquire within. The answer is always there. Once you unwittingly connect to their energy, you will feel like entities of darkness picked you for target practice! Not pleasant, but needful for some to realize the difference.

EFFECTS OF MALEFIC ENERGY

Anger and greed are related to hate and to every other vice. Humans so inclined, suffer from a weariness that haunts their restless nights and plagues their dreams with entities of strange esteem.

The vital and desire body that normally overlap, in despotic natures interlock and take on a foggy, murky density. A pitiful sight. If not transformed and redeemed by the Spirit of God, such individuals become disembodied entities after physical cessation, hover in the smothering mists of the earth atmosphere and stalk the living. Is it worth it?

Truth is ugly, irritating and offending, but when understood it becomes beautiful and soothing — a precious pearl. We cannot change the pain of unfoldment and inner growth, but we can bear in mind: there are degenerate personalities and callous mortals reduced to sorrow, but no degenerate souls. Even though soul can become the victim of the lower mind, the Radiant, Immortal Self is beyond corruption. Of course we should like to hear things more inspiring and uplifting, than what concerns the carnal man, but how otherwise can we become whole? Without facing ourself in honesty and truth, God-Realization cannot be attained. And though we may choose to look the other way, we know the warring world is sick — physically, emotionally and spiritually. And since single individuals comprise the whole, the burden rests on all of us. The way out is from within.

WORDS FROM THE WISE

"Every sentence of Pythagoras, like most ancient maxims, has dual signification,". . . explained Iamblichus in his Life of Pythagoras. This "dig not fire with a sword,". . . "this symbol", he says, "Exhorts to prudence." It shows "the propriety of not opposing sharp words of a man full of fire and wrath — not contending with him. For frequently by uncivil words you will agitate and disturb an ignorant man, and you will suffer yourself. . . For, he says, "it is difficult to fight with anger, for whatever is necessary to be done redeems the soul."

"And this he says truly. For many gratifying anger, have changed the condition of their soul, and have made death preferable to life. But by governing the tongue and being quiet, friendship is produced from strife, the fire of anger being extinguished, and you yourself will not appear destitute of intellect." — From Isis Unveiled. Science, Book I, Page 248 (The Theosophical University Press, P.O. *Bin* C,

Pasadena, Ca. 01109).

THE ISLAND OF TRANQUILITY

Irritation, unhappiness and frustration are helpless feelings related to stress. Stress is the cause of physical illness and mental havoc. There is no need to feel out of control. You can deal with stress on inner and outer levels.

When tasks become too important and pressures mount, step out-of-doors. Look to the calmness of the hills, and as you deeply inhale the carefree, soothing energies within the air, edginess dissolves into peace. Look at the peaceful, immense scenery of Nature, let your eyes scan the vastness of the clear blue sky and follow the fine line of the distant horizon. And in comparison to the natural Wonders of True Greatness, your trying duties will diminish in significance, and stress abate.

Now let your thoughts and footless spirit glide along the fleecy carpets of drifting clouds; and by the insweeping Breath of God flowing through you, you regain buoyancy, quiet strength, composure, and inner calm. - The Island of Tranquility is real. Assessible each time your thoughts turn to God. Once you touch base, you will strive to maintain your newfound vitality, inner constancy and peace.

Persist to think goodness, beauty and love. Do not affirm inharmony nor deny it, but recognize divine purpose in all conditions. Turn your *good* ear to God; listen intently to be taught and directed. Attain to humility, self-appreciation, self-forgiveness and never turn back. The past cannot mock you when you have let go of it.

Your inner bodies respond to influencing astral energies that intensify what you sense, desire, feel — and stress. Daily introspection enables you to tone down and to control your emotions and release all strain. And even though we flow with the stream of Spiritual Life, at times we must learn to swim against it to maintain balance and to gear our forces into more constructive lines. The way out is from within. And when all of us have found it, perhaps then the face of the world will dry its tears and smile again; and the soul will pour forth ever more light.

HEALING FEAR THROUGH LOVE

Where anger prevails there is fear. Where there is love and trust fear cannot exist, since you cannot be governed by love and fear at the same time. When Love permeates your thoughts and actions, it swallows up the very idea of fear, yea, death itself! Whatever you are afraid of, bring it out, face it, let it happen, let it be and let go!

Of fear said Krishnamurti: "Now, do you know what you are afraid of? If you do, then don't run away from that fear. You must not escape from it, you must face it; and the very facing of it helps you to be free of it. As long as we are running away from fear, we do not look at it; but the moment we stop to look at fear, it begins to dissolve. . . "

The Inner Voice once said to me: "Go as though you were unafraid and you will find you had no fear." And so it was.-

Dante's Inferno speaks of going to the *center* to get out of hell, and not through side-doors barricaded by fear. A mind in submission to God grows healthy and fearless!

Between the persona and God stands *You*, the Majestic Self. This True, courageous *You* is beautiful, perfect, noble and dauntless, and resembles your other self in form. Strong and righteous it stands suspended in the Light. Through *It* you enter inner transformations. The All-embracing Self knows nothing of fear. It knows only Love. Its counseling inflections speak to your higher senses: 'Fear not, *I Am* with you! You are never alone.'

You are the Thought of God manifest. Therefore God is conscious of you every living moment. When fearful, hold fast to this truth. You are *in* God, and God in *you* — here and now. Grin at fear, show your teeth! Stop giving in! You must *want* to do a thing more than your dread to attain it. You cannot hide from life because something *might* happen, since what is meant to be will happen wherever you are. Begin to trust the Great Partner within you. Discern between the imaginary and the real. When you experience *beyond* the senses and respond to inner energy, you will find fear flushed out of your life. You *can* heal yourself.

EXAMINE YOUR FEELINGS

Whatever is not Love, is anxiety, fear or indifference. Though fear affects the physical body, it is not an illness but an emotional hang up you may take off the psychic hook. When you analyze your most dreaded feelings you will find they are shadows without substance, which the underlying *fear of death* created. Every fear has its roots in the fear of death. Fear is associated with loss: loss of control, possessions, love, including loss of life.

Now, persons' biggest problem is that they fear losing the body. You may rest easy! The body you will have at the moment of death is already within you. It was your vehicle before you entered this world and you are using it every day. The life you live before death is the same life you live in after death. If we placed more emphasis on the spirit than on the body, the body would grow increasingly healthy and content, and we would no longer fear death. To be worldly wise and physically fit do nothing for the soul. What does the *transient* gain in Eternal Life? Your body is the vehicle of the True You, the deathless Self. It enables the finer Self to live in the dense atmosphere of lower worlds. At death the coarse garment is exchanged for one of finer substance in order to endure the pure ethers of Higher Worlds. It is just this uncomplicated. So why should we fear the continuation of life? It takes more courage to be born into this world than to rise out of it! Much more on this subject later on.

The mind only fears when it feels cut off with nothing to support it, until it shifts gear to the illumined state and finds its deathlessness in God. On earth, only the *appearance* of form is concrete, all else hangs in the balance ready to change without notice. The True Soul fears nothing in life nor in death. So long as you cannot face your mortality, realize your timelessness, and that you are the very Presence and Expression of God, there will be strange forebodings and unfounded fear of death. People are afraid of themselves. But when the Sound and Light already within you are recognized and experienced, you will know only Love.

DO NOT THINK FEAR

Escape from reality through drugs and drink are futile. The mind abides by its own repetitious mantrams and you will have to sober up sooner or later to face the same fear. Fearfulness robs you of life's abundant joys. Happiness, laughter and appreciation are as important to the mind as good nutrition is to the body.

Fear attracts fear and belongs to the consciousness of limitations. Do not think fear! If you cannot face it, blank out the thought. God is everpresent. The air you breathe is God, the kiss of the wind is God, and the light you see by is God. Can you still be afraid? God is in the center of your every conscious and unconscious moment, the Silent All-Abiding Presence. There is nothing at all to fret or cry about!

How many fears and phobias can we count? As many as we can conjure. Fear is a grueling feeling and finding a sympathetic ear not always the best solution. When it becomes apparent nobody cares, you will find the courage to do what you must. I would like to reach out to every anxious heart in this moment, hug it dearly and tell it not to be afraid. I would like to tear asunder the web of your dreadful illusions and remove from you every desperate, anxious feeling. And though I know it must come from within *you*, perhaps it is done!

God heals from within. If you permit, He will extract your fears like venom from a snake — which you can feel. And then it will be as though you never knew a single, fearful moment in your life. When God removes your fear and panic, you will see the conglomeration of a shapeless blubber standing outside of yourself, dissolving into the nothingness from which you drew it. It will be the last clammy experience you will ever again know.

Fear is venom to body, mind and soul, but it can also

awaken you to God-Realization. Though on opposite poles, weakness and strength are of the same energy. When you understand *why* you fear, it becomes your strength. It is far less painful to face the cause and heal it, than to be out of your mind with fear for a lifetime.

You are not alone in your plight. Everyone on this planet harbors a fear of some kind. Your fears and anxieties do not count for anything, only your conquering them does. You are a hero for all your life! You truly are.

Fear itself is unreal. It only becomes real when you persistently magnify it. People are programmed to fear from the cradle to the grave! All the news heralds is infilled with fear-inducing suggestions and will rob you of inner peace when you dwell on them. But will mean nothing to you when you see the world and its populace for what they are, and withdraw your attention. Suggested drugs suppress fear and keep it in incubation. Self-suggestion is equally futile and does not affect the cure. You unseat fear by facing the cause.

DEALING WITH LONELINESS

The high pitch of anxiety is part of loneliness and desolation. Some call anxiety unnatural, but may be plagued by it subconsciously since it is part of the hectic life — as are high blood pressure pills. It is said: 'no man is an island'; but since soul is an individual unit in the Body of God, man *is* an island. A person can be with thousands of people and still feel desperately alone. Loneliness prevails until you realize the Presence within you and allow It to fill the empty space. Then you will be happy, joyful and content and feel no longer alone. A glorious sense of destiny will replace aloneness.

To withdraw from life leads into deeper depression, at best to reclusion. Since reclusion interrupts the active rhythm of life, the recluse will find himself on that same lonely road in a future life, until he grows out of it and rejoins the human race.

Love, sharing and innate goodness are the unfailing antidote to loneliness and fear. Fear is within us and nowhere else. Fear based on physical causes can be corrected by the medical man, unless the patient develops dependency on him too, and is back to square one.

SILENCE THE PAST, LIVE FOR TODAY

Whether pleasant or troubled, the past should be left to itself. For if it was bad you will sorrow and if good, you will dwell on it with longing and try to incorporate it into the present. It hampers your progress. Look to the brightest day of your life yet to come and all that is yours to gain. To sit in self-pity is within everyone's power. Life goes on no matter how we choose to feel. But God can be very convincing. He either moves us back into the mainstream or allows us to sit alone to work things out.

I've known persons with extraordinary sensitivity and intelligence who suffered from psychological scars and great anguish, from no more than a wrong conception of themselves and from fretting over the past, that coming to grips with themselves and issues at hand clarified and healed. While others more readily recovered when they felt wanted, loved, needed and worthwhile, and permitted to share their life with others.

Genuine caring heals many wounds. To be patient and listen can do wonders for people you consider apathetic. And those who desire to be appreciated should make themselves more endearing to others, instead of riding on their nerve strings. Now, we don't have to always be happy, we may be sad! Experiencing the depth of human emotions brings you in touch with the Inner Self that will guide you to your highest attainable happiness.

Fear and guilt are akin. Guilt is more often a fear of delayed retribution, a sense of Divine Justice looming over one's shoulder. We should let go of the idea that something is out to get us, and begin to understand that only our own can find us — in *any* world.

Fear is natural and unnatural. Regretfully, some parents condition their children to fear by constant threats of consequences. Then, when the child grows up it cowars to everyone, is anxious, fearful, and has problems adjusting to a productive life. The need is *Love* and understanding. Soul's greatest need is to realize God.

Now, when the child is left alone it becomes afraid, but the moment the mother picks it up it feels loved and secure. This is natural. And though the child has the ability to manipulate the parent from babyhood, it is developing its personality. But when conditioned to fear the youngster dreads to go places, this is unnatural. Now, a youngster raised in the fear of hellfire and brimstone rather than in the Love of God, will be easily intimidated, wet the bed and fear darkness. It can either grow up to be a religious fanatic or a guilt-ridden schizophrenic, and will in some cases turn into a radical, cold-hearted brute. Subconscious picture images haunt man's mind and dreams, until the Spirit of God blots out the lie.

Since the nature of unredeemed man is merciless, he gives little thought to Divine Mercy. Man believes in a strange wrath he calls Divine Justice, because it identifies more with himself. By and by, he will learn that any wrath descending on him is entirely his own.

ROOT OUT FEAR

Fear issues out of child abuse, possessiveness, hate, greed and deliberate wrongdoing. Express the opposite and you change the polarity of the energy current and your mind and heart will grow peaceful and content. Instead of being constantly involved in the squabbles and emotional turmoil of other people, including that of your own children, become the watcher and impartial witness to what goes on in *your* world and within yourself. Freedom from fear is found through self-honesty and inturning, never through meddling, fretting or propagating gossip.

Let prejudging pass. Withdraw your energy from anxiety causing relationships, personal and business. Disallow your thoughts to cling to them, fling them far from your life. The delusions of lower world reality with all its many loves and hurts are not life itself, but an interval of time through which you pass. The more unincumbered you travel, the freer you will be. The invisible manifestation of fear is excess baggage. Time has arrived to discard it. There is nothing tragic in life, even less worth a tear. Our negative attitude about life and about those who share it with us—is the tragic thing.

It is widely taught that what you fear is your teacher, but what can it teach you when you are scared out of your wits and do not understand the lesson? And *how* can it teach you when you do not befriend it? Precious Seeker, befriend your dread — it will set you forever free.

FEAR CONQUERED

Now, some fears and phobias are rooted in our distant pasts and resurface to be confronted, conquered and healed. On our long journey back to God we died every imaginable death, and a faint recollection of *the way* we died can at times be recognized in our phobias and fears. For example: fear of heights *or* depth is associated with falling, with airplane crashes, being thrown off a cliff, etc., fear of crowds, elevators, confined spaces: smothering. Fear of ships, water, storms, etc.: drowning. Fear of fire: explosions, war, guns, being shot or burned to death. Fear of poverty: hunger and starvation. Of thirst: desert, hot sun, poisonous animals. Of cold: freezing to death. Not tolerating tight clothing around your neck: death by strangulation or hanging; or expiation from diseases of the throat or respiratory system. Eating disorders and food phobias: death by poison or overdoses of medicine. The subject is endless.

I knew a person who trembled fiercely when she saw a puddle of rain water. . . and recently a man told me that when he died he would love to *freeze* to death, because it felt so wonderful! A mother took her five year old son for a walk along an embankment by the river. He suddenly stopped, tugged on her hand, and pointed downward saying: "Mommy, see there. . . this is where Barnie and I died in our last life. We drove a big truck that rolled over the edge into the river and we both drowned!" - Though past traumas can leave their scars, they can no longer affect you when the *cause* of your phobias and fears has been recognized and understood.

A BRIDGE TO CROSS

A woman in deep distress came to me. When walking or driving across *any* bridge she would be seized with panic when arriving at midpoint; freeze in her tracks or at the wheel. This fear affected her so profoundly, she panicked by the thought of getting into her car, since wherever she had to go there was a bridge to cross. As she had to go to work each day to support her small children, the predicament was dire.

A glance into her distant past revealed a colorful scene of a lifetime when she was a little girl eight years old. She wore a long, ruffly dress, and a floppy, yellow straw hat covered her locks and frizzy coiffure. The colorful ribbons in her hair ruffled by the warm summer breeze. It was in late June of 1846.-

I found her standing at *midpoint* of an old, bowed bridge, and as she leaned across the rail, it broke in two. She fell into the turbulent water below, that swallowed her up to be no more.

When after this revelation I looked up, a wondrous light played across the young woman's face, that seemed to dry her tears, all strain had disappeared. She thankfully parted.

Within a week she called to say that all fear had left her, and that ever since that day she never again felt anxiety or apprehension. And that she went out of her way to cross other bridges to see if her loss of fear was real! And so it was. Though it made me happy beyond words to find the young woman free of her lifelong fear, I profoundly believe it was not my vision of her past which healed her, but her own courage and fortitude to *face* her dread and let it go.

TRANSMUTING POWER OF LOVE

You may transmute fear into Love. When you love

grandly you will find Love knows no fear. Fear is the energy of coldness, Love is the Force that warms your heart and limbs and heals the mind. The energy of Love instills Its Fearless Emanations to your heart and transmutes fear into courage. Love spurs you on to live, to dare, to reach beyond the stars — and to conquer!

When afraid, a mere glimpse to Love sets Its Power within you into motion. Cling to *It*. Say to yourself: *the warmth of Love is all there is. It is my reality!* — and you will feel instantly relieved of anxiety, jubilant and warm. It is a very real happening.

Though of One Force, Love and fear are opposites. Fear does not diminish the Power of Love, but Love always swallows up fear. To love *truly,* means to automatically relax in God's Greater Power and to release every anxiety and tension into *It*.

Soul and God are two parts of the same whole. The only part in existence that can occupy the same space are soul (or *You*) and God. Therefore you are always in God and God is always within you. There is nothing left to fear. You were born of Greatness, how can you be anything less? We have need to let go of the *image*! The crux of the matter is: people are engrossed with/ and attached to spiritual *images,* but not with the Root of God Reality Itself!

We should let go of Trinity or Tri-unity and connect to the *One* who is all three. There you discover your inexhaustible supply of hidden strength and the Wellspring of limitless Power from which you may draw any time you wish. When you trust the Fire of God's Own Light and surround yourself with Its Living Flame, then out of fear inner strength shall rise; and fear can no longer vex you in life or in death.

When you know God and have entered His Worlds while living, you no longer dwell in the apprehension of the masses, wondering if somebody is going to *save* you, you know how to get there by *yourself*. Man's woeful and fanciful ideas of salvation are born out of his fears, insecurities and imagination. And all of it untrue. When we accept what is freeing, we no longer lend our thoughts to unrealism.

Whatever life brings, within yourself you are always whole, always! You lack nothing, because nothing is missing!

To take a nonemotional approach to problems and issues enables you to move with greater ease through the many different levels of consciousness that comprise life; and not to overreact to the energies you encounter day by day. When we speak of changing ourself in order to live a fear-free life, it means to change our *attitude*. For the Divine Self is unchanging, you see, conditions change, the Inner Self does not.

Open your heart wide, let peace flow in. Let it abide. Whatever lingers in God's Light for even one surrendered moment, is by the Spirit of Its Fire transmuted into Its Own Likeness.

WISDOM OF THE ANCIENT TEACHER

The Golden Sayings of Epictetus, at XLIV-LXI, convey his teachings: "Above all remember, that the door stands open. Be no more fearful than children; but say as they, when weary of the game, cry, "I will play no more"; even so, thou art in like case, cry, "I will play (fear) no more", and depart. But if thou stayest, make no lamentation."

And Epictetus proceeds: ". . . God has placed by the side of each a Man's Guardian Spirit (Reason), who is in charge to watch over him — a Guardian who sleeps not, nor is he deceived. For what better or more watchful Guardian could he have committed to each of us? So when you have shut the door (closed your eyes) and made darkness within, remember never to say you are alone, but God is within your Guardian Spirit, and what light do they have need to behold what you do? To this God you should have given your allegiance.

"He has delivered thee to thine own care, saying, I had no more faithful than myself: Keep this man (or woman) for me, such as nature has made him — modest, faithful, high-minded, a stranger to fear, passion, to perturbation. . .

Such will I show myself to all — "what, exempt from sickness also: from age, from death?" Nay, but by accepting sickness, accepting death as becomes a God!"

4.

The Law of Consequence and Action

It is wonderful to pray and to feel the Love of the Indwelling Presence, but prayer does not change the Will of God. Man reaps what he sows. Re-embodiment enables him to repay his debt to life, thus to himself, for he *is* life.

Reincarnation and Karma are interrelated and of One Immutable Law, which operates in any world and universe within the Jurisdiction of Cause and Effect. This Law is impersonal, dispassionate, exacting, knows no favoritism and holds no vendetta against anyone. It restores inharmony to harmony by returning to each the energy of his own actions.

Though latent within all things, the nurturing force continually withdraws itself from the snags of mortal confusion and in its innocent course reawakens in man the energy in need of purification. This Superprinciple is the Gentle Nurturer of souls. It takes no pleasure in man's grief, but inadvertently grants him the wisdom not to degrade his divinity or to manipulate life. Once this unbending Law is understood, nothing from within or without will have the power to move you to offend *It*.

Good or bad, each pays his own debt to God. No personal saviour will do it for him. Every man encounters the consequences of his own actions and feeling the cause through the effect he must stand as bold facing them, as he stood committing them.

The Force has nothing to do with calculations or material thought, it simply moves out what restricts the spirit in man from progress. It ignores every tear and petition for mercy. No stain goes unnoticed, for where can man hide from the Force that dwells in him as life? To break the Law of Right Action means sowing to the wind and reaping the *Cyclone.*

Over the course of time we made restitution for deeds long forgotten, that upset the rhythm of universal peace and shaped our destiny. But destiny does not shape the future, it merely provides us with a more solid foundation to evolve into Godhood. Therefore we should not think of our burdens as punishment, but heaven sent opportunities guiding us into Divine Enlightenment and to be sure — out of convention. Man prays for forgiveness to avoid the consequences of his actions, the Law knows no deviation from *Right* and is always fully satisfied. Since life is eternal, *It* does not care if your debt is repaid in two lifetimes or in a thousand more.

Every cause invokes a consequence. No energy can assail you in any world, unless you yourself have set it into motion, sometime, somewhere. Your sense of error also awakens you to recognize the Law of Justice is within you, and that Love, Mercy and forgiveness begin and end with *You.* Wrote Albert Camus: "I tell you a great secret, my friend, do not wait for the last judgement, it takes place every day."

There is no God that deals out punishment. Your good actions become your saviour, malefic deeds your judge of doom. Self is saviour, judge and jury, that will either lift you to the highest heaven or plunge you into the sorrowful regions of undoing. And for all here mentioned, the Judgement of God is acute, but His Mercy greater. No one is safe from the Accuser, save the humble in heart and penitent.

Whatever man *was* and *is* reflect in his world. His life experiences and karmas are fashioned by the way he thinks and what he thinks he is. To suffer karma as each of us has, is nothing to be proud of or reason to demand pity, and is no better than disease; both prove our insufficiencies and lack.

The Law of Consequence calls for accountability. Individuals who keep saying: "I'm okay, you're okay, and everything you do is okay!" — will rue their lack of foresight when the Wheel of Life shifts gear and the karmic heat is on. Then laissez faire attitudes awaken to facts. We do improve as time moves on.

The Law of Consequence weeds out the thistles of ill emotions from the garden of the soul. It helps you to refocus your attention from hurt and bitterness to Love. Nothing is so bitter to us than the cup of Karma, and nothing sweeter than the Honeycomb of God. Our karmas should be accepted with grace and the bliss of God with quietness in heart. You need not shout it to the world, when you are truly inspired from within it will shine from your whole being.

PERPETUAL CYCLES AND NOWNESS

Life is a circle, a cycle. You do not know where it began, nor when the cycle will end for you, at least not for this time. There is no past, present and future in God, only *Nowness*. In example: when you attune yourself to a forthcoming event, you experience the future *now*. When in one illumined moment the Spirit of God moves you beyond the borders of time and space into Reality, you realize the *nowness* of that moment. For that instance your world, past, present, time, and space no longer exist for you.

In the realization of nowness, you begin to live the karma*less* life, for your thoughts are then *in* God, in all you do, which leaves no margin for deliberate errors and neutralizes the affect of lesser energies.

The Energy of undeviating Justice constantly frees itself from psychic entanglements, which cause pain to him who spun the web. The Old, Original Law of 'an eye for an eye, and a tooth for a tooth', is still in effect; which man feels acutely, until his heart and hands are clean again; free of blood, free of hate and free of thievery, possessiveness and greed.

Only the Brilliant Fire of the Holy Ghost can burn away the dross of karmic accumulations. Then the road which leads ever upward becomes clearly visible. It is sad to see people play the lottery of fate to the hilt without knowing why. Suffering from addictions to emotional excitement, drama and self-destruction are also man's karma.

Consciousness never sleeps. The interplay of actions and consequences of the day continue in your dreamstate. Since you are *what* you are wherever you are, you cannot be different in dreamstate than when you are awake. And while you create more karma on subliminal levels, you also work it off.

Now, even good actions have negative outcomes when underlying motives are selfish. God is not deceived. For instance: a person may be taking care of a loved one, in hope to receive a large bequest, to find he/she was left no more than a few regrets and good wishes, while the inheritance was left to someone he considered less worthy. To give to get is a sad scene. Nothing sets people apart, except some ask for diamonds, others for God.

Whether karma is bad or good, *both* bind man to the fetters and fetishes of Rebirth. Good actions that result in misery create new reactions and karmic conditions. Thus, when good actions meant to set free become iron shackles, they weld giver and receiver to the Wheel of Undoing.

UNDERSTANDING RETRIBUTION

In matters of health, whether you believe in Karma or *ancestral inheritance,* it's all the same. You never suffer the burden of another's actions, but only what you yourself set forth. The quality of his energy follows the doer from life to life. Whether to do wrong was imposed on him by other authorities or willfully committed by himself does not matter.

Your body and its limbs are instruments of spiritual

power. Use them for abuse in one life, if the deed was horrid enough, the particular limb involved may be lost or altogether missing in another existence. Scientific torture of animals, as well as humans, manifests dreadful consequences. More on this subject in a later chapter.

It is tragic when a limb is taken off by mistake, but the Law of Retribution is infallible. Once a person went to the hospital for the removal of a gangrenous leg. By error the surgeon severed the healthy leg, and the person became an invalid. Gruesome, yes, but Karmic Justice. What you abuse you lose. Have you ever used your hands or fist to brutalize another? To breaking bones or to butchering live animals? Or used your fingers to extort money or to sign a death warrant? The Law of God will hold you responsible. Consequences bring every lewd act to light. You've heard people moan: "How did I ever deserve all this?"

Our dilemmas seem unfair because we do not remember our past actions, else we would avoid what we must face. Once you enter the Spiritual Life, pastlife transgressions come to full remembrance. Then you will understand the reason for suffering and how to improve the future.

The energy of pastlife sexual perversions, overindulgences and self-abuse, manifests in another existence as debilitating nervous disorders, since the vital fluid in man's nervous system is the energy of procreation and regeneration that suffered abuse. When purification sets in, the same force attacks and destroys the network of nerves vital to life. The Spirit of Karma readjusts the energy in man and will drive him on until his lessons are learned.

Once the Immutable Law of Retribution is better understood, you will see that Its healing properties do not inflict harm, but restore the human being to balance and reason. Pleasures that gratify the senses do not always lead to a self-established hell, but at times to the womb of spiritual death. The fate of the soul can be extinction. Individuals who refute the Law of Retribution and reincarnation are much like the man who cannot relate to life and says he is alright.

Now, we cannot say that all that comes our way is karmic, since carelessness and daydreaming can also cause accidents and hurt. These however establish other future consequences. Every hurt stands to be rectified. Old debts dog our footsteps and reappear to be paid when least expected. What you are going through is not so important as the lesson you realize and remember.

To gain liberation from self-bondage we should enter conscious states beyond the reach of Karma, where the Lord of Light destroys cause and effect and darkness can no longer control the appetites that defile the soul. Instead of enlarging our ordeals we should look at life for what it *can* be and magnify the good. At times you may feel you must make changes, but to make them first in your attitude might prove less costly and solve a multitude of problems. For it will reduce the negative polarization and initiate healing your life.

The Spirit of Retribution answers the doer in the same ruthless, dispassionate manner he set forth to break Its Law. It disregards the opinions of those who find it unthinkable their own energy dispersions should find them again, but are unable to explain their suffering. The unswerving Law of Retribution has no regard for religion, race, color or caste. No priestly forgiveness can shield from *It*, priest and penitent suffer alike.

LIFE, THE GREAT TEACHER

To know *why* we suffer allows us to better cope with incidents that shake the very core of our existence. Petitioners of God should realize He is already in the center of every circumstance and lesson. Nothing is so sad than the emotional trauma of persons who cannot find a reason for living and marvel why so many milestones block their way. To say: "Well, it's supposed to be that way!" depicts an uncertain, fearful character, religious opinion and acceptance of doom.

To consider the necessity of cycles gives new meaning to life, and the understanding that life will give us no more than we poured into it for multiplication. Can we still say that lack is of the devil and good is of God? Now, we cannot hide from the agonies of life, but we *can* beat a wide path of Love through it, that others too may find the Light and feel the Peace.

THE IMMUTABLE LAW

No matter how trivial, all actions bear significance. The error of omission bears as much rebuttal than the act of commission. Your silent thoughts, good and bad, are as karmic as physical actions. Thoughts are flowers or weeds in the Garden of the Soul, and we already know what happens to weeds. Again and again, they are purged and uprooted until they are gone. So it is with our karmas. Justice and Love are the Law of every universe and world. Man's first responsibility is to himself, his duty is the conquest of the lower self.

The Law of Consequence is the Law of *Action*, of opposition, a Force of equal vibrations. It counteracts opposing vibrations with precision. The purer and stronger always overcomes the weaker. But we must act to survive.

The Cosmic Scanner sees all, hears all and records all. Rueful promises find no reception. The karmic record within you instantly absorbs the energy of your motives, thoughts and deeds; and when life has ended this record is taken along for the Judge's perusal. Wrote Omar Khayyam: "The moving finger writes; and having writ', moves on: nor all the pity or wit shall lure it back to cancel half a line, nor all thy tears wash out a word of it." But God endowed us with reason, foresight and *conscience*, that silently remind us of the consequences *before* we act.

Actions below are felt Above, even as higher activities are felt on earth by degrees, as energy travels within the shoreless, Infinite Circle of the Body of God. Thus higher energy must meet its lower manifestation, interblend and counteract again and again, until lower energy becomes bright and shining as its Sacred Source.

In the interim of incarnations man's inner, spiritual bodies are also strengthened and perfected, unless through constant disobedience these bodies weaken, become ill and disintegrate as does the physical vehicle. Then the soul belongs to the spiritually dead and the primordial spark withdraws into the Sea of Light. So we here understand, though the Light of Soul is immortal, not all will enter the Kingdom of God as an awakened, God-conscious soul.

WHAT CREATES DESTINY?

The karmic record of your life is impressed on the Astral Light. As the nutriments of God sustain the life of the body, karmic picture images cast upon the bloodstream affect the body and the blood. "The life of the body is in the blood," says Leviticus. To cleanse the blood on physical and etheric levels, a complete change of heart and attitude must take place concerning all things. And a turning from lesser ideas to the Divine Ideal of God.

Ideal is Grace, Ideal is Life. When we look to the cause of karmic pain, we should also look for the cure that is found in the Divine Physician, the Holy Spirit. Mainly, we should get off the fence and decide in what we're going to believe.

What we do, desire, and love becomes our liberator — or the adhesive force that fastens us to the Wheel of Rebirth. Desire for happiness, desire for reward, desire for riches and acclaim, jealousy, hatefulness and whatever else, compose the cement. We should seek the peace inner harmony grants. We do not suffer from sin, but from ignorance. Some things just cannot be prayed away!

Thread by thread, man's loving ways and heartless actions weave the pattern of his destiny, he returns to untangle. Even though cleansing and regeneration continue in Other Worlds, it is in our power to make straight our path. The Muslims have a great saying: "Live as though you lived in Eternity. Live in this life as though you died tomorrow."

When mortal hopes are dashed you sit on the scale, unsure of how it is going to balance. As a rule you would look within. Then there are moments when you feel ungrateful and at loss, because even though you seem to do all that is right and true and have given your best, the negative polarity of life leaves you at loose ends and struggling. But this also brings you to realize that longing for right is not enough. *You* must take the initiative and *go* to the right, nothing else can suffice. We already know what happens to those who stay in the middle of the road, they get run over! And that is just what the conditions of life will do to you unless you take charge.

You can do it! Go ahead, Gentle Friend, *Do It*! Take your life by the collar, shake it up! Take control and do what *you* want to do. Set your priorities straight. Close the door to other people's opinions. Live *your* version of happiness, let it happen — and a thousand Unseen Hands will come to your aid!

Every obstacle is a steppingstone to inner growth. Karma is the nurturing principle of life. Suffering its effects moves us to become conscious agents of Divine Will and clearly, into the direction that leads *beyond* negative and positive worlds — to God.

KARMIC STAGES

First we deal with primal, or *Original Karma*. Our life was comparatively karmaless, or without sin, until we received the gift of mind and reason, began to think, desire, want, act, react and to experience life. Our reactions to conditions and happenings decided our karmic future, our destiny and fate. While acquiring lessons, the energy of each motive and action good and bad, correlated the record that became the deciding factor of each succeeding life in the drama of involution and evolution.

The second is *Fate Karma* on which our life experiences are based. Meaning, we reap the fruits or seeds we have sown in another past. This we collect on every level: physically, emotionally, mentally and spiritually. Past inharmonies and individuals to whom we are indebted confront us again, until conditions are worked out and amicably resolved. Thus we should not part from anyone in anger, but should wait until a relationship, or a business partnership has been peacefully settled. Seneca wrote: "The greatest remedy for anger is delay." Cardinal Newman advised: "We should ever conduct ourselves toward our enemy as if he were one day our friend."

The third is *Reserve Karma*. Since it is not possible to rectify our errors in one short lifetime, they confront us along the way; as they are dealt out to us by the Lords in charge of our karmic pasts. Thus Reserve Karma is reduced but not stayed.

The fourth is the *Karma Of The Now*, we create every day, which we may rectify presently through restitution, forgiveness, admittance of error and so on. Or we may let it be stored up as reserve karma to be worked out in a future existence. Observing the way we conduct our present life, it takes no magician to foretell what will confront us tomorrow.

Thus, each works out his own salvation and is given ample time to do it in. No other blood redeems but the blood of the Self, that is nailed to the cross of flesh from which it may rise into freedom if it wishes. When man surrenders his thoughts and life to the Sovereignty of his being, he will know himself and his Creator.

Man lacks self-honesty and sincerity, whether it concerns his belief or other matters. Deceiving, he deceives himself. In my young days I belonged to theater groups and often studied the behavior and mimics of people. In later years when observing the character of individuals, I noticed people were still saying their lines, playing their acts to the hilt. We are actors and *re*actors on the Great Stage of Life. When we cease to *react* we find nothing is real — save the Reality that moves all things.

KARMIC LIGHT

God loves the soul. Man is his own avenger. When conditions call for readjustment Karmic Light reactivates the energy and sets it into motion. Most importantly it teaches man to sow good seeds (thoughts), and to become the master of his fate. The Karmic Force leads man through the desert land of earth and the fiery furnace of life to make of him a gentler, more compassionate being, that he may find his God.

Predestined by necessity, and by our own free will, we set the Law of Consequences into motion. Some individuals can only accept its Judgment as long as it applies to someone else and not to themselves. This is the nature of their religion to which they are entitled. When after much ridiculing and anatomizing the subject man finds the God he worships will do nothing to mitigate his misery, he will begin to look for the answer within himself.

Some lifetimes go by smoothly to rest the soul. But a life will again manifest when an accumulation of malefic energy comes into focus to be purified all at once. We wonder why a seemingly *good* person suffers from cancer, or why a kind, gentle soul suddenly breaks down with feebleness and mental vegetation. The cause is rooted in the individual's past.

Once the Law of Balance has been broken and the energy recorded, it is too late to reorder your life and ward off consequences. There are many forms of cancer, the worst is that which eats away the soul. Pain belongs to the world of pain. What good is mortal satisfaction when an individual is ill beyond hope and left to his misery? No tear, no prayer, no saviour will alleviate it. The Law of *Right Action* is Inexorable, Unchanging.

Now, when trouble appears on the scene we wonder why, but accept the good without question. We are really never satisfied with anything much, not even with Nature. When a river runs crooked we dig a new trench and reroute it to straighten it. When a mountain is in the way we move it elsewhere, but it never occurred to us to remove the mountain of our karmas, that, if we don't, will finally fall on us.

Every day is filled with the energy of new actions and effects to causes that constantly test our reactions and create new destiny. Whether minor or major, and by Virtue of the Indwelling Lord, nothing can happen to any soul it has not brought upon itself. Now, we can let Karma run over us, or use its Golden Opportunities to develop a strong, upright, honest character and "build more stately mansions to the soul." How well we cope with life depends on us.

And who is to say who is good or bad and what shall befall him? Good and evil belong to the Universe of Mind. God has nothing to do with our dilemmas, good or evil, for God is *purely — God*.

> "Shallow men believe in luck, believe in circumstances. Strong men believe in cause and effect."
>
> - Ralph Waldo Emerson -

5.

Consciousness — The One Life

When we give our inner life priority and ponder our needs, we can bring them into outer manifestation. Once negative energy is moved out, the mind penetrates far beyond its own barriers. It begins to harness the vital forces that free of dependency and move us to think and create on higher levels.

Thinking issues out of what we experience, judge, compare and analyze, and according to the way we were conditioned by the ideas of other minds — and tradition. Now, when we don't understand what we hear, it is easier to create a conflict and throw it all out, than to examine what we perceive on deeper levels. Even while reading this book you may feel at odds and not too kindly, if the message does not comply with what you trust and believe. Is this not so? But to be your own person you *need* to feel exactly the way you do — to think for yourself to determine what holds true for *you* at your present stage of spiritual growth.

The mind is the instrument by which you work out earthly problems. But the final solution to human dilemmas is not to strive for peace of mind, but for peace of soul through which true contentment manifests. How do the conscious, subconscious, and Superconscious mind work? How does the mind react to their subtle influences? To follow is a brief delineation on this subject.

THE DIVINE SPARK

Consciousness is *One*. It should not be thought of in parts, but always as a whole. Consciousness is the limitless Being of the *Absolute*, a Boundless Sea of Brilliant Energy of which the divine spark was *born*. Therefore, the Superconscious and the divine spark are inseparably one. In this realization we do not look to subdivisions, but to Its highest manifestation. When you stand in Truth, there is only *One* consciousness. Even though it branches into billions of appearances and forms, *One* is all there is.

Consciousness is the Body of the Lord, the Ocean of limitless Light. Soul is the incarnation of its Sacred Parent, Formlessness embodied as form. The awakened soul no longer recognizes tri-unity or Trinity, but the Deathless Being as itself. The Light of the Brilliant Sound is the *Image* and True Reflection of God, and the Sound Current the means by which the Abiding Worlds of Love and Joy are reached and entered.

The influences of inner and outer forces move man to act and react, and the consequences of his actions subject him to various levels of this mighty, Spiritual Atmosphere, where good is rewarded and duality and contrariness are effaced. But oppositions enable man to gain a clearer perception of himself and to attain *Self*-Realization.

LEVELS OF CONSCIOUSNESS

Once you have entered into the Audible Lifestream, God becomes the undercurrent and motivation of every thought and action, and the Valiant Force directs your way. But even though you live in Higher Consciousness here and now, you can only experience it by degrees, according to your inner perception.

Now, we can envision the immensity of consciousnness in layers or as a ladder, scale its brilliant heights or glide back to the bottom rung of creation. Though man has free will, it seems he has little choice as to which way he must go.

The problem is, many of us blow with the wind and are like half-masts, half in and half out, never realizing Truth on either side. Through fickleness, the anchor gets quickly uprooted and the individual becomes a floating raft on the sea of life. As long as the mind swashbuckles to and fro, there will be Karma and hell to pay.

Consciousness *is*. Beyond conscious regions lay the Superconscious Spheres of Celestial Worlds. All levels of life are supervised by lower and higher controlling entities, that range from Mighty Lords and Spiritual Giants to Superior Energies that supervise Light Systems and keep the worlds in running order. Other Beings of High Esteem carry out the task of comforting, healing and nurturing lesser life waves, and others yet create, recreate and uncreate the enormous panorama of soul's fantastic imaginations and often insidious delusions.

On denser conscious levels the beat goes on. And the pitious redemption of abused energy will continue until earth itself becomes cleansed and reborn. Then all souls shall enter their merited state. Those who remained enmeshed in vice will sleep until a new universe and world beckon to rebirth and shall enter new cycles of repeated involution where old Karma appears in a new guise to be rectified.

The Conscious Mind registers all you perceive through sensing, feeling, seeing, hearing and touching. The personality is the actor and reactor on the stage of life, the mind is the tool that makes soul its slave or master. To live orderly, soberly and to use innate power rightly is the way to control the driving forces and to overcome limitations. To control your world is different from desiring power. Individuals who crave power do not desire God. Thus they remain powerless.

As the unborn child pushes its way through the mother's

womb into the world, so the conscious mind — the lower part of soul,must push its way through the psychic fog of the physical universe back into the sunlit worlds of God. Soul was always free, *is* free, and will be ever more free, when it pulls the mind into the Brightness of Divine Light. Freedom belongs to those who claim its liberty and live it!

The Subconscious Mind is the memory bank of all you deposited past and present. These thought energies determine and compose your present and future conditions. Thus your subconscious mind can be a reflector of bitterness and frustrations, or of happiness, health and stability that reappear in your condition. The subconscious records the vibratory energy of mental emanations and plays it back to us until the day comes when we can see every falsehood we deposited as truth — as *untruth*. We can erase the old record by depositing energetic vibrations that make *true* statements. Then, having removed the cause of our problems, old deposits readily dwindle away and life is restored to the happiness God intended for all.

Impressions and thought forms mature in your subconscious mind to reappear in your life when the cycle is completed; often not until after many lifetimes. But we tend to blame resurfacing problems on everyone else, including God. Now, when inharmonies are seen as untruth and you immediately shift your attention to what you know *is* Truth, the negative chain breaks up and dissolves.

Copious volumes have been written on the subject of the subconscious mind. Worldwide seminars endeavor to teach you how to clean out the mental clutter. But this only works up to a point. Firstly, we came down to earth to work off our karmic debts, which are unavoidable since we incured them and no mental reconditioning can efface them.

Secondly, mind is what it is: *mind*, the instrument of soul and Spirit. Though when disciplined its powers are enormous, it can only rule its own world until it comes under the Dominance of Spirit. Therefore programming and *re*-programming of the subconscious is futile, brings passing results and do nothing for the soul; since the practice exerts *will* over matter instead of Spirit diffusing it. Only when the soul has pulled the mind through the Third Eye center and mind has become its precision tool, can it be said that the old record is slowly being blotted out. It has never been otherwise.

Of course, we know we have been conditioned to negative thinking since the day we were born, that left its mark on our self-image, which holds true for some but not for all. While the karmic life of one individual may warrant negative or depraved conditions, another may be born into a milieu of happiness and plenty. Either soul must develop a positive self-image, which however can only be strong, healthy and free of egotism when it learns the Ways of God and plumbs its spiritual roots. Until then the mind will pull the personality back into its humdrum of repetitious thinking.

Negative thought creates a veil. When dense enough it begins to release its own momentum and the individual feels as though all the sadness and depression of the world has gathered in his corner. Man creates this hypnotic veil by persistent negative self-suggestion and by accepting the negative autosuggestions of others.

Be unique! Do not cater. Dare to be different. Do not fall prey to gainsayers. Keep yourself *divinely* insulated against the attacks of psychic scavengers and you will feel rested, bright-eyed, well-healed and you will have energy to spare. It is in your power to keep your world clean and clear of intruding energies.

The cells of your subconscious incubator know neither yea nor nay and automatically accept what you feed into them. To be happy, reinstate your vibrations to the Center of Truth. You *are* Truth. In everything see Perfect Light and all things as a manifestation of Spirit.

The Superconscious Mind is the Seer of all things; the Perceiver and Receiver of your thoughts, words, motives and intentions, which It regrants without reservations. Abiding by Its Own Law, It can only refract what *you* affirm as Truth, whether this is a fearful existence, a nervous breakdown, good health and happiness.

You are the generator of all you encounter. Thinking good, wonderful, productive thoughts, decreeing *Love, Life, Power, Perfection* and *Divine Order* for your life provide your dynamic keys to vibrant health and Superconscious Power, that will move you across the old threshold into a great new life! Then you will realize Consciousness is God — and *You*.

The Force of Divine Consciousness is the cohesive Love that binds all things together. Yet it is not the Supreme One, but the emanating calm, Shining Sea of Spirit that glistens in the Brilliance of His Great Light. This Emanation exudes the Force that is free of the sentiment and emotionalism that drive religious beliefs into battle for their God and people over the edge.

All things evolve out of Consciousness, they only differ in degrees, to various strength and correlations of density and lightness. Thus the different sheaths of man's inner bodies, including the physical form are composed of God-Element, that, when seen by inner sight resemble luminous star matter. And the stars, planets and worlds on end evolved out of this same Principle Pleroma.

THE DIVINE CHRIST SPIRIT

Christ is the emanating Principle of the Power of God. Existing as Consciousness and Force, the Energy of the Spiritual Ego. Christ is therefore no man, and no man is Christ. This Divine Christ Spirit shall in time withdraw from lower worlds and recede into the Ineffable Spheres of Love and Mercy. Then the earth world and lower universes shall be no more.

Once we become immersed in Its Sacred Stream, we realize *Nirvana* is not the ultimate goal, but a point of attainment on our long journey back to God. Neither is the seventh heaven of the spiritualist the end of the voyage, but a resting point in the interval of time. The Pure Worlds of

God that lay beyond heaven and hell have yet to be attained; and are conquered by that special breed of souls who are unafraid to plumb the depth, breadth and heights of their own being.

Eventually most souls shall reach the pinnacle of Spiritual Heights and merge with God. However, not becoming *one* with God as widely presumed, but reassimilated into the Magnificent Being of the Sacred Father.

We often wonder why it takes so long to receive God-Realization, why we sometimes go around in the same circle, or *Cycle*, and why we cannot reach our goal directly? Because lessons are to be learned along the way that build in us a strong, reliable character and a solid spiritual foundation. In matters of God, as in life, we are the apprentice before we become the journeyman and then the master.

Consciousness is not intellect, though intellect is the offspring of Supreme Intelligence. A completely unlearned man can become a Spiritual Master, while a superintelligent man may never reach divine unfoldment, since his worship is geared to fine words and eloquent speech, but not to the humility Spirit requires. Robert D. Owen wrote: "The worship of words is more pernicious than the worship of images."

MANY MANSIONS

As you begin to live above the energy of human strife and yield your energy to higher causes, you will no longer dwell on the grand or ugly of the world. For you have attained the state of inner harmony and balance, where nothing can bear down on you that was not predestined.

You will perceive some happenings as needful, but illusive shadows and realize more and more you are the inlet and outlet through which Divine Power flows. Thus you become the do-er, the knower and the discerning thinker, the great director of your life.

Soul moves progressively inward, through many mansions of consciousness. From the lowest to the highest each is more expansive than the last, until you pass through the final gate and won the just fight. To attain positive results in your life you should develop superconscious thinking. Superconscious thought moves energy into prospering directions. All of life moves by Its Energy.

YOU ARE IN CHARGE

In whatever circumstance you may find yourself right now, is the mansion or room *of your choice*. You *can* change it! Nothing can keep you from moving out (or on) to occupy a more peaceful space if this is what you truly want. There is no such a thing as "I can't!" But there is always that famous: "I don't care to!" which is also your choice. Granted, life can be ridiculous, to say the least, but even if you see no immediate solution — don't give up. Anyone can do that without effort. God commanded man to "till the ground". So you simply change your *attitude,* move into that new state of mind and activate it to the hilt with joy and happiness. As energy follows thought, all good will follow. It's much like buying a new house, furnishing it, and imbuing it with *your* vibrations and making it *home*!

You can awaken this new state of mind with new, wonderful, forming ideas, this is how dreams come true, you know. Now, you can remove yourself physically, but wherever you go you take your thoughts and feelings with you. So you change your mind about old or present conditions, about inharmonious relationships too, and move into the territory of a happy, more fruitful life. Only when you have given your very best and you can see no solution to manifest peace should you remove yourself physically. Turn from harmful people. You owe it to yourself. Happiness is the Thought of God for you, nothing less will suffice.

People with attitude problems would do well to distant themselves mentally from perplexing conditions. From a more relaxed viewpoint, nothing is as dire as it appears. But at times we find people would rather suffer their miseries than giving up material conveniences, since it would mean standing on their own feet.

And too, individuals that *do* gather up the courage and

move to new quarters may find they are no better off. Their new surroundings still feel unlovely and peculiar, because their negative state of mind remained with them. You might be surprised how sunny the worn down homestead becomes when you begin to love, appreciate and understand yourself and change your attitude about life in general.

Though your old walls may have seen a thousand tears and sniffles and listened to the moans of the heart, your vibrations of joy and happiness will make it a blessed place to be, and make of old stumbling blocks a fortress of Light and Peace. But without willingness of mind, soul can do nothing, for mind reigns in the material world and soul in the boundless state of God. And if the room is poor, it can then be no Mansion in the Father's House — even though it exists in it.

Consciousness means activity on every level: physical, mental and spiritual. And even if you decided to sleep your troubles away, consciousness remains alert, never sleeps and life goes on all the same. So you may well gather up the forces, envision a bright future, *and make it happen*!

There is no retreat from life here or Beyond. No sooner you move energy into action, substance takes form on visible and invisible planes. Whether out of duty or love, man works for what he gets. Nothing is freely given. Life is a constant exchange of energy, flowing in and out of itself. It is up to each and every one of us to create our own happiness.

CONSCIOUS SENSING AND SOUND

All of creation is imbued with the Dynamic Vibrations of Divine Love. All life is sentient on conscious and unconscious levels. The water rushes and rambles downstream and feeds the lives within its tenement by mothering instinct. Flowers turn their face towards the sun, sensing the warmth and strength of the Light. The outstretched branches of trees feel the force of the wind; plants sense danger, animals answer to scent and sound. Now think of

Soul, the True You. Your sentient nature can touch every level of consciousness Above and below. It is sentient for always.

Soul smells the Perfume of Spirit, perceives the Unseen Presence and energy vibrations of earth and Cosmos. It hears the Sound of its inner worlds and responds to the Call. All of life is constantly nourished by the Brilliant Sound. If the Sustaining Source withdrew, life in every universe and world would cease. All would dissolve into matter, and matter would again decompose into atoms and return to its primordial state. But since the Holy Sound is the Living Force of God, life is forever.

Now, when your energy declines and you feel spent for days, it is often because you need conscious attunement to the revitalizing Sound Current. But even as the earth must be barren before it can become fruitful, so it is that souls become barren too, that the Fruits of God may manifest; which are life, exuberance, vitality, health, peace and deep joy.

The Power that illumines the limitless Ocean of Conscious Life, is the Order of Peace and Love that emanates from the Center of Itself. Every human being and every living thing are constantly replenished by the Force that resides within each form as a sun. When you become weary and tired, turn your thoughts inward and rest under the Umbrella of your Shining Sun-Self for awhile. Consciously absorb its energizing rays and see them flow through your whole being and you will find yourself restored to balance and strength.

So long as you believe in the solidity of matter you are controlled by it. But when you look at things as being subliminal, they immediately become plyable, flexible and yielding, you see, then you can shape things to your liking. You can help yourself greatly by transcending the mind *beyond* the restlessness of earth into the High Reaches of Spiritual Life; where you rediscover your independence and that nothing is freer than the *Soul*.

CONSCIOUS UNION

Life prepares us for conscious union with God. It is the greatest blessing a human being can receive while on earth. The realization of conscious *Oneness* spells one simple, dynamic word: *Love*, and Love is what you're all about! It brings you to the point where incompleteness gives way to Completeness, that the individual will emerge victoriously from all that kept him bound. Conscious union with God is a *gradual* attainment, received after many lifetimes of ardent preparations, thus rules out the now or never attitude of religious thought. This Divine Union is the end of courtship, but wedding between soul and God. The decision of this brave, forward thrust is critical. For in the split second of inner receptivity, when man opens himself wholly to God, His Spirit has already entered. Divine Union is consumated as bursts of Blinding Brightness flash across the face of the soul by the impact and Splendor of Awakening Light. From then on nothing remains the same and soul can never turn back without great suffering. The Heavenly Spirit that is here, there and everywhere — has incorporated it into Its Being.

The magnetic moment when this privilege occurs and the *conscious* soul and Superconscious Spirit reunite, is a great event and celebration in which all heavenly forces delight. Words do not suffice to explain the happiness. But until this momentous occasion is met, inner conflicts resurface as human conditions, life after life, death after death.

The realization of God is the state of being in which *facts* replace beliefs and fruitless point of views. In this Consciousness Christ is God-Principle manifest to the soul. '*I Am Consciousness, I Am Light, I Am God Principle* flowing through my total being.' It brings you to realize: *I Am* born of the Radiant Uncreated. Therefore, I am not earthly — but heavenly. And this *I Am*.

To shed the worn out husk of old beliefs can be unsettling, like moving out of a comfortable homestead into the cold. The old belief felt warm and good since there was nothing to worry about but a hell, maybe a heaven, that by some act of grace would be provided, perhaps denied. Besides, a personal saviour would take care of it all. But now you are faced with genuine responsibility to yourself and to others for your every word, thought and action. You also realize that God will not help until you have crossed the limits of helping yourself. Whereas before the protective cloak of indoctrination forbade the intrusion of Higher Ideas and possibility of your deeper awakening to God, this has now changed.

I used to say: "I love you God, though all hell lay inbetween!" When the Voice replied: "Come hither!" and I followed the Call, the raging sea was stilled. It proved I was the captain of my ship, that was mine alone to navigate back into the Harbor of God, and by no one else. A weak soul is dominated by others, a strong soul finds its own way. And I could not exchange what now was mine, for all the vague hopes and broken promises of old beliefs, and unsure destinies, nor for one glance back to the endless, wasted hours in which I tried to manifest what was not in my power to bring forth. Wishing, hoping, and in blind 'faith believing' were replaced by the Reality of God — on my way through many mansions.

THE SOUL

Until soul can accept the help of God's Holy Spirit it remains a pawn on the chessboard of life. It is either manipulated and moved by the will of others or can move itself into sound directions. The secret of independence is self-honesty, tolerance, mental balance and unswerving trust in the Power that directs our lives.

The principles of soul are simple. Soul exists because God loves it. You *are* because God *Is*. The divinity of soul does not refer to the personal ego, but to the spark of Empyreal Ego residing within.

Thus, the immortal part of soul is the *Spirit* of the ego that permeates the ethereal filaments and the form of man. Soul is nothing you possess, *it is what you are*.

And so, we find spiritualized souls and others who hold no interest in regeneration, who can become so hardened as to never regain the divine estate. We should seek the Initiatory Light that mellows the mind to responsiveness and opens the channels to the Sound Current. Then as one body is imbued with heavenly likeness, so are the corresponding forms simultaneously regenerated, including the physical body. We should desire to know God above all else.

THE HEART OF THE MATTER

Matter, (your body) is the vehicle of the soul, and soul is the vehicle of the manifested Spirit. Thus matter is the shadow of Spirit, so to speak, but spiritual in substance as it is composed of celestial molecules and atoms. There is no dead matter anywhere, here or beyond.

The Divine *I Am* is your true, permanent Self, the personal 'I am' is the transient lower ego or personality. In the true identity of soul, there is no birth, or death, or rebirth. There is only *"I"*, for God cannot be born or reborn. Birth, death and rebirth belong to the unfinished self, the personality.

When you awaken to God you find you are not the body, emotion or pain, but the soul. Experiencing conscious union with God, you become fully aware that you are no longer the soul, but the Light Itself.

TRUE POWER

The nature of soul is consciousness, that evolved through the consciousness of every lower kingdom and form, until it entered the human body and became endowed with the divine spark. The survival of soul is nothing supernatural but natural. Thus it is nothing to be prayed for, but should be pursued through right living and spiritual being. The only place you can ever be truly safe, secure and free is *within*. All becomes so simple when it is right.

Everyone wants power for whatever reason or intention. True power is of the soul, because the indwelling spark is the Parent Light and only channel through which true power and knowingness manifest. Thus God is His Own Channel, none other is needed, and *Soul* is the True Disciple, not the personality or man. Wrote Pittacus: "The measure of man is what he does with power."

True power issues out of the Sound Current. Power means nothing when you don't know how to use it and it becomes a destructive tool. What good would it do if you possessed all the power of the universe and could not control your energy, circumstances and life? Concerning power, the Invisible Master once said to me:

> "You cannot have power until the lesser self has been mastered and made pure; until then you have only energy. You must desire power more than anything else."

THE NATURE OF THE SOUL

The nature of the unfolding soul is not purely divine, since its fabric still belongs to the universe of matter. However, the divine soul is birthless, deathless, eternal. Even if ill-fated, it never dies, because God cannot die. The seeking soul must be redeemed by the 'Power of the Blood' — which is the *Word* or Power of the Sound Current, and not the blood of Jesus the man. When soul no longer seeks the cross, it will find its crown! Then it will draw its strength and vitality from the Cysterns of Eternal Life and separate itself from the maelstrom of mundane living. For it has found greater pleasures, a deep interest in the Spiritual Life and its Home in God.

The primordial Nature of God is *Neuter*, therefore the *essence* of soul is neuter, sexless, neither male or female. Once merged into the Conscious Bond with God, there then occurs a gradual branching off from human sexuality. This does not imply the human becomes sexless, for he is human, but that the total being, human *and* divine become more and more spiritualized by the Neuter Aspect, that at the same time transmutes sexual energy into Divine Power.

In lower worlds 'He made them male and female' — for

the sole intent of procreation. If all were of one gender there would be no humanity nor forms provided to embody incoming souls. Without *positive* masculine energy infusions, there could be no foilage, no beauty in nature and no animals to enjoy. Thus would be no ascent of man or species. Involution and evolution would end.

Now, when married individuals turn from sexual union because they feel they are too good or too *spiritual*, they are nowhere near Truth and asking for trouble. The energy will find an outlet. Many become victims of self-abuse, perverse activities and paranoia, not to speak of the shambles their irrationality leaves behind.

We might also consider another just as important fact. When the body is no longer capable of procreating and the *lust* of sex — that essentially begins in the mind remains uncontrolled, impudent energies devoid of ability to recreate, congregate in various parts of the body. When crystallization sets in, they manifest as tumors and cancers, and not necessarily in the reproductive organs.

THE PROVERBIAL SLUMP

Unconcerned with his fate, man aligns himself to the flow of astral vibrations that keep him restless and harrass him from within and without. The pressure of these vulgar energies keep the personality immersed in the lowlife mores of evil, until this is all it knows, and loses the way that would lead out of the circus.

We follow blindly the dictates society ascribes; drink, make merry and dance to the lowest tune of the pied piper. Until we grow deaf to the Inner Voice, blind to spiritual being and suffer from barrenness of soul when the Light has finally gone out of it. But when soul decides to get out of its transient entanglements, it will remove from the mind all lesser allurements and pull it up into the Higher Ideals of Inner Life.

By nature of the divine self we feel the pressure of the Force urging us Godward to reunite with Our Source. In this we have to face Truth in many ways, that will challenge our old beliefs and habits at every turn to move us into right directions.

As we move deeper into God-Reality we begin to release our grip from the unreality of a personal God, *personal* saviour and personal power, because we now move towards the Infinite Lord. When you know God, then you no longer need the crutch of saint, guru and master, for you are free and have it all.

The consequences of swashbuckling back and forth from old fantasies to newfound Truth can be nervewrecking. But by and by, you find stability in the Inner Teachings of the Invisible Lord and realize the only part of you that can truly be happy and satisfied is the *Soul*.

Every one on earth is a spiritual being, even though not all wish to accept this truth. Because man is intuitive he responds more readily to the energy of love than to the verbal and silent demands of others, who infringe on his privacy, right, will and freedom. And it is certain, when souls of like esteem meet, there will be a spiritual bond between them that nothing in the world can divide. Millions of individuals around the Globe are reuniting in brotherhood, advancing together towards their Infinite Goal; because the Electronic Lifestream of Divine Power pulls them upward and inward to hasten the ascent.

God and soul are inseparably *one*, that is to say, the essence of God and soul comprise the unit. Soul seeks God because He is its Parent. When its latent powers awaken, soul is then all powerful. Regardless of mortal conditions and diverse circumstances, soul does *not* belong to the minority but *Is* the Majority, for it is all of humanity and all humanity is itself. And it *will* survive and reach God no matter what may be said of it, and no matter how often the preacher who tries to save the lost and fallen — sends it to hell.

True, faithful souls submit to no one but their Maker. In God, soul grows all wise. True souls accentuate the positive side of the human spirit and envision a great future, while others envision failure and dismal conclusions. No matter how severely superimposed pressures may tug and pull to strip the soul of its innate will and freedom it grows by them and will not budge an inch, nor bend, nor compromise its principles.

You *are* God's Best Beloved, Blessed Reader, destined to become as strong as your Divine Roots. Can the lower mind forever bind you? How long can psychic manipulators oppress the soul? until they finally touch and set off the *dynamic* spark that has the magnitude and explosive power to destroy the world. For it is God. Once the soul has bathed in the Living Current of Sound and Light and has been cleansed thereby it becomes the Current Itself. Then man is no longer the mortal weakling the ignorant surmise, but has become the Power. Soul is energy because God is Energy. Energy is the Force of Creation and of the Soul.

"TO THINE OWN SELF BE TRUE"

. . . then thou canst not be false to any man," said the Great Seer. When you can behold the Radiant Image reflecting from the center of all things, you will then see through matter as well as through people. Demagogues declare it is wrong to feel, to intuit' and to heal. . . and that you should think as little as possible! Which gives them the edge. Not so! Feeling, loving, simplicity, intuitiveness, exuberance, independent being and clear discerning thought are the way of the soul.

Morticians of society and spiritual leaders insist their actions should not be considered, but their *point of view*. Would we not agree that man's actions *ensue* from his point of view? While claiming to have direct and specific instructions *from God* on how they should run His universe — and *You*, their sins climb out of their pockets and down from the pulpit to announce themselves to the world. People who operate outside of the Law of God and outside of the Law of man are heading for trouble. When the hollow laughter of the world recedes into a faint echo, perhaps they may wish to have placed their esteem on more solid ground.

Bookshelves are stacked with volumes that advise how to

submit yourself: body, mind and treasure. Time seems of the essence to talk it over and pen down how *not* to submit, to maintain your individuality and self-control. Our message is strong, direct and clear: *The direct Path to God, the Way!* The Spirit of God is the Master.

Now, anything that defies convention and untruth inspires sharp protest. If by any measure the power of the pen sets the record straight, expressing what millions of people think but are afraid to say, they call it "anticorruption hysteria" — since man's lower ego loves surrender to anything that will keep his job, false self-image and bank account in tact.

Whether we like it or not, you have an overriding responsibility to yourself. When you take care of yourself and bow to no man, you carry out the Will of God. Earth-bound thinking, repulsion and attraction are the hallmarks of the lower mind and are left behind when the Invisible Lord infills the soul with Truth and opens the Portals to His Heart.

THE WAY TO THE KINGDOM

Your unlimited freedom is recognized when you begin to leave the body at will. Out-of-body movement is not difficult or mysterious. When you go to sleep and often while daydreaming, the soul separates itself from the body and re-enters it upon awakening. The difference is you should be able to do so while fully conscious. To the seeking heart it is no great feat. Since it deeply desires to know God it will enter the experience without fear.

The encounter is natural and manifests to everyone when progress warrants it. Then souls are carried inward by the Sound Current and enter Its Worlds. While in soul-body you are very alert, your senses are clear and bright. You know exactly where you are at all times and bring your findings back into every day reality. The experience attests to what is and makes an end to disbelief and clash of opinions. Truth needs no defense. We need to rediscover our roots in the Father. Not imaginative ones, no — *real* roots. God is only a myth to those who don't know him. And you will find, His Light need not shine on you through someone else. It shines on you directly. The proof you seek is within you.

Though the velocity of out-of-body travels is such that at times you feel as at a standstill, you feel comfortable, joyful and secure as can be. The ground beneath your feet is compact, but at times you are more airborne since you advance by the force and shifting energy of your spirit and will. The freedom is immeasurable!

Soul travel still belongs to lower worlds. Timetravel ends when you move beyond Spiritual Highlands where True Soul Awareness begins and movement is no longer necessary. Fully aware, you are conscious of any world you turn your thoughts to, therefore in all places at once; for this is where God is — everywhere! — even as in similar way a developed individual can appear in more than one place at the same time while on earth.

Timetravel is no more than a shift of consciousness from one place, plane or world to another. Now, you can shift your energy current from here to Peru, or to sunlit heaven worlds, receive a clear picture image and perhaps find yourself there for a few short moments, that is, as far as the shift of consciousness goes. But beholding and short visits differ from leaving lower worlds behind entirely.

Now, the purpose of out-of-body consciousness is to become God-realized, since "flesh and blood cannot enter the kingdom of God". Then indeed will you have conquered the greatest milestone of all, and nothing will ever again bind you below or Above. Freedom is within yourself, it is the only place you *can* be free — no matter where you are.

DREAM, DARE AND DO

God Realization is an experience you must live to know. From then on you will be able to speak from the heart of experience and your every word will carry power and ring true. Other individuals can readily discern whether what you speak of is *absolutely* true, or if you memorized it from a book. Because there is an interconnection between all souls where Truth is everpresent. Many who teach the Way cannot enter the High Country because they are afraid to step into Its Freedom. How can they, not knowing God — teach others?

The Love of the Invisible Spirit makes total transcendence possible. Living in both worlds you begin to balance your energy and shift your force from one conscious state to another. Until we can enter inner worlds consciously, we will always draw inaccurate conclusions. Fearful souls linger at the Promenades of Cosmos, and never move far enough into the Lands of Light to know the difference, but it is a certain start.

Why should we become mortified when the body becomes weightless and we feel disembodied, when in the end we will leave it the same way? Our true nature *dwells* in the weightless state. Would it not be better to go through the experience and find there is nothing to fear than to fear the final event for a lifetime? We should stop looking at the scenery through the windows of the soul, do and dare — and walk right into the sunny scenery of Our Father's Country.

To the seeker whose sincere interests have turned to God, out-of-body experiences occur spontaniously and under the **Super Vision** of the Guiding Force. A brand new life and worlds of Unknown Love begin to reveal themselves to him, for which the individual will risk all, give all and for which every other dream is gladly forfeited. Then the soul yearns to return to its inner worlds again and again. It will pursue God with all its love and strength, and all the fortitude it never knew it had comes into play. The battle between Light and Darkness has been won, self-mastery attained, and every milestone to God conquered.

Throughout this book, we speak of *You*, the timeless soul, the most precious of all beings. My Dear Reader, if you are not yet aware of your splendid worth, please do so now!

6.

The Art of Creating Abundance

The universe you live in is permeated by living vibrations and composed of spiritual matter, that you can control, form and mold according to your needs. Since soul itself is a manifested vibration, and you are *Soul*, you can accelerate its creative power to hasten results or remain on idle. You are a being of Love, Intelligence and Power. Your creative ability is unlimited, and you can imbue your practical life with equal beauty and abundance.

The secret to creating abundance is impersonal giving. Love has no conditions and you cannot outgive God. On deeper levels the thinker must become the knower, for in knowingness there is no division. Then nothing will be impossible to you. The keys to creativity are trust, hope, enthusiasm, envisionment and change. When ambiguous, our thoughts and wishes are in opposition and we keep searching for solutions instead of living the answer! And what are you going to get when your efforts do not match your dream? You cannot live on expectations, but you *can*-make dreams come true. God never says *No*.

DREAM AWAY

Daydreaming creates wonders, but people who enact their fantasies get caught up in the net of illusions. Fantasy directs thought to outward things, daydreaming is creative on inner levels and manifests desired results in your outer world. Whatever you wish for, live it, be it! — whether it is material or God. You shall have it.

Where some wish or *envision* too hard, others do not envision enough. But have you ever noticed when you finally ran out of patience and gave up, how your wish suddenly manifested in your life even though you no longer wanted it? When you remove your attention and release your dream, creative energy goes out and manifests form. True creativity never clutches after things, it lets go. People who cling and hord usually end up liquidating out of need.

CREATING EFFECTIVELY MAKES DREAMS COME TRUE

When desperate or under pressure you cannot create anything, since your attention will shift to lack and thereby defeat the purpose. To create effectively, relax, let go and employ patience.

All great minds were evolutionists and reincarnationists. They knew the secret of creativity and succeeded because they beheld a greater vision, not only for themselves but for all mankind. They succeeded because their thoughts were constructive, therefore creative. They held no interest in wishful emotionalism. Their minds were far too attained to the work at hand and inventions that fully captured their attention. Thus they kept their minds fixed on each task and saw them through to the end. Their innovation carried them to the heights of achievements. You can do the same.

Your good should be envisioned, anticipated, invited and accepted with the same inner joy as though it were already present — before it can be yours. See the *clear cut* image of your desire with unwavering trust that it will manifest. And it is certain, when your ideals magnify the best in you, you will attain what you creatively set forth.

This is why the Ancient Adepts placed no importance on possessions. They not only used this method, but became the thing itself they wished to produce. They knew the mystery of materializing substance whenever it was needed and in this same way they manifested supplies to the poor and needy not only in deed, but also by projecting to them abundant, all-supplying *thought*.

Envisioning high ideals and ideas replenish the soul and supply its earthly needs. Lofty ideas enable you to work with a happy heart, instill to you inner calmness, new incentives and the purposefulness that makes life worthwhile. Your creative thoughts attain to the high spiritual ethers that lay *beyond* positive and negative worlds, where you recognize the Giver, the Source of all actions and control of all things. But experiencing the heights of creative worlds, you might also decide to disregard what you previously set out to gain, and seek treasures permanent in nature, which include health, deep satisfaction and peace of heart. In the consciousness beyond time and space all things are made new and your material stability will reappear on its own accord. Incorporating spiritual thought into your mental patterns you begin to create in the consciousness of *Now*, rather than in weary, lack producing states of mind.

KNOW — AND CREATE

When you think of the energy expended during working hours and how *hard* some things are to get, we might take time to think a little less and create more. When results do not coincide with what you set forth, you may be certain you will receive something much better, while othertimes you will find your creations manifesting all at once.

Before you enter contemplation, clearly define the form or the condition you desire, and *follow through* on this current to build the archtype.

In order that your objectives may become perfect externalizations, you begin by clearing the mental screen of all images. In other words: make your mind a blank, from which you will envision and project. To push negative thoughts out is useless, since another string of thoughts will replace them. Simply raise your thoughts higher and the mental force field will be clear. Uplifted thought moves from Ideal to Ideal by which aspirations are fulfilled and come into fruition.

THE LIGHT THAT NEVER FAILS

Now, as you look to the blank screen of the mind and shift your attention to the vast sea of creative energy, you will feel increasingly removed; and begin to concentrate on the slowly dawning Light of the mental world. If you do not see this Light, be not dismayed, it is present whether you see it or not.

You will now perceive a vibrant stillness all about and the soft emanation of a dazzling brightness begins to surround you. From this vantage point in limitless Creative Spheres you begin to use your imaging power to mold and shape *Above* what you wish to manifest in your world below. If you form the mental picture and *clear cut* image of your objective it will appear in your world when the creative cycle is completed. The process is much simpler than it sounds. I have employed this method all my life and it works!

Now, when you cast your mental images upon the Creative Sea, you must also envision them in full detail. See the scenery, people, or whatever your objective in vivid, living colors and in action as though you were watching a movie. Think it, feel it, hear the conversations, infuse everything with vitality and life; and then step right into the spectacle, into the scenery, and get involved in the activity.

Keep moving, feast your eyes and dream away. You are now in soul body, but the moment you think yourself back you re-enter waking awareness. This is dynamic creativity in action. It will prove to you that all things you *truly want* are attainable. Nothing is impossible when you disallow others to dishearten and dissuade you. *You are* the answer. You can live it beginning right now. You can go as far as your willingness can take you. There is no limit to what you can achieve and you can only fail when you cease to try.

Creative visualization also applies to your deeper, spiritual life. While in soul body you can ask the Guiding Force to take you deeper into Its Kingdoms. This It will do.

Your desire to meet the Invisible Master can be fulfilled. When you envision His Radiant Form standing at the Door of the Soul, it will bring you into His Presence.

THE KEY WORD IS SILENCE AND TRUST

You may create as many images as you desire, but *one at a time*. Remember too: energy creates *and* dissipates! So you should not speak of your joyful creations to anyone, then "the Father who hearest in secret will reward you openly." Human nature is envious and selfish. You will find, when you shout your secrets to the world, the world will put a lid on it and you will materialize nothing. When you no longer desire the approval of others, it will be easy to keep silent and you will reach your goals unhampered. Do not go back to remodel your creations, let them be correct the first time. Know what you want, act on it and commit yourself fully to each task. Concentrate on *your* success and not on negative characters who say you are a failure and try to fasten you to their sinking anchor. Rather than stress producing envisioning and constant desiring, keep end results in mind. Every now and then, bring them back into clear focus — and let go.

In doing so, you cast your nets (or thoughts) to the *Other Side* and walk upon the Waters of Spirit (energy and trust). It's quite simple, when you dream away and *let go* of the thought. Then your energy will go out and create for you. Creative Energy sets up an all-productive magnetic field in your life. The more your thoughts rest in God, the greater your surrounding force field will be charged with spiritual power. Place no time limit on your projects; nature works in her own methodical way. Wrote D. G. Mitchell: "There is no genius in life like the genius of energy and action."

Some call visions devilish and imagination profane, yet they are using it every day in one mode or another. Only scepticism can haze man's sight from beholding the pure, clear images of God. When you can see good in all things, visions become divine. And even as God spoke to Moses: "Thy good shall come before thee", so will your good appear before *you* when the mind is free of derision, and you will behold all that is beautiful and guiding. Spiritual sight attunes us to Wonders we may have otherwise never known. Divine Truth is perceived within. You learn within the soul. Only then can the mind cease its reasoning and wrangling, and submit to the Spirit of God for inward changing to receive its good.

I AM IS ABUNDANCE

The energy of visualization is creative vibration that molds substance. Malicious vibrations destroy. You, as *soul,* are the attributing principle of all substance. The things you want are already in your life. When you can realize that Abundance is always here and now, you will manifest the 'impossible dream'. You should not think want or need, for your thoughts will attract both. All good comes to you when you come into harmony with its principles. In my experience I found, when you no longer *need* the world and its things, trinkets and people will beat a path to your door.

Before you enter the vibrant solitudes of Creative Spheres, know *I Am is God*. Then say to yourself: *"I Am Abundance!"* It is the Key Word that opens the channels to receiving it and brings you into unity with the Creative Principle.

"I Am Abundance, I Am Success, I Am Creative Principle Flowing Through Me, I Am God Harmony, God is I." From the center of these dynamic affirmations abundance will pour into every avenue of your life; when your thoughts are free of doubt and your words are spoken with authority and in full trust. Why? Because they draw energy from the Central Sun of Creation, that forms the powerful protoplasm which is the basis of life and matter. You may be certain whatever good you 'cast upon the waters' will return to you as does everything else.

We already know man has to 'earn his bread by the sweat of his brow'; but sometimes you sweat profusely and nothing at all lives up to your expectations nor need! And though failure can be quite constructive, weeping never endured and not trying again or not at all is graver than both. To be rich, you must think rich, fertile thoughts and establish a *continuity* of clear thinking. It is the way by which you remain in unity with the Principle of Abundance and with the Father's All-Prospering Thought for *you*! This is the secret of every success. I can tell you it works!

TO HAVE OR NOT!

Feast, famine, occasional outright poverty, the school of swift kicks and veiled help of the unwilling, quickly taught me how to manifest substance from within. Lack, pinpointedness and determination pushed open the door to higher creativity. Even though reluctantly at first, the good I sought had no choice but to appear in my outer world, for I applied unrelenting *Trust* and necessity gave wings. As I never believed in halfhearted measures, I flung my thoughts higher than the sky and anchored them securely in the deep, magical Life of Spirit to let them rest. In turn all good imbued my life with such enormous bounty it might have astonished the wise. But I also knew to revert my cornucopia of blessings back to the Loving Source, thus into my work.

Since I never believed in giving out but a slice of bread, I threw in the whole bin. Though at intervals supplies would run low and some days were drier than the desert, another avalanche of abundance already made its way around the corner. At times, instead of projecting more creativity I would simply sit down and make a balance sheet, figuring out how I would distribute the next profusion of Good. By and by, the wisdom of Archimedes held true for me: "Give me where to stand and I shall move the ground." And so will *You*.

To receive and keep over one's immediate needs becomes stagnation. Your assigned bounty must benefit the whole. I never sought success itself, but to give my best to tasks at hand that would pour out more Light to others. This of course grants a great deal more of inner satisfaction, than success as the world concedes. Somehow I outgrew the need for worldly things, but craved to know the equanimity and peace that would be mine in life and beyond death. And even though I sang unhappy tunes at times and grumbled all the way, when I searched out the cause of hurtful things — the finger pointed back to my own attitude. So, who is perfect?

But I did learn, that instead of throwing out my thoughts and let them toss about like aimless corks on the troubled waves of life, I could correlate them into full-fledged scenes and dream away. This removed all weariness of mind and created what I desired and in my view — deserved! If I didn't like myself, what would?

Haphazard thinking, unorganized thought and half-idealism create unwanted conditions. But you know, sometimes you come to the fork in the road where you are forced to think right whether you want to or not.

Eventually you will find that neither negative *nor* positive thinking are the answer, but that spiritual knowingness is. Negative thoughts bring negative results. Positive thinking merely swings the pendulum in the opposite direction. And by nature of the negative polarity that rules our world, the pendulum must swing back and thoughts become negative again. But spiritual knowingness is all-creative.

Now, if your thoughts are inconsistent, hazy and uncertain, so will your life be. It is within your power to let your thoughts soar high and to infill your life with vitality and purpose. In this world of shifts and changes, little can affect you when you say to yourself: "I can do anything; I can do it well and do it now!" What harm done? Hold this ever before you: you are original, extraordinary, and unique. There is no one else like *you*! When you believe in yourself, thus in God, no one in all the world can deprive you of the good you deserve, but you must *feel* deserving before it can be yours. And *it will be yours* in measure of your acceptance. What is it within us that makes us feel insignificant? Certainly not God Who loves you and says: "*I Am* is you, you are perfect, dynamic and successful!"

DREAMING AND WISHING

Now, some people have no ambition for success, while others kill themselves in the process. True success is never hurried, but gathers momentum when you have inner peace. Some fritter away precious time and whine "O promise me!" or "I wished I had!" unknowing *they* must create the condition to gain the desire. If energy does not go out, what can return? You can make your life beautiful and fruitful, but if we think it is not worth it, who else cares? And if your life is happy and free of cares and the heart is not filled with God, it is empty and wanting just the same.

At times people complain that they lack education and are therefore poor. Now, if circumstances denied you education, then think of the scholar who works from nine to five, and of another individual with barely formal learning whose natural inventiveness made him a millionaire. The difference between the two is creative thinking and sound reason, called common sense. Though by itself reason is blind, inner seeing and sensing endow the mind with superior reasoning power.

Creativity is birthless, deathless. When you say you can't, you are already defeated. Best of all, creativity frees you of dependency, since you realize you don't have to beg for what is already yours. Tokens and gifts have fangs. Gifts turn into emotional flogs and place you into unwanted indebtedness. Very few kindnesses are genuine and Godsend.

Creative energy permeates all life. As it flows down from shoreless spheres it is received by Cocreative Spirits and the elements of nature, by the soul, and manifests through creative minds on earth. No force can block its flow, no magic can reroute it, because *it is*.

In creativity alone is man free to do as he wishes, and his creations determine his character and the conditions of his life. Once the mind assimilates the creative power of the soul, to think and act negatively becomes a double edged sword. For man's contradictory energy will then be equal to the power of the forces that now do his bidding. Emotions must be kept under control. An awakened, but unbridled individual can destroy whatever comes into his range of fire. For the Light that awakens also stirs up and invigorates the latent, negative energy, that, if not lifted up, becomes a devil on the rampage.

More truth can be found observing the *inner* life of a person, than in his behavior and words. No book could ever reveal as much. A book is an echo of the inner man by whom it was written and what he is reflects from every page. If we would read the pages our lives comprised, we would be amazed how far we have come out of our pasts, how close we have drawn to God — and how much more is yet to conquer.

LOVE IN ACTION

True success means to be useful to the whole. Everyone on this planet has something to contribute. What can be more valuable than the gift of yourself? — the loving, sharing and understanding extended to others? Self-giving brings us into the peace and vibrancy of Spiritual Life. Selfishness moves us from caprice to caprice. Self-giving imbues our inner forms with celestial radiance and moves us into the creative stream of the Sound Current.

What may seem to you a small, humble token, often holds great significance in the Unknown. I remember an incident during the last war, when an old woman handed me a crust of rye bread, she generously spread with rendered goose-lard, since there was no butter. Now, this might gag the spoiled palate, but is a delicacy when you are starving. More than fifty years later I still remember it clear as anything. I blessed that stranger for the all my life. And I recall times when in mortal danger, how persons jeopardized their safety in exchange for mine. How much more than my thankfulness must be their blessings in the Unknown. But I've also met the other kind that squeezed back out more than there was to give. It's always the motive and what the *heart* extends that truly count. A token from a great heart is always crowned with blessings.

Life is energy in motion, a perpetual outpouring of creative Love that flows back into Its Own Being. Nothing remains on throttle. There is always something to do and see to, but also a time to relax your efforts, when you sit by the Heavenly Candle to receive enlightenment; or go out of doors into the flourishing atmosphere of nature to bathe in the revitalizing, moving Force of God.

Each day of your life is a new episode in the increment of time, that dissolves the wreckage of yesterday's futile self-promise. Each new day should be met with new enthusiasm, optimism and *realism*. Yes, optimism is a very necessary condition in our life, as is the objectivity and realism to see things clearly.

To be truly creative and successful, let go of every element of self-hypnosis and of the vulnerability to negative influences. At daybreak, when the world is new and bright, face each day with new resolve, with a healthy outlook and highest expectations of good. Make time for yourself. Become increasingly aware of the creative force within you, that gives concrete form to your noble wishes and creations. *Accept* the clear vision of a love-filled, healthy, prosperous, uplifted life. In every moment acknowledge God's Presence: "*I Am God. . .* the Holy One in midst of thee." - Hosea.- And so let it be.

And while you dream to distant points beyond, I would like you to become *do-ers* in the rarest sense. When you pick up the creative thread and take no thought of what is left behind, you enter the Radiant Realities of inner worlds. Where by *your own* sight and power you behold a clear illumined image of the goodness that is yours in the *Hereness* and *Nowness* of God. Then you no longer hope, wish nor dream, but you are the soul fully conscious, that can shape all things to come. You realize the Grace that directs your life, in the finest interpretation of an ever deepening Truth.

"Sometimes when I have come to work empty,
I have suddenly become full, ideas being in an in-

visible manner showered upon me and implanted on me from on high; so that through the influence of divine inspiration I have become infilled with enthusiasm, and have known neither the place in which I was, nor those present, nor myself; for then I have become conscious of a richness of interpretation, an enjoyment of light, a most keen-eyed vision."

Ennead.- Philo.-

THE DARK SIDE OF PROSPERITY

Prosperity will bless the man who along with his good qualities can overcome his deficit of greed. To some individuals money justifies everything and they will risk life and limb to gain and maintain it. Covetness and greed steal away your strength and peace of mind. All things belong to God since they are part of His Creation. Man can claim *nothing* as his own, not even his physical form belongs to him, nor the things he worked for. This realization should instill in us gratefulness and appreciation for all that is extended to us for use. Nothing should be taken for granted.

We are stewards of substance entrusted to us. A good steward will have more than one who squanders it away. If individuals who complain they never had nor have enough would add up all that went through their life, they would find they had more than enough and to spare, but needed better management. We might need to develop *the art of using things*.

No matter how many property and land titles an individual holds, a sharp curve in destiny can remove it all at once when a lesson is to be learned. At such times the rug is constantly pulled out from under the person. On occasions, the individual must lack the most essential things in life, until he learns to recognize the *Giver*, instead of worshipping his goods, name and fame. When by fate or natural catastrophy all you own shatters and breaks up around you, what has been gained?

TO BE IN THIS WORLD BUT NOT OF IT

True Abundance is found in the Affluence of Spirit. Material good is transient as the matter of which it was formed. Earthly good is to be enjoyed, not clung to. For man to remain materially solvent he must remain an open vessel through which Abundance can perpetually flow and must be wholeheartedly capable to envision abundance for others. Mental sharing is as necessary as extending material aid, for it magnifies the Ideal of the prosperous spheres that are everywhere around us. Block the flow through selfishness or greed, and benevolence begins to overflow until the vessel is drained dry and the individual finds his assets diminished. People hate those who help them because givers flog them with their tokens and treat them shabbily, and the disgusting, emotionally abusive giver who feels his own nefariousness rebounding, hates the recipient of his 'charity'.

Now, oppression of others and greed are not necessarily rectified in the same lifetime, but become karmic debts to be repaid in future existences where the individual may find himself in poverty — questioning the reason. Abundance refers to every level of man's being: physical, emotional, mental and spiritual. It is unlikely that many reach that all-abundant state, especially since abundance has different meaning to different people. Abundance is God. To souls that realized God fully, no other abundance is sought. As you walk towards God, earthly baggage drops away, for you recognize your Source of Unfailing Supply.

Some claim: 'when you have money you can demand service', but what will you demand when the Hand of Fate plucked your pockets clean? And though the materialistic credo is: "Money is might!" — the possessor of Spiritual Truth *commands* with the Power that runs the material universe and governs all life. It is *power* that propels the soul Godward and materialism that keeps it bound. Along the way of spiritual growth it is not how *much* you learn that counts, but to understand what you know.

Covetness, anger, jealousy, greed and fear of loss, block prosperity. When good dissipates through illness or other mortal calamities, we begin to look within. Luxury breeds vanity, contempt and the perversions of drink and drugs. The body gets sick from negative drain and chemical infusions, until eating even a small portion of a meal becomes the *luxury*. What good is gold to the impoverished soul?

Used rightly, the acquisition of material good adds to man's blessedness. However, some consider money evil, instead of looking to the good it can do in their world. Whether out of fearfulness or a sense of Divine Justice, horders often bequeath their goods to charitable orders, or forfeit possessions otherwise to atone for their insurrections, lifelong deceptions and dishonesties. Thus they seek to cleanse away the stain of guilt and greed to gain Mercy. But no matter what we give away, it will not bring us to the Foot of the Invisible Lord.

Only in Him can soul be made blameless. To withdraw from materialism means nothing. God must become the *one* deep need and desire. For one is of earth, the other of the Spirit. Man is what he is, no matter *where* he is and can be no more after death than he is here and now.

THE KARMIC BALANCE SHEET

Material loss is not always due to greed, but due to individual karma, which can represent a long, drawnout process. Persons are placed into the individual's life to whom he is indebted. An individual may have great earning capacity, but funds dissipate no sooner than they appear, because out of unknown love and for obscure reasons he cannot say *no* to those who ask. Whether loss occurs due to greed or free will, both are karmic. A person does not *become* greedy and selfish, he merely awakens to the characteristics he carried along from another past, that he may now correct. Some persons eagerly want to shower others with their love and goods, when in fact deep inside they *feel* they owe and can't help giving.

And some are leaners. Fainthearted souls tend to rely on God for everything: for comfort, purging of sins, for every small detail and decision in their life. To them, the 'daily bread' does not come easy, since they forget they must go out and earn it. God's Gift to man is life. What man does with it should be his gift to God.

The divine spark within us is the imaginative faculty through which we contact Our Supreme Father and find our way back Home. Human as we are, when things go right we take the credit, when things go wrong we blame God. And if we were to give up anything, God would top our list. But man forgets that the Valiant Force that gets him out of trouble, is the Force of the Diamond Light and Brilliant Fire that gleams and shines in the sacred center of his own heart.

When we rediscover the wondrous constructive power within us and apply it to our lives, we will again learn to depend on our innate courage, inventiveness and intuitivity. Then we will forge ahead in the Trust and Love that is the very foundation of life. Only because man leans, his extended begging bowl to God or to his fellows remains empty. Save for tokens of formidable haranguers, who on second thought peer to the coin to see if it is still there! Only what man himself sets forth can return to him for multiplication.

We should rise from our place of smallness to the lofty heights of innate greatness, God imbued to every soul. We are citizens of Eternal Worlds, nourished daily by God's Quickening Love, in which we breathe, move, think, and grow rich in goodness, bounty and achievement.

> "Good is for those who strike boldly upwards, their eyes fixed on the heights, putting off those garments of defilement in which their fall has clothed them. Many times it has happened; awakened from my body into my true self; becoming outside all other things, but within myself beholding beauty beyond wonder, then, more than ever assured of communion with the Highest, established therein attainment of activity, raised above all things less than Supreme."
>
> Ennead, - Plotonius -

In the measure of all things, true success means succeeding in each given task. Nothing is unattainable when the Hand of God begins to mold it. Nothing is ever begun or finished, creativity is eternal.

We shall now delve deeper into the mysteries of life; explore our reason for being on earth and illumine the subject of Involution and Evolution.

7.

Rebirth, the Drama of Involution and Evolution

Reincarnation and Karma are interrelated and of one energy and Law. Rebirth was the doctrine of Jesus and has been taught throughout the ages by every true spiritual teacher, and by the christian forefathers. Karma consists of evil as well as righteousness and the energy of good and evil is caught up in the karmic net.

Re-embodiment is best understood when it becomes a personal experience through sudden flashbacks of past-lives or inner revelations. Since no two experiences are alike, so was mine of a different sort:

> The intense illumination of a Blinding Light flashed across my face, and in that instant scooped me out-of-body. It swept me into Eternal Worlds and brought me into a place where I could see and know all things. For that moment I became the Light and all the joy and pain of weeping creatures were part of me. And then my many pasts, the present and the future unrolled before me as an endless scroll and proved I lived before and will live on. Subsequent the vivid scenes and panoramas of the past receded, as did the Guiding Light.

ANOTHER PAST

In my book 'Journeys to Worlds Beyond', a friend described his spontaneous pastlife regression: "I must tell you of an experience, that I had when I was about twelve years old while helping my mother make grape-jelly. I was stooped over an earthen jar, using my hands to crush grapes. Suddenly I became transfixed by an indescribable sensation that gripped my whole being; there are no other words to describe adequately my feelings; the nearest I come to a description is that I felt intense quickening and a clearing of my whole being. It seemed as though a fog had momentarily parted, almost giving me the solution to an old problem — almost I could have named the country I looked upon. In the hundreth part of a second I looked, and lived, and then the rift closed to span no more. Although I was left with the baffled, helpless sensation of knowing there was much more to be experienced, this is all I retained, could grasp and examine:

> A sunlit scene in a sunlit pleasant country and myself barefooted with a white garment about my middle and shoulders, treading grapes in a circular vat. The purple juice was splashed to my knees, and then I was shut out, I was no more. The most vivid thing about this experience was that I was intensely aware, beyond hesitation or doubt that I have lived before; there was no befogged staring at the thing, for I moved as a babe to its mother's breast.

"I know the experience was authentic, the thought I am here because of my imperfections ever urges me on to live nobly. Like iron I must pass from fire to anvil and from anvil to fire before I am fine steel. I live in conditions that were part of my own making when I was last here; whatever I do to make earth a better place will be to my good when I return. . .

THE GOLDEN LADDER OF EVOLUTION

Reincarnation and Karma is the Mothering Law that corrects the soul and directs it to rightness. Every experience is built on a previous one. Past happenings take on new form. People are placed in our way to whom we are karmically tied, and problems keep repeating themselves until lessons have been learned and inharmonies resolved.

Each soul returns to the conditions of its own making, to unload the burden it heaped on itself and responds to the conditions it enters. Even as the wind moves its appointed way and worlds revolve in the perfect symmetry of Cosmic Space, the immortal soul follows its predestined path. Inevitably it finds freedom from the yoke of lower encasements and returns to God. By the Inexorable Law of Rightness, proud and haughty souls fall from their exalted estate, while humble souls find entrance to the Lands of Peace and Light.

In every lifetime a finer character is built. In each life the soul becomes more deeply aware of God and its divine heritage. Knowledge gained is never lost. All you learned before comes again into full recollection, unless the Lords of Karma deem otherwise. Whatever has been temporarily withheld will resurface after the debt has been cleared away, and you continue where you left off.

Though we can become aware of higher life from early age, inner awakening seldom occurs until the greater part of karma has been worked off. Otherwise foresight would help us to avoid what must be faced. If we doubt the possibility of reincarnation, Revelations 3:12 gives proof: "Him that overcometh will I make a pillar in the temple of my God, and he shall go out no more." What did it mean? Go out *where*? You must go out before you can come back!

Life then, is a cycle of learning, but you can govern its speed. Some work tirelessly to unravel the Mystery of God, while others find it less complicated. Re-embodiment is a golden blessing, for the human form is the only abode in which soul can meet its Lord. Life is not all sorrow and sadness, happiness abounds everywhere when you have found it in your own heart.

Emerson described the ascent in this way: "We awake and find ourselves on a stair, there are stairs below us, which seem to have ascended; there are stairs above us, many a one, which go upward and out of sight."

WHAT WILL YOU TAKE ALONG?

Since man reaps what he sows, karma is his inheritance. Sowing begins in thought, reaping takes place in body and mind. Since it is imperative for the development of the soul to go through every experience to regain its divinity, it cannot be achieved in one short lifetime. This applies to saints, to buddhas as well, and to all.

In the course of millions of existences you have been every color, belonged to every race and creed, and suffered every imaginable death. Life after life you extracted and deposited the energy of every meaningful happening, good and bad, into the soul record, that is reawakened and activated in the duration of cycles. There is no interruption at death as often believed, you live in the *One* conscious state *always*.

Though in each lifetime we change locations, vocations, and live in other realities as well, the soul never changes its immortal identity. In soul is no night, day or twilight, no past or future, only *Now*.

Some individuals claim two incarnations to the soul, others say millions. As for myself, I know with certainty I have moved in and out of this world and other planets uncountable times and remember occupying various forms. Even though some recollections leave me but fragments, others produce vivid, detailed, colorful panoramas and scenes with all participants actively involved.

LESSONS WE LEARN

Where your treasure and desires lay is the world and place you will be born into; for the energy of your thoughts and desires gravitates to the magnet that are your unfulfilled dreams and wishes. The lesson to be learned is Self-Mastery.

To get off the treadmill of reincarnation we need to redirect our energy from the transient to the Permanent Life. Now, when treasures shatter, mundane pleasures move out of sight and there is no one left to love and care for, individuals become depressed, even suicidal, since they have nothing left to cling to but inner barrenness. To dwell on suicide long enough creates a strong thought form that can manifest in some other way, when some stranger attacks and fulfills the death wish. This is evidenced when people are found knifed in some alley, strangled or shot to death for no apparent reason. Now, there is no use being depressed, life goes on just the same and there is certainly much more to live for than die for! Life goes on.

Many lessons are learned through the pain of physical attachments, but often depravation opens the door to Wisdom. While individuals claim material bliss brings peace, they lay awake nights worrying if one of sharper wit might undermine their ephemeral peace by trick or trade. Material man does not rule his world, it rules him.

Like the worship of any god of man's imagination, the money god is an earth entity of man's creation that grants his pursuer his desires. Money is good and you should have enough and to spare, but it should never become the chief objective for which every higher principle is sacrificed. It is the pursuit of excess that throws the soul into spiritual poverty. Greedy young investment bankers caught up in the inside trading scandal are good cases in point, as are religious vandals who feather their nests with the assets of the poor in heart.

Desireless living is the highest state man can attain in his life, none other can bring him to God. For his mind must first dwell in God before he can lose his desires. Attachments and desire keep the soul earthbound. Endless commercials feed your desire for luxury, entice you with delicacies to buy, eat and overeat. Man becomes ill and suffers the consequences. The next commercial tells us we're too fat, so we join the latest diet fad or hop off to the steam room to sweat it off! While the Finger of Karma keeps recording. . .! And too, tenants who take care of absolutely *nothing*, as some landlords, will find in the next cycle will be more than rent to pay and collect! The Immutable Law of

Karma permits the insensitive and uncaring to live in identical conditions they provided for others, of uncleanliness, foul odors, broken down appliances, and more — that all may learn to abide by Its Principles and Rules.

DEATH, THE REVOLVING DOOR TO NEW DESTINATIONS

To analyze the psyche and subconcious part of man anyone who deals with the subject can do. But to enter the Subconscious Life in fact, in order to properly understand and guide the conscious self takes expertness, courage and is quite another matter. And so it is with death. Unless you lived through the inevitable event through out-of-body consciousness while living, it will remain a mystery and dread.

When soul takes flight at death, it takes no thought of the worn out form and of what it left behind. Since it now has entered another world, prepares for a new life and to join another field of action; to re-enact an old play in the Grand Theater of human drama. The revolving door of death may lead to new directions, but always back to the place where the seed sown may be harvested.

For everything that dies something comes to life and all that lives reaps the energy of its own actions. To say to the Judge of Death: "I am sorry, I just didn't think!" or "Bless me Father. . ." or "I was drunk and had a blackout", and other regrets, fall on deaf ears. And are met with a cold, dispassionate look when the Judge unrolls the scroll of the past, that, since you wrote it, gives accurate account.

Now, to convince himself of his honesty, the money-grubber repeatedly claims to have accumulated his good through job loyalties and a lifetime of hard work. But the soul record, laden with indebtedness may show he cheated his employer, pilfert accounts, skimmed off where he could and lined his pockets. You can deceive others, but not the Lords of Karma.

Karma and Fate mean the same. Every deed, every thought has a purpose and a destiny and some haunt the doer wth a vengeance. Until we come to God, learn to become emotionally detached and gain spiritual balance, every mental and physical action calls for readjustment of energy equal to our deeds and silent motives. The slightest impulse manifests a reaction. We know right from wrong before we err against ourself and others.

The heinous acts of tormenting animals, disecting the fetus in the womb, the low grade lust of artificial insemination, commercial sales of human fetal tissues and spare parts for medical use; the deliberate unkindnesses we extend, failing to aid a fellow human or animal in distress, bringing children into loveless homes, buying and selling human sperms, death persecution by mortal law, how much more could be mentioned? Negative Karma is all around us. The choice is ours not to participate! Moreover, mortally rich achievements are not always morally and spiritually right. How much you accumulate is not the issue, but how it was begotten.

All social functions and every charitable action *not* rendered in selfless honesty belong to the moorings of the spiritually dead, since they are infused with desire for acknowledgement, praise and vainglory. Greed, desire and vanity becloud the mind until the veil becomes so dense the thrill of materialism appears to be the permanent and the things of God an illusion.

ATTRACTION AND REPULSION

Some transgressions affect individuals deeply. In the case of the man who raped a woman and then cut off her arms and legs, no matter where he wanted to settle the townspeople turned him away. They were repulsed by him, angry and unforgiving, because they perceived him from the soul; which weighed heavier than their opinion of him. Harsh as their judgement appeared, it was just.

Inhabitants of lower worlds are ruled by the Law of attraction and repulsion, where like attracts like and opposites repel. Each individual gravitates to vibrations equaling his own in any world. In the foregoing case, and though the man was released from prison, he had not merited his return to human brotherhood. In the next life the subtle undercurrent of his evils will still be felt and met with rejection — for unknown reasons. However, he will again be eligible for acceptance, after the animal passions in his blood have been purified in a form equaling his passions. Thus he temporarily enters a lesser state of consciousness, which is called: transmigration.

Now, some individuals are so imbued with meanness of spirit, that though alive, they are already dead in the Eyes of the Lord. They are no more than a corpse infilled with crude energy. Their greatest satisfaction and deliberate conquest is to draw Light-bearers into their useless life, much as the arsonist destroys for secret pleasure.

The pain and abuse inflicted on man or animal is relived and suffered by the offender in body and mind. Abuse of mind energy results in severe mental illnesses, even idiocy. Vindictive, calculating individuals who lived like vampires on the vital nerve energy of others, as those who project their sexual energies at will, often suffer paralysis or other diseases of the central nervous system in a forthcoming incarnation; and other forms of regression.

When there is no hope left for the progression and redemption of the lesser self, the subhuman entity re-enters the Primordial Element. Slow and methodical as is the way of Nature, the very last lifetime is spent in mindless vegetation; coupled with physical deformity and with little awareness of much else. Such individuals recognize only loss and the powerlessness to do anything about it. It is their self-willed estate. There was plenty of time and opportunities granted to change the current of their energy — and fate — into forward directions; but continued indulging in degeneracy, sodomy and other evils won out. Even as when the energy withdraws from the vegetable, it wilts and rots away, so does the Light of Life, energy and intelligence shrink away from the incorrigible and spiritual death occurs. Then nothing can undo what has been done. The choice to do better is ours. Should Truth feel disconcerting, as Truth always is, is it not better to know the facts than rambling through life unaware of what may confront the soul after death? Our world is beautiful, nevertheless earth is the land of the dying and the dead. Some individuals are geared to cram their life all into one day. Where are we rushing to? What are we running from if not from the unknown Self? When Love, happiness and peace imbue the heart, you shall know heaven on earth. The Father Who loves us has not changed — have we?

THOUGHTS AND CONSEQUENCES

All life is connected to God and all souls are interrelated. Every happening and action begin with thought and thought energy creates our conditions. Since energy is immortal, the thoughts we project manifest events far into the future. Whether thought is well posed or unstructured, it goes out into the atmosphere, ignites other thoughts and sets them into motion. If the energy is strong enough, it will congregate and result in riots, murder and self-destruction. Heavenly, selfless thoughts form into noble ideas that manifest goodness and inner healing to the whole.

Thoughts incite actions which redeem man or leave him sorrowful. Slothfulness, usurpation and the oppression of others throw the soul into most humble conditions in the new life. That it may gain gentleness of heart, learn self-restraint, humility, patience, and develop a greater appreciation of others. Domineering personalities are born into surroundings where conditions are constantly changing. Under unstable influences the individual is pushed from pillar to post, until broken down in his/her once strong will *and* health, he becomes the charge of others; who likewise deprive him of his psychic space and independence and unkindly silence him each time he complains. Thus he/she is taught to respect others instead of *demanding* for himself. Thusly he/she learns spiritual honesty and more importantly the virtue of silence.

Now, there is no reason to hate anyone, posing as the avenging angel! Karma takes care of it. Besides, why despise a person and end up paying for *his* ignorance? Hating burdens your karmic record. When the actions of others and pressures of life no longer upset you, you have broken through the psychic maze, and you have conquered the greatest milestone of human limitations.

God has given you the gift of *choice* and every choice you make bears its price. Some learn readily, others slowly, but all learn. There is nothing fearful in life or in death, when one lives gently, honestly, loves grandly and forgives wholly. When we can see our conditions as hidden blessings perfecting us, we begin to understand our purpose for living on earth and to appreciate the beauty of life. Then all questions concerning life and death receive the answer.

It is not predestined for all souls to meet God in their present lifetime, for all are not ready, nevertheless He should be sought. To realize God within is *I*, limitless, valiant, brave! — you find the *True* is always the Inner Image. People believe what they *need* to believe at any given time, and cannot believe more than they are ready to accept.

The preparation to receive the High Charging of the Light is a very gradual process, that does not occur until lessons have been acquired in every state of consciousness. There is no need to ponder how much you have attained, but to yield to *Becoming*.

Enlightenment affords the insight that there was no fall of man, but the descent of Spirit into matter. Spirit manifested as soul and soul became man. Involution and evolution began. To conceive higher ideas and *experience* them is a gift of God, merited through enduring the rigors of inner unfoldment. Earth tries you in its fires. You may whimper, or brace up to it and dance on its coals. When attached to God, the fires will still lap and leap high, but they can no longer touch you, for they are held at bay by the Waters of Spirit.

The many who claim the pain of learning is of the devil and scoff the illumined way, prove the devil is but the spirit of ungodly minds. Numerous are the dark nights and desolations of the budding soul, but when Morning breaks and all is flooded with Light, Love and Joy, you will count all things endured worthwhile.

Margaret P. Montague wrote: "Once out of all the grey days of my life I have looked into the heart of reality; I have seen life as it really is — ravishingly, ecstatically, madly beautiful, and filled to overflowing with wild joy and value unspeakable. For those glorified moments I was in love with every living thing before me. There was nothing that was not alive was not a miracle. . . my very soul flowed out of me with great joy."

THE PREDESTINED COURSE

To understand the present is to know what preceded it. Destiny is not created for man by God, but the result of his own actions. Under the Law that holds every soul accountable all are equal. Justice and Impersonal Love are the Law of every world, universe and light system.

Predestination operates under the Principle of Divine Order. In the cycles of duration every meaningful event and every condition have been preordained. Even the amount of food and drink you intake, as your number of breaths have been premeasured. The hair on each head, feathers of every plumage, each leaf on a tree, each grain of sand have been counted. And what you take from life too soon, you must reinstate. I.e., when overindulgence makes you ill you will eat less, thus balance the scale.

Too, we might keep in mind, you cannot die one second sooner or later than the appointed time. Here we see that the trauma of accident or suicide does not release the soul into Higher Life until the natural cycle has run its course. And that these also had to be experienced by the soul; except that the nature of the death wish, as other murderous thoughts are subject to retribution.

There is no mistake in the Perfect Pattern of Divine Law, whether in experience, form or sex. Each receives a vehicle best suited for his development. Since motion, impulse, motive and determination are the nature of life, man and creatures act, interact and react as they must at any given time.

Thus some are wild, some brute, others gentle, kind and loving. And each individual and every creature is at its appointed place here and now and carries out its prescribed task. Seen in true light, there is no ugliness or beauty anywhere, nor any disarray in the patterns of Nature. If you would observe, even scatters of hay fall into exact geometric patterns. Birds have nests, people have homes, animals chart out their own territories and protect them. To each is assigned a smaller or larger space in the symmetry of Universal Life and all life is destined to evolve into the Order of Divine Consciousness.

Soul, as all other species, is attached to Its Divine Source by the invisible, umbilical cord of the individual ray. Thus each enlivened creation from atom to Cosmos is imbued with the Force of the Current that gave it life, and enveloped by an invisible and sometimes visible radiant, ethereal mist that issues out from within.

While predestination does not allow man free will, he is not a victim of circumstances but fell into the predestined path by his own free will. However, he has free will to change himself and fill in the blanks, when open keys or new opportunities appear. Even here he must use discernment and not jump into things by a sheer rush of determination to better himself, neither for the sake of progress. When we take a close look at our planet it is self-evident how human ideas, inventions and willful destruction have subtly shifted the Globe off course, transformed the scenery, and the benevolent elements into a furious force. And though we would wish to retrace our steps, some things can no longer be altered or wished away.

Sometimes decisions are made *for* you, and othertimes the force of circumstances leaves you no choice but to decide your own directions. Either way is predestined. One door closes, another opens. Old conditions are left behind and new destiny is being made in the ageless pattern of evolution. By and by, the herculean soul becomes wise, and frees itself from the world where nothing stands still, not even for one fleeting moment.

HOLD FAST TO GOD

Man neither decides his destiny nor the hour when he shall change his cloak. Yet his birth is timeless, his transition deathless. Karmic results, good and bad, are natural effects to causes we set into motion. The Law of Life is unforgiving, inexorable. Only God can diminish the grief. To realize God does not remove the debt, but grants to live a freer, happier life. So long as we live in the physical world we subtly carry the burden of the whole. Where lay the answer? In the Radiant Spirit of God, that alone can emancipate the soul from the land of death and grant Eternal Life.

NO ESCAPE FROM PREDESTINED EVENTS

At times you may wish to escape to a more peaceful, productive environment. But the Force may place obstacles in your way to prevent your relocation until you have worked out conditions in your present surroundings. Nothing happens per chance, and everything by choice!

No matter how far you roam karma will bring you back, or move you into circumstances worse than the last until the debt is paid. Divorced people remarry for the same reason, because the conflict between them has not been resolved, until they can part in kindness, understanding and friendship. Then it is over. Now, you may also be held back from other destinations to receive your good, when others karmically indebted to *you* must repay a debt in kindness, caring and support.

Whatever you encounter, the most important moment of your life is always *now*, and every moment of your life deserves your best and full attention. Instead of seeing adverse conditions as woeful, we should seek out the lesson they present. When you change your idea and belief about things, you can change your whole life around.

INFLUENCE OF THE RAY

As much as following the predestined course, man must express the Angelic Ray upon which he entered his life and conditions. If the quality of the Ray is Virtue, he will express it throughout the greater part of his life. If tinged with moroseness and afflictions, body and mind will suffer, since his own energy marked it that way.

Should the ray spell talent, it will be fully expressed. And should the Life-Ray be imbued with the radiance of healing and compassion, he will heal the sick and comfort the desolate.

Now, when the ray bears the markings of dishonesty, the results will be a thief, robber and so on. If it bears the character of wildness and uncontrolled force, man will pilfer and murder whether he wants to or not. The subject is endless. So it would seem man cannot help for what he is, except that initially he himself tinged the Clear Light with the qualities he now re-enacts and must again qualify. At times a soul may also come in on a malefic ray, not because it was merited, but to test and try it to the last, to bring out the magnificence of spirit, which terminates all re-embodiments into lower worlds.

If the nature of the ray is stamped with genius, it will produce a protogee; if musical, he will express it and excel. Should one be destined to become a pianist or organist, the fingers will be longer for that purpose. Born to be a champion runner, body and legs will be fashioned to accomplish the feat. Our predestined lives are by choice. What we intensely wish for becomes our reality in a future cycle and is realized in the realm where the seed (or thought) was sown.

People pride themselves in their professions, when in fact these are their *karma*. Whether you are a doctor, scientist, artist, researcher, priest or anything else, your present is built on yesterdays dreams and unfulfilled hopes of the past. Our present life experiences guide us to know what we can expect to face in the next round.

The Godward Way leads to ultimate freedom. The human state is not a lowly one, but exalted, which the angels and lesser gods long to enter to attain Ultimate Godhood. I have experienced other worlds more glorious than ours, where God is met. But to realize Him *fully*, we, the soul, must begin at the base of evolution — the earth world. For here the Hand of God has sown the Holy Seed or *Soul* to germinate, and life on earth alone can lead us through the throngs of every necessary, liberating encounter in order to experience God on *every* level of consciousness.

It is ignorance to claim to be the incarnation of another personage. You are always the abiding *Self* and never someone else. No one can reap the good or suffer the malady of another personality. Karma, Predestination and Transmigration are the balancing factors of *One* Energy and Law. Hold fast to God, allow His Spirit to set you free.

AMERICA, THE HOME OF NATIONS

Countries, continents, the earth itself and nations are subject to predestination and change. America is the Mother and Cradle of every nation in the world.

It is no mistake that immigrants find homage in Her Bosom, their journey was predestined. By virtue of Her constitution, by the unshakable faith of Her people in their God, America radiates an outreaching Love that shines into the farthest corners of the world.

America is blessed and protected from scavenging nations — try as they may! And all who abide in Her Land in good trust, enjoy the prosperity created through their labors and manifold skills, in a rich tapestry of cultures. America the beautiful — the Shining Spirit of the Race and the Mighty Spirit of the Globe overshadow Her.

And it was preordained, that by their very ability and good efforts immigrants found a better life, that some risked life and limb to attain. Thus they hold a deeper devotion and appreciation than many natives for the Land in which they may live safely and without fear of political reprisal. Only those must turn back whose destinies did not allow them to remain. Fate is infallible.

Here they are free, though some of their young, even as our own, have yet to demonstrate a deeper sense of gratitude for America's warmheartedness and readily extended Bounty.

Persecuted in their homelands, they must learn the deeper meaning of unity and true brotherhood that are the Heartbeat of America, though disgruntled natives may disagree! "Liberty and Justice for all" — is Her Credo, and the Hallmark and Mandate of Our Most Sovereign Lord.

By all America gives and extends, though Her Earth may bear the bloodstains of many, Her Destiny will be as it must — to lead! Regardless and inspite of internal turbulence and consequences suffered, mistakes by a young Nation finding its way; She will remain safely in the Hand of God.

TRANSMIGRATION

Though the thought of transmigration is unpalatable to the discerning thinker, it does not alter the fact that some suffer its fate. In *lower worlds* man is the crown of creation, but this crown had to be earned. Evolving consciousness passed through all lesser forms and species before it became embodied as man and endowed with the faculty of reason, *Self*-consciousness and clear thought.

The message is not new. Passed down from the Sons of Light to the Masters of the Orient and from them to the material west, they taught and proved how individual consciousness moves through the eighty four lacs, or eight million four hundred thousand *forms* of life. They called the Wheel of coming and going, the Wheel of *Awagawan*. These eighty four lacs consist of billions of individual energies, of mineral and plant life, insect species of every sort, every kind of animal, forms of atomic life, of land, water, fire and air, and beings above and below man such as devas, demons and much more: all of which are clearly perceptible to inner sight. The erring soul is at times required to regress to lesser forms, that equal the energy of the crime committed, before it can again evolve to the human status.

Nothing sets man apart from the animal, except his outer form and the sanctified spark, their needs are alike. When man's reasoning and actions persistently fall below the animal level, the effects of his evil acts and volatile energy throw him into corresponding states after death, where it is best purified. Clearly then, man's lesser nature returns to an embodiment appropriate to his karma, until balance is regained to evolve inward and forward. Few face this fate, only rare cases enter annihilation.

The crude self meets refinement by experiencing the intensity of harm and pain it inflicted on other humans and on other lives. Whether this takes place in human form, animal, insect or some tree, the Law does not care. It is then not unusual that we meet people who act like animals and animals that act like people. Re-embodiment and transmigration may not be what we savor, but it is the Way of Spirit and Nature. We should know that during transmigration the divine monad is not within the temporary form, but removed from it, as even the soul is seldom directly in the body. Unless the course of regression is destined to end in annihilation and guardianship is withdrawn, the higher part observes the drama but remains unaffected by the pain. Though the divine spark within the soul is immortal, not all souls reach immortality; for the Radiant Force must enter the mind *and there remain* before the lesser self can be transformed and enter the Immortal Aspect of Soul. Without the realization of the Sound Current and Its Redeeming Light, man remains in darkness.

As soul commits its way to the perpetual evils of the mind, it loses the luster of its spiritual fire and as the flame burns down it loses its spark. Then the soul is no longer divine but material and regression begins. As the nature of soul is timeless, the stay in lower predicaments can be endless.

The purpose of transmigration is not concerned with body or form, but with the evolution of consciousness. Even as Nature is constantly changing its patterns, transmigration is part of the evolutionary process. After death man enters the state and world to which he properly belongs.

WHY RETROGRESSION?

When immorality, cruelty and hatefulness become the way of life and by reason of irredeemability individual consciousness no longer warrants life in human embodiment, retrogression to lower species occurs. Thus it eliminates every destructive tendency of the mind. If man descends to subhuman levels, his own animalistic conduct has sent him there and he will endure until the full measure of his debt has been cleared. Those barbaric entities called "humans" who inflict severe distress, pain and *scientific* torture on helpless animals, may consider this fate and stand reminded that the Breath of Life is the same in all.

The rise and fall of consciousness is witnessed in all of nature. Individuals who find the idea of transmigration uncouth, need to take heart and enter the Spirit where they can prove it to themselves. For until then anything read or said about the subject remains mere theory, heresay, speculation and a subterfuge of words.

If it were up to man there would only be an *either/or*, heaven or hellfire and brimstone. But God redeems no matter how long it takes for man to forgive and change himself, and to take off his blinds to see the Light of Truth. People need not be concerned with heaven or hell, both are transitory states, but with their fate.

In lower worlds, Karma is vital to eternal progress. The workings of Karma give ample proof that there is no injustice other than the injustice of man. We ascend or regress by choice. Since the descent of consciousness began in the *Neuter* Aspect, it can readily be seen that It can also move back and forth through Its Own Nature of exalted and lesser states. Even as the True Adept can look at a thing and become the thing itself. Man is given uncountable opportunities to correct the mean and spiteful things he so willingly performs.

Though Truth sets free and grants peace of mind, it is not necessary for anyone to believe in reincarnation. But the individual should ask himself *why* he is here today and why he suffers. The fabrication that God created man because he was lonely, is as ridiculous as man's idea of devils with pitchforks. When heart and mind are free of human darkness, prejudism, anger, dishonesty and hate, the Truth of God appears on its own accord.

Living in a dense form, enjoying the excitement of material life, people believe life on earth is all there is; only because they are out of touch with the Wonder and Reality of their inner worlds to which they are destined to return.

The physical dissolution the human dreads is in fact his reinstatement to innate happiness; that will fulfill his greatest hopes and fondest dreams. The cycles of birth and death are sequential. Each new form is fashioned according to the individual's previous state of mind, which can be angelic, human, or a lesser manifestation.

For all the lives we lived, we evolved from primitive manifestation to intellectual being, and moved from other heavenly planets into the era of the earth world. And now it is expedient to find ourself in God to end our transient existence in the world of form, where things are born, die, and reawaken to evolve into Eternal Life.

MORE LIGHT ON THE SOUL

When soul descends into lower worlds, which includes the astral world, it takes on the garment of the region it enters. As a matter of survival the vehicle or body must correspond with the ethers of the new atmosphere. But as the enveloping sheath and the body are coarser than the soul, they not only hold it down but weigh it down as well. And more, when mind actions weaken the soul, they revert its attention from its divine estate and drag it down to the material bottom. Until soul opens all channels to God, it swashbuckles from life to life and from form to *re*form.

Sincere and steadfast introspection and seeking the Presence of the Radiant Lord, ends doubt and wandering around in circles. Soul wants God. Mind revels in the pleasures of the senses, somehow the two must meet. When you regain your natural stability in God, you will then pull the mind into the Light of Peace and the struggle will be over. Nourished by the Sound Current there will be no more tiredness and gloom. You will feel whole and centered and find the Holy Sound has produced changes in you.

In time the cycles of self-manifestation will end for all. External forms shall pass away and the inner forms of man shall take on yet finer, multiple vestures. Then souls shall return to the Holy Port, the Great Journey has ended.

No sermon, no man alive on this planet, whether he claims to be in or out-of-the-body — can provide your emancipation, it is an Act of God. An illumined teacher can lead you *to* the Gate of God, but only *God* can open that Gate and permit you to enter. Be not deceived, Best Beloved of God, out-of-body experiences can be fanciful and do not mean to be *In* God, but are moreoften on the outskirts of Divine Reality. Believe in God with all your heart, love and strength, and in nothing you cannot prove to yourself. Believe in *Yourself*, the Self is God. Then you will make the *conscious* connection with the Force that sustains you momentarily, hourly and for always. And in golden moments you will realize you have touched the Face of God and entered His Kingdom.

GET OUT OF THE CONFUSION

It seems when we are troubled we try to shed the burden by confessing to man, who is fallible as we. We dab and sprinkle ourselves with holy water, worship at pagan grottos and are baptized and rebaptized. But the mind remains unclean and unchanged, until we are reborn in the Sound Current that washes away the stain.

Stand-ins for God who endeavor to save us and claim to possess *ultimate* power, alienate more than they try to convert. They may take up the space of God but never His Place. And isn't it sad, while the preacher calls erring men to a salvation he himself never knew, and *allows* God to forgive them, his sins sneak down from the pulpit and expose him. Where will it end? No more honorable are the *saved* who broadcast their sins to the world, thus attest to their guilts and bondage. And when the 'faithful' feel the high pitch of emotionalism and the energy of astral spirits it invokes, they call it the Holy Ghost. It never occurs to them that He comes into the silence of the humble in heart.

By and large people are afraid of God, of life, of death, of themselves, but mostly of the opinions of others who might deny them social acceptance. Viewed from a higher vantage point you behold the confusion of lost human beings fumbling their way along the promenades of ignorance; clutching after each other's arms, doctrines, *and* thoughts, in hope to find right directions. But conditioned to domination and fear, no sooner than man beholds the Illumined Door, he bulks in terror and fears it is the wrong way.

IT BEGINS WITH YOU

A trillion tears will not change the fact that God does not care what happens in worlds below. But since His Light imbues the soul, you are never alone. The Spirit of God cannot be manipulated by emotional outbursts, rage or beggary, but it will certainly touch the one who longs for Its Grace in dead earnest, and draw him into Its Heart. Yes, you are loved! But to *feel* loved you must first enter the state where Divine Love exists. We have great need to get out of the psychic whirlwind tour of spirits and lesser magic, and cease wending our way in-and-out-of the spiritual traffic to know where we are going.

Man, a god by divine heritage stands alone. Equipped with the Sword of Spiritual Power he must learn to cut loose his binding, fearful ties to earth and choose whom he would serve. We tend to believe earth is paradise, while the Wheel of Involution and Evolution keeps grinding away, snatching the unknowing into its spokes in order to restore soul's empyreal garment to ideal perfection.

In midst of racism, oppression, starvation, sickness and death all over the Globe, can we still say this is paradise? It is rather a tossup of a pair of dice to gauge who will be victor tomorrow. Our issues are no longer black and white, but to know the difference between *wrong* and *right*, personally and collectively. Can any country beneath the heavens be Shangrila, where racism influences the judicial system and justice can be bought? Wars among nations and dissension between individuals are no more than a struggle of wills.

The energy of Retribution and Transmutation works slowly and affects individuals and nations for centuries to come. For: "Though the mills of the gods grind slowly, they grind exceedingly fine." Except by the pen of man, the Old, Original Law of God has had no revision. It ever remains, that: "Whoso sheddeth man's blood, by man shall his blood be shed." Gen. 9:6

God hides His Secrets in the heart of every man. In the course of a lifetime, many shocks and madnesses assault man's body and mind, to condition and sensitize his inner being and his nervous system to receive the Empowerment of Spirit, in which he is reborn a God.

8.

Cults and Religions

Love unites us here and everywhere. The Essence of Its Truth is the Forging Force that links us soul to soul. In the endless chain of stalwart seekers who yearn for freedom from duality, some have the dauntless will to break the bonds of physical, political and spiritual oppression.

The Spirit of the Age and closing era demands Truth in every department of life. It does not abide in the trappings of convention, tradition or organization, but in the Impersonality of the One Law, that decrees Liberty and Justice for every soul. Out of Caos—Peace is born—out of man's wreckages the Immortal Phoenix shall rise!

Of the many fearful who would not dare, there is a handful God can rely on, who know the Truth and report it clearly, no matter what the cost. The following is written in Love and not in contempt, with best intent and respect to all beliefs, concerning points vital to our well-being, physical, material and spiritual future. When we attain to the Highest Good, we will have the immeasurable blessing true Liberty affords and shall maintain our freespirited nature.

It is simple when all agree, but controversial views often stir up deep emotions, that nevertheless will favor the perfect picture when the quake is over and pieces fall into their rightful place. I do not seek approval. I speak from the courage of my innate convictions and offer the benefit of another view, as the scrub buckets and fringy mops are pushed along the expansive corridors of learning — attempting to clean up the ground floor.

WHAT IS A CULT

Anything that incites a following to a system whether of ceremony, rite, ritual or belief is a cult. When man begins to worship his Creator "in Spirit and in Truth", he will have no further need to congregate. But to appease our sociable nature, we ally ourselves with those agreeable to our state of mind, and defile our faiths by goading and forcing others into the narrow mold of our creeds, only to find them anxious to throw off the yoke.

Organization destroys the true religion of the soul, since it denies man the right to think and act freely to find his God. The issue then is not religion, but the Spiritual Freedom it denies to follow one's own conscions and inborn trust in God. Wherever you find organization you find power struggles and dissension because the lower ego seeks satisfaction.

Since the soul is the incarnation of its Father, it has its own religion. All religions are a call to God, but not all show the Way. Man should disassociate himself from those who tell him what to do, how he should do it and in what to believe. When abiding by the Law of God, the individual will then abide by the law of man, instead of taking up permanent residency behind the bars of already overcrowded penal institutions.

Freedom of spirit is a priceless pearl and always exacts its dues. Many have dearly paid dearly for it. When you have *become* free, your expression of freedom will make its own statement. You can either go through life permitting others to decide for you, or decide for yourself. A free soul rules its mind, for it is in submission to Divine Will. The inborn freedom of soul is boundless and by innate instinct it will defend it to the last. Persecute a man, take away his rights, throw him into prison or into the sea, and he will do his best to get out of it. He will yearn for liberty and maintain it, if nowhere else but in his thoughts.

But while in human form, man can never be *absolutely* free, since he must abide by the system of his world to survive. Only when he regains his freedom in God, thus knows to leave his body at will, nothing will have the power to keep him bound.

ANOTHER VIEW

This writer is not influenced by any other than the Inner Light, that spurs the pen to pull the massive rope of the gonging, droning bells that call to Freedom. It grants the space to think on one's own terms and to express conclusions that are here shared.

Revelations, inner growth and the satiric glory of initiations into the Order of the Spirit were well earned. Thus not bestowed on me by sect, or creed, nor by any mortal who as myself did fall from Grace into the world of matter; but by the Higher Grace of every man that manifested to me as the Radiant Light.

Religion is what is in my own heart — and the Force that caught me up into Its Vibrant Life to know the Spirit and the Breath of every living thing, of bush, of tree, of animal, fragrant blooms and mountain rocks was within me and I in them. To realize the Spirit of Creation and precious life of everything in one short moment, is a revelation ineffable.

My shoes more often full of holes, I ran barefooted through dewy mists of meadow, wood and vale, and felt the prayerful breath of the evening wind caress my face and ruffle up my hair. Grasped after the dancing lights of lightning bugs and glowing fireflies, and searched the starlit tapestry of heaven in longing for the Unknown God. Stepping high with Love and the heart infilled with the transcendent music of the spheres, I could not doubt that this was God, or at least as near as I could get right then.

And othertimes I beheld the forms of little prismatic colored creatures in their fullest splendor, some golden-white with yellow polka dots and others azure blue, some brown, that played along the wooded paths beneath the towering pines. I beheld the mist of angel-likeness that rose out of the nature of big trees, and other forms locked in their trunk that wept. And understood the whispers of nature's encompassing, brooding peace that welled up from the meadow and out of evening mists. Where the soul could sit in silence and realign to God and feel the flowing Force and Harmony of Cosmos moving 'round about and through the soul.

I heard the joyous sounds and silent sighs of bush and tree and listened to the busy dialogues of crickets, ants and bees. And saw the gigantic forms of Weather Angels, that leaned over the tops of billowing white clouds, and so much more!

I experienced the Reality of Celestial Worlds in many ways, and entered Realms Bright where Love and Peace reigned uttermost, which held forever true for me; that reading books or scriptures could not for me provide. And I, much later on remembered what was gathered up in distant pasts. And again picked up the Golden Thread to the God I sought of long ago as soul, that disallowed the entertaining of all false and wayward mutterings, of ignorance and sophistry.

The Christ I found was Spirit, Impersonal of religion, cult and creed; that Christ was the Love and Light of every faithful heart, but moved with Superstrength to purify the dross! Thus I cannot say the God-Man died for me, for as already proved, myself as any other human must die to lustful habits that incarcerate the soul; to wordly cravings and to the little self. Thus learn to die to live. For had the Valiant Jesus died for me, the grave would have gulped up my memory of other pasts. There would be no need to live on earth *today*, to rectify past insurrections.

CONSIDERING THE FACTS

Jesus did not make Peter his successor, for he was neither trustworthy nor dependable. Much less did Jesus establish a church in which he held no interest, but to which christendom contributes its original roots. And is especially untrue since Jesus ascended over two centuries before man began to build his pagan monuments to Him and honored Him with the bloody sacrifices of the innocent.

Paul was the originator of christianity, not Jesus. Jesus taught the doctrine of Rebirth, Consequences, Sound and Light, that His avid confessors of today vehemently disavow and call 'devilish'. Jesus taught that God is to be worshipped in *Spirit* and in Truth; which opposed the pagan worship of idols of the priestcraft, including the practice of necromancy, spirito-enjoyments, and side-shows of miracles. The German poet Nietsche wrote: "There was only one christian and he died at the cross!" Jesus was a Jew. When he dwelled in Spirit, the Divine Christ dwelled in Him, when He went about His daily duties He was Jesus the man.

The Wondrous Spirit that graced Jesus occupied the forms of the saviours before Him and It dwells within *You*. Unfettered and Boundless, It dwells in Its Creations but is not possessed by them. People worship their evil gods and goddesses and profess a God they never knew.

There was no Judaism before Moses, no Sikhism before Guru Nanak, no Taoist before Lao-Tse, no Moslems before Mohammed, who died in the year 632 and was the last of the True Prophets. As already proved, there were no christians before Christ. But no matter how great a prophet or saint, they remained bound to the universe of mind, until they could consciously enter the Sound Current. Christianity was not fully established until the hammer of oppression fell upon the humble: to be a christian or die! And the bloodfeud continues in our day all over the world to install one dogma after another.

SIGNS OF THE TIMES

Neither Zoroaster, Buddha, Jesus, nor any other Liberator before them claimed Saviourship or Divinity, nor did they hold interest in religion. They taught those who would listen how to redeem themselves, their message was brotherhood, peace and forgiveness. Nowaday masters and pseudo gurus demand your unconditional surrender to their wanton personalities and warn their integrity should never be called to question! All beg of God — what can they do for *You*? While religionists sanctify their threadbare relics and wallow in their demonic lust for power and sexual perversions; instead of showing the humble how to worship in the Temple of God *within*. In this world where everything is bought, sold and resold, people will adulterate and sell their divinity to gain their objectives.

In the breath of sacrificial prayer they "plead the Blood of Christ", and avow salvation and forgiveness by the very blood they shed for the glory of religion, which will exact its karmic dues, blow for blow, strike for strike and blood for blood. For, for every drop of blood shed, willfully, naturally or accidentally, another must be shed to redeem it. The Law is Unchanging, Inexorable. And: "O, my God, I am heartily sorry" — and other paternosters will find no reception. The Winds of Karma swallow up their words.

TEACHING SYSTEMS

Jesus did not leave one single written line. We only have what He supposedly has said. What was handed down to us from the sayings of prophets, apostels and masters, is what *their* teacher or god had to say to *them* and does not replace what you yourself must experience in God to become free. Nothing else can hold true for you. Though Jesus was the Great Teacher of His Time, the same Presence that dwelled in Him is your Guiding Force today, that leads you to the Door of the Soul where the experience becomes possible.

When the search is sincere, the Spirit within will guide the seeker to the right source and will stir him away from harmful edicts. What the Grand Christ initially taught became a mixture of diverse beliefs, revisions, abridged editions and conjectures of personal judgments. World religions are composed of belief systems, therefore opinions.

The soul must turn to its Chief Source to gain True Enlightenment. You must *want* to be with God if efforts would prove fruitful. Until man begins to trust the Spirit within he will always need something or someone to lean on. And when he retorts: "But — the scriptures say. . ." he cuts himself off and can progress no further than what he reads.

Teachings that *illumine* and are vital to spiritual unfoldment can be found in the voluminous Library of the Theosophical University Press, Pasadena, Ca. - A golden legacy of excellence has been left to us by the Spiritual Giant and literary Genius, Madame Helena Petrovna Blavatsky. Her writings were compiled in part from the Secret Doctrines of antiquity which she ardently tried to preserve. See *"Isis Unveiled", "The Secret Doctrines", and "Collected Writings".*

"The Nag Hammadi Library", and Egyptian Teachings of Hermes Trismegistus, will incite in the seeker a longing for spiritual maturity, and speed up the search to enter the experience of the Far Country. (Available from the Theosophical University Press, P.O. *Bin* C, Pasadena, Ca., 91109).

ONE TRUTH FOR ALL PEOPLE

Truth is seldom comforting but necessary to face in order to evolve. The Spirit of Light calls out through every age to emancipate the seeking soul, but obscures itself from hearts wedded to creeds and cults, that spring up like weeds out of the phantasmagoria of incontinent minds.

Innate truth eliminates all questions, every *why* and wherefore of God. God placed His Light into all people. There is but *one* Truth, manifested *as* man and *through* man and is therefore realized within the individual self. "Truth has no special time", wrote Albert Schweitzer, "the hour is now, always."

In God are no dualistic teachings. God is not understood nor met through belief, acceptance or devotion, but by entering His Spirit. Questions and answers belong to the lower Universe of Mind, wherefore we ask amiss and answers received are incomplete.

The authenticity and core of ancient teachings derived from the Brilliant Sound Current that dropped its Unwritten Word into the hearts of Holy Men and Holy Women, who attained conscious union with God. Therefore no religion or cult can claim to be the originator *or* the keeper of Original Truth, since it is not bound in volumes.

Recorded texts were kept in ancient mystery schools and withheld from the profane. Violations of secret codes or abuse of secret knowledge could invoke severe punishment, even death. We might pose the question: why should he who cannot control his own energy receive spiritual power? To harm and destruct?

Though in our day part of the teachings are public domain, those unprepared will read but not understand. As in days of old, sacred teachings are given him who *earned* the Holy Trust, by inner revelations, which the receiver instinctively knows how to apply and not to share with *anyone*. They are given to him in such a way, he couldn't interpret them to others if he tried, though he himself thoroughly understands, and if he could, wouldn't. For what good is Divine Knowledge to him who lives for the pleasures of the world and has only sporadic interests in the things of God?

Western luminaries who claim all teachings are but sprouts and shoots of *their* particular wisdom, will find Truth deprive them. While it continues to shine brightly on the clean living, humble saints of the Far East, who accredit their deep knowledge to none other than the Lord of Light, and remain silent as westerners plagiarize their texts. Blessings and joy vanish, spirituality declines, when we offer others the husk, instead of the soul-nourishing kernel of God.

Many spiritual teachers are sincere, but not all are brave enough to submit to the Transforming Light. A true teacher is not found in the market place of greed, for his life magnifies the Light he seeks to convey. He adheres to Divine Truth and lives it.

Word fencers and philosophical meanderers claim, to be a spiritual teacher you must have immense metaphysical knowledge, which is decidedly untrue. Only what you speak from the center of your innermost encounters with God will have meaning to others. Speaking from the inner life does not depend on texts or a litany of well-chosen words.

Above all, it should be remembered that *you* are the focal point of Light, wherefore your guidance comes directly from within. Time and time again we must clear the mind and look within, where the Radiant, Immortal Spirit shines down on Its creations and delights to bring us into reflection; and by our cognition of the Sound Current into the direct encounter with God. How more blessed could we be?

LOOKING FOR THE TEACHER

The Spirit of God is your Teacher. But you will also find that the teachings of illumined men and women who speak from the heart of inner experiences are alive with Truth and infused with spiritual vitality you can feel. Of this spoke Krishnamurti in Lutyens biography: "I maintain Truth is a pathless land, and you cannot approach it by any path whatever, by any religion, by any sect."

Learn as we will, it remains half truth and will slip our mind until we *enter* the experience. Only then will we know and never forget. Nothing taught is ever new to the timeless soul, accept in form and interpretation. It only seems novel until we reawaken to it. Then we say: 'O, I knew that all along!'

When looking for directions we should use discernment, take nothing for granted and make certain of the truth. Some teachers only speak from book knowledge and out of material need. You can find yourself wrapped up in the psychic veil, drained, sad in heart and weighed down to the bottom line of depression. Such individuals manipulate what they know — and *You*, to suit their needs. If they were God-realized, there would be no need to be a mouthpiece for stray entities, nor for the emptiness of spiritual mouthing. Persons who follow cults complain they feel dazed and passive, that they are moved by a strange energy and no longer themselves.

A teacher who speaks from the Heart of Light and projects his realization from worlds within, will illumine others that they too may learn to love with innate capacity and he will guide them to the Kingdom within. His teachings will lead out of the desert land of lower consciousness and certainly out of indifference towards God. Understanding, cheerfulness and a great sense of humor are the characteristics of spiritual souls. I can't imagine a person anywhere who does not have the innate desire to be happy. Can you?

At one point of spiritual unfoldment God will take you up and show you the spiritual teaching systems of Cosmos, that will stretch out before you as a gigantic, uprising map, reaching into Infinity. An incredible sight! Here you behold the value of every teaching, from the lowest to the highest last; and find there are lessons to be learned in all. And, they tire us out — that we would reach for the Truth that sets free.

Now, how can anyone teach you the Way of the soul, who speaks of your soul, my soul, and doesn't know he *is* the *soul*? It is when individuals admit they do *not* know, they begin to understand the Law. At times we encounter persons who are cynical, yet they hunger to know. But until cynicism, suspicion and distrust are layed to rest, true knowledge remains out of reach. The worst obstacle to Divine Learning is pride, prejudice, austerity and opinionatedness. When you look at a thing with a bias, you come out with a bias. Speculations have no value and half-knowledge is worse than no knowledge at all.

The Spirit of God cannot teach a man who claims to know it all, no more than It will absolve him who feels he has nothing to be absolved for. Nor will Spirit teach a person who considers constructive guidances as a personal reprimand. Spiritual progress depends on man's readiness to accept Higher Truth. Now, we may deem ourselves more advanced than another struggling soul, who may live purer than we and closer to God, and perceive aspects of Divine Truth we might not see at all.

HOLD FAST TO GOD

Aspirants of the Illumined Way are often avid readers and will get quite enthused over a subject until someone comes along and says it's all wrong. Discouraged they lay it down, browse around for something else or forsaken the subject matter altogether. Where is the answer? You should let God guide you. No longer look to the edges, Blessed Reader, but turn within to the center where men and women become gods and Gods become man. Where the Living Teachings of the Lord are clearly perceived and His Truth becomes part of you.

By natural instinct every man seeks the Perfect One. Until he meets the Sacred Beloved, he will run from one teacher to another and remain unfulfilled. There must be *trust* between soul and God. Faith does not suffice. But I say, if anyone believes in a godly, virtuous being, who teaches him to be a better person, then as long as he believes let him believe and be made every wit whole. But let him first believe in *himself,* for this is believing in God. Every soul has illumined moments it cannot forget. But most, rather than pursuing them, push them out of their mind.

And this I know: there is an invisible string that yields down from God to which you are attached. Every now and then you can feel the tug, the string is being pulled upward and you are being brought up higher. You cannot hold on to both ends. You must let go of one or the other. You cannot have God and the world. Yet you must live on earth, abide by its laws and nourish the root of the tree, that the crown may attain heaven. For both are your origin and while in the body you cannot be separated from either, accept during temporary suspension.

CULTS AND RELATED GROUPS

It is no secret that throughout our country many families

suffer and grieve over loved ones that joined the mad menagerie of cults and were brainwashed and murdered. In man's subconscious need for God and search for the Unknown Deity, his frustrations turn to accepting substitutes, such as cults and new world saviours that spring up from the egocentric fancy of uprooted souls; who claim superhuman power; and offer their special brand of *salvation* and hallucinagenics for a quick trip to the Kingdom! While eloquent discourses of 'the only way' serve as attention getters and *secret* truth can be had for a membership fee; with the comment that only the *privileged* stumble upon their truth!

Piled up psychology and swarming literatures offer the *only* way to God through the cult leader and unconditional love to those they subjugate and *seduce*! There is no Holy Sap in all their works, human ego feeds the whithering vines. In one text the cult leader expressed, that whoever does not accept their energy will bear the consequences and he who does will be blessed! *No*, my Friend, you must not accept anyone's fallout! You *may block it* and return the energy in the same bombastic manner you received it! You are not harming, but returning what does not belong to you.

The corrupt energy some people project from conscious and subconscious levels depicts the malignant force to which they became attached through the cult. To return good for evil is not always the way it is done. Much more could be said. By and by, life teaches evil individuals to reroute their energy.

Great claims are made how departed saints no longer intercede, but that the saints of *their* persuasion are always with them; while Christ they say is dead! This does not take from the Radiant Truth Jesus of Nazareth demonstrated when He dissolved His body and ascended, while the bones of the antichrists and authors of pen-hatched doctrines lay decomposing in their graves. The *True Master* never dies.

And though some claim the God-Man was unlovely, I've

beheld His Spirit in many forms. The Lord of my visitations is brighter than Light, taller than a tower and most fair. I am not a christian, but know what I know. Nothing holds true from individuals who never beheld the Blazing Radiance and Fire of His Brilliant Light. And when the Spirit takes them into consideration, *It* will relieve them of their sullied robes and spoofed authority and place their breath elsewhere. With the respect that accords them: they are the soothsayers and tsetse flies — and the saints said worse!. . . that seduce the seeker into the sleep of doom, hoax and illusions.

To secure supremacy, the "master" projects his image on the mental screen of the follower's mind who then has a vision of him and worships him as his God. It's a change of pace for the lonely and for those who just stopped in for a fresh breath of spiritual air. . .

BELIEVE IN NO MAN

No mortal is your master, for the Master is no mortal! The liberty pseudo masters take covers a broad *sensual* spectrum and they will go as far as you let them. It is amazing how many individuals willingly trade their freedom to subserve another mortal, who, though well fed, himself starves for the Bread of Heaven and will have enough to atone for in the end. Some cultists speak of morals and ethics they never sought to emulate and point out: "We no longer wear robes and sandals and therefore do different."

Beloved Reader, the Holy Law of God does not change with man's fashions and passing fancy. It stands Majestic, Invincible — forever. But when the faithful wise up and decide to leave the cult, they are threatened to lose the "master's" protection, they should have been spared from the start. God never withholds His Love and Protection, no matter who or *what* you are. Wherever you find organization, trouble abounds. And, as has been proved, when one leader pushes the other off the earth-bound throne it is not in an amicable way. Mud slinging and public slander become the holy order of the day!

DEPROGRAMMING

Well-meant deprogramming is no more than an additional traumatic experience for the young and no better for the wear, since deprogrammers *force* the already abused into the furrow and squeeze of *their own* indoctrination and belief.

To further menticide young persons who are already too weak to exert their free will, only deepens unseen scars, which can become a long healing process and can remain with them for life. To indoctrinate anyone against their will to *any* belief, *violates them*. It does not reflect the clear, pure Image of Divine Law, but the indoctrinator's own ignorance of God and unredeemed ego.

We should unlearn what we know and begin anew, in simple, honest and direct worship of Our God. Then, and then only, will we be able to *know* God and love others with a full heart.

WONDERS, MAGICK OR NATURAL LAW?

People get rather upset when a 'miracle' is wrought by any other than their pastor or priest. When indeed, all wonders are the manifestation of God's Natural Law. There is no difference between the magic feat of the heathen, fakir, witch, warlock, voodooist, priest, guru, master and the humble in heart, except in the degree and purity of energy in which that wonder or 'miracle' is performed. You are using the same power.

Whether by natural ability or Superconscious attunement, all employ the Force of fire, water, air and earth, and the force of will, save he who learned to get himself out of the way and permits Divine Power free reign to flow through him — to do Its own Bidding.

Those labeled 'heathens' and heretics are a special breed of souls that have their own wonderful way of reaching God, which is unobstructed by any arbitrary influence. Thus overpowers the practice of those who hold up the flaming torch of damnation at the gates of hell. Rather than remain soldered to creeds, we would do well to become re-educated in the Fiery Love of God and Strains of His Spirit, and turn to Our Source in the infinite cleanliness of childlike *trust*, humility, and brevity required of the Gods.

In 'Isis Unveiled', Theology, Book II, page 500, Madame H. B. Blavatsky cites: "How true the words of Paracelsus when worried by fierce persecution and slander, misunderstood by friends and foes, abused by clergy and laity he exclaimed: "O ye of Paris, Padua, Montpellier, Salerna, Vienna and Leipzig! Ye are not teachers of the truth, but confessors of lies. Your philosophy is a lie. Would you know *what* Magic *really is*, then seek St. John's *Revelation*. . . As you cannot yourself prove your teachings from the *Bible* and the *Revelation*, then let your farce have an end. The *Bible* is the *true key* and interpreter. John, not less than Moses, Elias, Enoch, David, Solomon, Daniel, Jeremiah, and the rest of the prophets, was a magician, kabalist and diviner. If now all, or even any of those I have named were living, I do not doubt that you would make an example of them in your miserable slaughterhouse, and would annihilate them there on the spot, and if it were possible, the Creator of all things too!" (Theosophical University Press, P.O. *Bin* C. Pasadena, Ca. 91109)

MONEY — SEX — SALVATION

Without Sound and Light can be no truth in *any* system and what we are and speak colors our life. Wrote Frances Bacon: "All actions take their hue from the complexion of the heart." Ask the religious law maker if he experienced the Light and heard the Holy Sound of inner worlds, and he will cover up his ignorance by quoting a litany of adverse scriptures.

Though all deny accepting money for spiritual services, spirito-materialistic empires flourish. Whether above board or beneath it, all make money, because it is not their professed love for God that moves them, but greed, occupation and business.

Religious societies claim to be supported by membership

fees and gifts, but workers draw their salaries and other compensations out of the same fund. Not only for time invested but also to satisfy their insatiable greed. Not to mention the tithe badgered out of the poor and faithful.

When the televangelist laments: "My back is against the wall, I have an eleven million dollar deficite!" he forgets, (unless he never heard of it) the Law of God demands a debt free life: *"Owe no man anything but Love!"*

Since when does the salvation of soul depend on show and money? Have *you*, the contributor, ever examined how many souls *your* money has saved? Not a single one! Especially since salvation is a continual process that endures over uncountable lifetimes. It does not depend on the weeping preacher, but on the qualifications and merit of the soul. The blind alley call to salvation is unspiritual; and the vagrant promise of heaven and hell-threat of salvation is only as good as the man who expounds it, since it only exists in his limited perception.

Motivated by profit instead of by the Ideal of Spirit, the sympathy hook of monetary beggary and the kalistic law that upholds it, makes religious innkeepers richer and magnifies the emptiness of the material world. While the money grubber stands on the misinterpreted Promise of the Abundant Life! As I said in other writings: 'Man uses God the way he uses people!'

Now, when you know God you're not going to retire to a life of plenty, nor could you endure living in a mansion, knowing how poor and hungry other human beings are. Your needs will be entirely different, as they are no longer of this world. And most who enter God-Realization while on earth — die poor. To boast the church gives to foreign aid is the worst excuse ever. Nothing given out of a full pocket has spiritual value. Ill-begotten funds corrupt the gift.

Passing the begging bowl and collecting funds under the nonprofit charter that milks the whole, the pious moralist admonishes others how wrong it is to accept gratuities. Organizations, divided as they are, might find it more honorable to come out from under the nonprofit charter and pay their taxes as any other law abiding citizen, instead of collecting in the Holy Name of God for theatrics, show and personal comforts. Where does it stand written man should erect lavish cathedrals, live in pomp, drain the poor, hang jewels on idols and build million dollar homes financed by the widow's mite?

Certainly, we are not living in an era of trading goods for services. And since money is the commodity, thank you(s) and gratitude are not bankable and only invite those who care less for God and more for themselves. What we are saying is: *Live* what you profess. Quit begging, badgering, wanting and needing — in the Name of God, and acting like greedy birds of prey!

Now, if the man made law of poverty would be upheld, then monies and bequests great or small should be declined. St. Matthew 18:8-10 would encourage religious legerdemainists to the following: ". . . freely ye have received, freely give. . . provide neither gold, nor silver, nor brass in your purses. . . nor *script* for your journey, neither shoes, not yet staves. . . for the workman is worthy of his meat." This makes absolete wall to wall closets of fineries and furniture trimmed in gold. To understand the Way and Law of God, intellect must be quickened by Divine Light and the mind illumined by His Spirit. Only then will man be free from vanity and greed, and then only will he qualify to serve God and to lead others into His Way.

THE SEX OF THINGS

The Most popular topic of today is sex. Some tend to treat sex indiscriminately, while the idea of the prude is: 'the body is ugly and sex sinful', since the blind do not see the purpose of physical-spiritual union established for man by his God.

To be whole, every inner vehicle must fuse in the harmony of body, mind and spirit. Even though a physical act, sex is a spiritual impulse, sanctified in the conjugal state. Would God condemn what He Himself set into motion as vehicle for the propagation of His species?

Persons who consider sex repulsive are likely to suffer from psychological disorders: low esteem, irritability, dissatisfaction with life and general neuroses; that can make them feel insecure and disconnected from others. Some claim to be celibate. Only after the soul has entered Conscious Union with God and moves deeper into the Neuter Aspect, does it unfold into *spiritual* celibacy and refrains from physical union; which holds true for a scant few but not for the masses. Overweened pietists and puritans should know: no human can claim celibacy as long as his dreams attest otherwise!

OBSERVING THE HEART OF THINGS

The action of sex in unselfish love was the original intent, rather than the promiscuousness of sex for self-gratification only. Now, when the human self feels remorseful we frequent confessionals and if this does not reconcile guilts with conscions we hang our sins on the public clotheline to tell the world how it is with us!

While giving charity and vocalizing our distinct disdain against infidelity, we close the drapes and retreat to secret passions, to incest, sodomy and other nymphomanias. Sodom and Gomorrah did as well — with less sanctimony! In addition, we are not beyond having affairs with priests and as recently viewed on national TV, being seduced by naked bishops at gunpoint — no doubt they are as human as we. By and by, we are learning to see things in proper perspective. And who, drunk with guile can absolve your sins? Much less be called *father*? Who forgives *them*? The prayers of the righteous get caught up in their own wailing. The virtuous words of moralists are quite impressive, though it's obvious some find it difficult to raise the mind above the cummerbund. Whether preacher, priest, seer, guru or sage, all harbor their own private passions and human frailties, thus they are not superior to anyone and should not be considered gods.

AWAKEN TO SPIRITUAL LIFE

Few on earth are pure in heart, for while in lower worlds

soul is constantly subjected to the influences of the negative power. But when man becomes attached to Sound and Light, he finds himself detached from all that deeply troubled him.

Looking for exemplary lives, the magic wand would trim its wick in shame if it peered the privity of chambers under vaulted roofs. The stone-walls of religious orders, as the private lives of ranting prophets could tell astonishing tales. No doubt we would withdraw our praise from those who demand our consistent reverence and remind us to rue our infamies. But we know there are exceptions, depending on the inward energizing of the consecrated soul. But most of them will do no more than following the rest, preferred to feeling insecure and disconnected.

We worship an obscure Ideal, but forget to search out the Essence of Its Heart. Last, but not least, individuals can pray for lifetimes, chastise body and spirit, work like trojans, and never realize God. For the being must become illumined from *within,* that then life would grow gradually purer. Celibate is only he whose heart and life are celibate, who lives encloistered by the Radiant Spirit no matter where he may abide. Only two kinds of souls are there: one who revels in self-production, the other who subdued his pangs of lust.

When man is alone he is himself. We call it privacy. Unmindful of the All-Observing, Unseen Guest, he abandons every principle. The message simply states: *Live* what you profess. We do not judge, but observe the action. And, independent of galvanized opinions, all are of the Light, regardless of sexual preferences. Some experience Its manifestation to greater degree and know God better, than their infernal hecklers and abusers who profess God at every turn. The Divine Self knows no division. All of the Light become ruled by *It.*

Whilst people's guilts punish them far worse than the Tribunal Spirits would concede, we merely lift the sacrilegious veil of virginal pretense and of blurred modesty from those who hail Eternal Life and love to all — but kill the life within their womb. Though life itself is indestructible, premature termination and dissection cause great pain to the unborn. And deprives the soul of a form, a body — and an incarnation it prepared to enter over many lifetimes.

If you are involved in awakening others to the Light of God, thus represent the Virtue of the One, Who is Father, Son and Holy Ghost, there are things you can no longer do in public or in private. Some options are no longer yours. "If you cannot keep your own counsel, how can you expect another person to keep it." -Proverb-

We cannot separate sexuality from ethics and morality, neither exists by itself. You are what you are, the *whole You*. Until these issues are faced, there will be trouble afoot and dissension at every turn. Self-honesty is a vital factor to mental health and spiritual progress. As every soul goes through periods of learning, let each do what holds true for *him*, but reserve his guilt for himself and not attack others because of it.

It is not in hope nor willingness human darkness transmutes into Light, but through the *Power Current* of *Divine Love* that will change the course of every thought and redirect your energy.

MYTH OF THE VOW

The claim that physical union robs you of spiritual power is untrue. To the contrary, it strengthens it, makes steady and stable. Affectionate, loving sexual union keep body, mind and spirit in needed balance and deepens the bond and inner harmony of the relationship. The subliminal stirring of sex is a spiritual impulse, but as bodily function not a spiritual act. The idea that it is the *duty* of woman to satisfy the sexual *drive* of her spouse is chauvinistic and crude, since some humans suffer from uncontrolled sexual compulsions. Such person's thoughts constantly attain to *enduring* sex, upon which they make everything else *contingent*. Thus inclined, they say: "You do for me and I'll do for you!" True love invokes a mutual, natural, loving response.

However, once the soul has entered conscious union with God, it will then by the Power, Mercy and Purity of this bond begin a celibate existence.

Man will never be satisfied until he meets God. To realize God means fulfillment on every level. God and soul are two halves of one whole. God is your True Soul Mate. The love between soul and God is rare, exciting, complete and ravishingly divine. A fulfillment of promise and love sought. And even though God loves you more intensely than any human being can, He will leave you to cry alone to test your faithfulness and loyalty. When soul meets God it is a Bond no power can break. For this is the bond no man can put asunder. Ad infinitum it is the *only* marriage made in heaven.

THE BURDEN BELONGS TO US

Over the centuries nonconformists as the reformed were persecuted alike, injured, brutalized, thrown into prisons and perished — as pseudo radicals offered their human sacrifice to God. Oppression of the human spirit bears dire consequences, that extend far into future existences. The enemy must be faced again until he becomes the friend. Freedom is not won by death, but by surrender to God.

Nations are men, men are people, and we, as souls, are karmically indebted and liable for the actions of the whole, as mass-karma demonstrates when people die together by the drones. The duty to redeem the wrong remains within us and becomes our karmic destiny.

Because God *is I Am* — is *Consciousness and Life*, whatever our brothers are, good or evil, *I Am* is also, albeit to degrees. The True Self includes all Life. Thus in the Unity of Spirit is no distinction, for the Infinity of Spirit is the infinity of soul. Until we recognize our unity with all life, see and treat it as *One* Soul, and as we would ourself — and behold the God-Presence as the center of all things; evil will dog our footsteps and disrupt our lives. Things will not change, but we *can* change ourself whereby uplift the whole.

WHY WAR?

Conditions that ensue from amalgamating religion with

politics and greed, as from religion itself, not only jeopardize our economy but the physical and spiritual future of our young. But as the saying goes: "It's nobody's fault and everybody's problem!"

No sooner than a just man endeavors to establish harmony and order, fanatics and money grubbers annihilate him. For the sake of warring and civil defense by which we claim to protect ourselves from *each other*, people are taught to hate, when the hated is even their own brother. To keep the memory of acrimony and unforgiveness alive, we memorialize the bloodshed of war and weep at the monuments of our transgressions. Thus we preserve the madness and history of false martyrdom and call it our legacy for the young. A tumultuous legacy of hate, indeed. Peace seeking individuals do not want to hear about these issues but are affected by them just the same.

While religious patriots kill each other "In the Holy Name of God", they express every attribute of satan. Have we forgotten to love? When still young, someone handed me this poem from an unknown author, that points to a better way: "I sought my God, but my God I could not see, I sought my soul, but my soul eluded me, I sought my brother — and found all three!"

The death-rattle of religious wars is the perversion of Divine Will. While power-wielders work through their sermons, stage acts, and twisted tales of God, avowing undivided love for their Lord, they rob the till and slay their brother in whom He dwells. If they would test their feeble strength against the Powers of Nature, it would shake them like a flimsy rag and snap them like a tender reed!

Warmongers are the crows that hover on the Branches of the Tree of Life and steal away Its Fruit. Thousands, nay, millions of young, blossoming souls are forced to give up their life in senseless battle — that others may have what they demand. Our young die for those who never sorrowed for anyone but themselves, who are indifferent to the suffering their infernal mandates provoke. The mouth praising God, their heart is a fuming caldron of iniquity, thievery, hate and spiritual treason. To them speak the words of John the Baptizer: "He that saith he is in the light and hatest his brother, is in darkness even now."

WHERE DO HEROES GO?

Contrary to popular belief there are *no* heroes in heaven. The Law "Thou shalt not kill!" (whether man or animal), holds true Above as below! And on June 29, 1987, the roman catholic clergy announced their sanction for the death penalty. quote:". . . some crimes warrant the same treatment!" unquote. How can the perfidious absolve your sins *or* guide you to God? It is not up to man to institute laws that condemn to death, neither to prolong life by artificial means. It is disconcerting to think man no longer has the right to decide his own destiny.

IN THE NAME OF GOD

Observing world events and researching historic records prove the wantonness and bloodstained character of world religions. Having myself endured the misery and horror of woeful times, and stared into the blank Face of War, gives good reason for pointing to unchanging conditions.

The colossal, gruesome looking *Entity* of War remained unmoved by the groaning, writhing agony of the dying. It didn't give a wink as flatbed wagons piled up with the dead rumbled down the narrow, cobbled streets of our town; and caravans of the tattered and wounded hobbled after them, battered, maimed, leaning against each other, some dragging along on crutches — trickles and thin streams of blood marking the ground.

The air was filled with anxiety. Panic-stricken individuals peeped out from behind the curtains, a few moved cautiously about. Echoes of rattling machine guns and the blood-curdling screams of the repeatedly raped and stricken pierced the periodic stillness of the night. Every now and then bombs came down en masse, in inverted X-Mas tree patterns that turned the distant horizon into daylight.

The ground beneath us trembled from nearby explosions and people were afraid.

In retrospect it invokes the thought that devotion, selfless love towards the whole and consecration to one's God were to be *our gifts to life*. But scanning the Globe we find none but anguish, sickness, suffering and death; while the Spirit of War lay like a cat in wait for the catch.

The terror, barbarism and persistent acts of persecution by the grim orders of the Great Inquisition are still at large and rampant all over the world; supported by the charity of do-gooders, mercenaries, religious flag-wavers, missionaries and misfits. While the Presence of the Invisible Master silently moves through the wasted harvest fields of earth and barrenness of soul to save the wheat *and* save the chaff!

Believers and unbelievers sign the blood-oath against each other, instead of trying to bridge the gap of religious controversy and to turn to the Beacon of Light that pours Its Merciful Love into every heart. The less concerned and lightless ignore the bloodstained ground and worship at the feet of Mamelukes and militants that run their warring systems and wanton institutions. We speak of peace and desire it but the world has never heard of it in its entire existence, not even for one Holy Hour. Peace will manifest when it takes root in every individual heart around the Globe. Is it possible? Evil is as evil does. Lust, greed and passion are the cause of every war. Try as we may, there is no fair trial within the system of the negative material world, since it exists outside the limits of Divine Truth.

The answer then for every soul is found in the Holy Spirit of God. Its Truth makes strong, steady, stable, and clean in heart and spirit. To love *Truth* manifests Its Grandest Reciprocation. When you feel loved the warring mind is layed to rest. Honesty, gentility and power are the virtues of the holy warrior. It is no clinger nor a weeper. Forged by the power of spiritual Love the True Soul has a heart of steel in every way. There is nothing it can't cope with or conquer. When you are joyful and peaceful within, thus at peace with yourself, you contribute to World Peace.

MAKE END TO WAR

Wars and weaponry are the use of perverted power. It is the mind that grubs and hankers after things, scoures the planet for its last treasure, and drains away its living resources to satisfy vanity and greed. In deeper spiritual observances you will find enough must die because we live. Warring is the congregated destructive will of evil-minded men, who should look to their higher part, the Soul, that is a citizen of every country, loves all creatures great and small, and every nationality, because in God it loves itself. Until we are able to love the Innate Self, we are unable to love anything else.

FROM BRIGHTER HORIZONS

Our advanced technology and explorations of outer space have drawn to us forces from Higher Dimensions and the Counsel of Superior Beings; who would teach us self-restraint and *how not* to act in order to survive. But we hide the evidence of their Visitations and pretend it never happened. Why? Would accepting their guidance and wisdom make an end to our atrophic teachings, believability and pride? Would it unseat our philosophies, bigotries, sophism — and broaden our limited perception of God?

Whether it is realized or not, true brotherhood extends into other worlds as well; and since we are *not* the Superior Race, we are subordinates of Higher Intelligences more powerful and evolved than we, thus inferior to them.

Other than the 'Greenhouse Effect', there is concern these days about what would happen if aliens invaded our planet, but we do not stop to think we already invaded *theirs*. Instead of being bent on star wars, we should befriend our Higher Brothers and contact them by *inner* means on Inner Planes — instead of alienating and ridiculing them.

We would greatly benefit by listening within and accepting the Noble Help extended to us from Brighter Horizons.

It is self-evident what our ingenuity, insensitivity and willfulness have done to our planet. Perhaps there is still time to turn the tide. For, once the blurred Face of Nuclear Death becomes discernible at the Great Disjunction, it will be too late to change directions.

WHAT IS RELIGION?

Spiritual systems are part of the universal scheme and beneficial until they arrest our attention and block the way to Higher Consciousness. The child must be taught in the ways of God if it is to have a sound, moral foundation when an adult. But freedom of self-expression must be allowed, that the child when a man can find his way back to God.

Since religion is an individual, inner experience, every person lives his own religion. How many can we count? Billions. True religion affects change in every department of life. In its fall, it becomes congregated, segregated, steeped in rituals, external worship, fanaticism and fatalism. Pure religion is the love, affection and holy bond between soul and its Maker. Whether or not people call it of the devil, does not subtract from this Truth. The true soul knows neither preacher, priest, creed, doctrine or script, nor *any* master, save the Radiant Lord within. It does not cower nor confess, nor bow to any one but God — and never compromises.

What Jesus taught is unrelated to the perpetrated myths admonished from pulpits. He did not teach Neoplatonism, nor the system of sacrifice Paul handed to his followers, which clearly belongs to the Old Judaic belief.

The Message of Jesus was Love, Perfection, Rebirth, and that the Kingdom of God is to be sought and found *within*. Without *Love* can be no religion. True Religion *is* Love.

The message of eternal life does not resound from dead-letter texts, but as vibrant Sound and Light flows down from the Heart of God into the soul of all creation. Its all-imbuing rhapsody and Holy Word is perceived by every happy, cheerful heart and heard in every universe and world. For a religion to be true, its teachings must be based on Sound and Light, allowing inquiry into the afterlife and teach the Principles of *Action, Consequence, and Rebirth* as fundamentals.

World religions insist life either ends in heaven or hell, some say at the grave! Would my Reader conclude we should believe suppositions that predetermine how it is going to be with us after death?

Only those can teach such doctrines who never found the Truth of God within themselves and never glimpsed His Brilliant Light nor heard the Sound; who not once observed the timeless wonder and luxuries of Nature, nor the Nature Beings that breathe life, vitality and beauty into everything. Nor beheld the glistening energies that stream from every bush and dart out wide from the top of every tree.

And if he who leads would watch the stars recede at dawn and reappear at eventide; and contemplate the Secret of the changing seasons, where all things come to life, thrive, die and are reborn, he would come to know the nature of himself and recognize the Nature of his God.

But we cannot propagate what the mind cannot accept — thus we amble on. The words of John C. Lavatar here well apply: "There are but three classes of men; the retrograde, the stationary and the progressive."

If individuals would glimpse the Reality of God for just one fleeting moment, they would cease plucking on the nerves of others and surrender to the Will of God. In this ineffable experience the words of the Ancient Saint resound: "Listen thou from me, O soul, to the secret of thine own being; thou wert ever with me."

ON OPPOSITE POLES

Religious spirituality differs from Spiritual Religion, as much as the uprising clouds of hyped up emotions are unrelated to the inspiration that is purely Divine. The latter is the quiet ecstasy of God in which there is no shouting, lamenting or kicking up your heels. And so, each in his own pace moves from stage to stage, until he has reached satiety, or meets with some disaster or misfortune, where he turns to God and makes the saving connection.

I've met persons who never saw the inside of a church, who were imbued with such radiance and so infused with heavenly Light I felt like taking off my shoes. And met others who reiterated their scriptures at every opportunity *"to bear witness"*, who were infilled with hate, bigotry, and the scorn of *the righteous* — and spattered forth their indignations and poltergeist messages without flinching. It seems to me, spiritual lovingness should be the rule rather than the exception. Suffice it to say, when we take our vaudeville act of electrical excitement on the road to raise anything — it should be our consciousness to God.

Individuals raising hell to their own level realize their deep fears. When asked to back up their allusions of heaven and hell, the kindhearted and *joyous* become increasingly irritated and take the antagonistic stand. For they must pause on issues beyond their keen, that have yet to become their reality. When you *know* the world you speak of, you do not have to craft your answers beforehand or quote from a book. For then you affirm with full authority: *I say!*

You have to *live* the answer before you can give it. All who sought have not found. And for all the times I said otherwise, my silent, long-term observations of their lives — that would have made a devil of a thriller — brought me to every foregoing conclusion. But no matter; 'er the bark may whither, the branches crumble or the leaves may fall, the Sap and Root of the Tree never change!

All scriptures are guide posts, pointing *here* and *there*, but the Divine Lord taught, *neither* to look here *nor* there, but to the Kingdom within. And thus spoke the Lord Christna to his disciple Arjuna: "Low men follow examples, Great Men give them. . . there is but one God. . . worship by deed predominates contemplation. -Bhagavat Gita-

The True Shepherd is within you. The Holy Spirit is your Teacher, the Divine Messenger that fills your heart with boundless and enduring joy, and guides you back Home to God. Anyone who wants with all his heart to know the Way to the Kingdom will find it. And anyone who truly found it and experienced God, is profoundly at peace. The Worlds of God are free of illusive fantasies. There is only endless Love and endless Truth. Sometimes what seems most difficult, is the easiest to obtain. *-PEACE-*

9.

The Power of Darkness

To better understand why at times the tidal waves of life wash over us, and then the sun comes out and gently dabs away our tears, we need to examine the mysterious, powerful force that commands our life and governs us.

The Negative Power is the Ruling Lord of the physical-material universe. As the Life Energy flows down from the Neuter Aspect, or Heart of God into universes and worlds below, the split or division into positive and negative polarity occurs at the lower borders of the Causal World (world of cause) that adjoins the upper Spheres of the physical universe in which we live. Here the Force becomes our Ruling Deity. Divided, yet whole, this Mighty Combatant Energy became Spirit and matter, positive/negative, male/female, that the Orientals call Kal (positive) and Kali — the negative feminine principle.

So we see, God is the Transcendent Source from which all energies derive and are born, the Center from which you came and to which you will return. While on earth, you are outside of the Temple of God and you can only re-enter it by going *within*. It is the place where negative *and* positive energies are neutralized. Though while in form, mind and soul are cleansed through suffering, transmutation takes place within.

Any world below the Pure Regions of Spirit is negative, not negative as in human terms, but negative as being on the opposite pole of the True God Worlds. While dwelling in lower spheres, soul is enshrouded by mind, matter and illusion. Thus its lesser self, the personality is negative or rather demonic, until it reawakens to God. Because of his limited perception, man is constantly affected by the illusions of his world, but once he has gained the illumined state, all things become relative. Then he sees the world, his conditions and people for what they are.

WHY NEGATIVE POWER?

For the unfoldment of souls it is the duty of the Negative Power to harass, plague and to keep them bound to the material world; that by their own inner strength they may awaken to God, learn to swim against the negative stream and become detached from it. Under negative inflections individuals lose their sense of harmony, but go in search of inner peace. Divine discontent has its virtue, in that it spurs the seeker on to find his God.

The Power of Darkness works best through religions, law makers, organizations and political systems, since there it can exert its pressure and demands through individuals who influence the masses. Positive power works in the same way, since it also belongs to lower worlds. Pro-life movements advance slowly, for the negative force is bent on destruction.

So long as individuals deceive, destroy, kill the living things of earth — and each other, they are its willing vessels. The Power of Darkness has its agents as do the Legions of Light, embodied and disembodied. Unredeemed human beings are its vehicles on conscious and unconscious levels. Influenced in their dreams, they carry out its lowly commands during waking hours — and pay for it! When man yields to the Light his nightmares will end. If one's character is cold and dead inside, so will his dreamy atmosphere appear.

As energies of deception plague the mind, man poisons the fields, water, air and earth and the fires of life. Polluting the sacred elements he slowly begins self-annhilation. Whether he lives or dies, the negative force does not care, it does not recognize death. And given that man does not abruptly change course and keeps rowing towards his inevitable end, it would seem he should take refuge in the Spirit of God that alone can restore him to reason and resuscitate him to life. God is always the cure. And though "There is no power but of God", its lesser effects are acutely felt.

WORSHIPING THE MOTHER

The worship of Nature is the worship of the negative/feminine principle and cocreative power in lower worlds. Her inner and outer forces and inflections constantly play through creation and through the sentient nature of man; manifesting etheric and demonic presences everywhere.

The reason we do not realize the *Father* is because we prefer worshiping the Mother. Since she is mostly portrayed as woman, some feel she can better understand them, but instead, she wraps you deeper into her veil of illusion and pollutes the spirit of all men. The Mother is worshiped as *Maria*, often confused with the Mother of Jesus. In truth she is the Goddess of Destruction. As the feminine aspect of the negative power, she is the Mystery Force of Nature until you recognize her for what she is: the power of harm, deceit and illusion, yet in paradox she is also that part of Love that moves the soul Godward.

The Stories of the Greeks say: "The Mother brought forth three deities" the Three Fates or "Daughters of Darkness", And that no matter how many souls came into this world, each was attached by a separate thread to the Fates. "One spun the thread of life, one twisted it and the other held the shears and snapped it when it pleased her to do so. One unwinds life; One ever weaves the shroud; One waits to cut the thread."

Out of the Mother's Bosom spring ravishing beauty, lofty moods, indifferent, uncaring attitudes, healthy and infirm forms, lust, greed, jealousy, murder and every other perversion. Her artful work from the finest thread of Indian summer to the smallest chip of granite in a mountain craig; fragrant meadows, thriving valleys, singing streams and colorful creatures, thrill and captivate the mind of man with the illusion of impermanent substance he deems reality. In her double-edged love the fields become fruitful and the harvest destroyed by droughts, floods and torrents of beating rain.

The Mother works tirelessly to perpetuate heavenly matter on earth, and creates new garments for souls to enter. In that alone she is the power behind the Throne of God. Thus she is the Queen of Heaven, the woman clothed with the sun, depicted to stand on the circle of a half-moon, crowned with a diadem of stars. I have seen her full appearance. She is strikingly beautiful. The magnetism of her illusion is fantastic!

The feminine principle is the eternal tempest, fury, builder and destroyer of her own creations; who exacts 'an eye for an eye — and tooth for tooth'! 'Er the winds blow and raging emotions of unbridled minds may fall, and the blood of man and animal seeps into the ground, she remains unmoved, unfeeling; — as those who are possessed by her, who act kind, meek and considerate, but are cold, ruthless and calculating within. Though the Mother is Cocreator of celestial substance, she cannot bestow divinity, nor breathe the breath of life into her creations. This only the Father can do. So we see: mind and body are created by the Negative Force. The brilliant spark within the soul is man's heavenly self and of the True Father. Thus man is spirit and earth.

WORSHIP OF THE IDOL

When efforts fail to reach the Father, we believe praying to the Mother will do as well, since the two are one. Though in essence they are undivided, worshipping the negative aspect is to your detriment and you will remember the bruises.

To reunite with the Neuter Essence of God is Law to every soul, This unity cannot be obtained through the Mothering Principle. Mother worshippers believe a feeling of joy and warmth, and an occasional vision are signs of right direction, but they are the illusions of *Kali* that entrap mind and soul. When apparitions or visions are accompanied by spirit voices that are as clear as your own thoughts, the devoted believe it is the Voice of God. Even the clergy falls into her traps. Whatever the heart may call upon, it remains joyful today and is depressed tomorrow, which is the way of the Mother but not of the Father.

Now, the Mother teaches her child bitter-sweet lessons. She will take it to the bottom line of poverty and pull it back up into transient pleasures, comforts and riches; only to withdraw them again as it suits her purpose. She will answer the prayers of her devotees, even slay their enemies, for she is Kali, the Power of Darkness. So long as she can keep man's trust and belief in her, she can keep him close to her bosom and tied to her moorings, to sorrow, suffering and death. Man cannot become God-realized until he turns his praise and the face of the soul to his Maker.

Many persons sincerely desire to know God, but do not want to divert from the worship of idols and negative nature powers. They believe the energy of stones and crystals will bring them power, wealth and healing. When such persons are in fact communing with demonic spirits no more evolved than they. If results appear at all, it is what man himself believed in that made them happen.

Nature spirits are entrancingly beautiful. But most who use them lack the ability to see them and to appreciate them for what they are. If stone-worshippers would perceive on inner levels, they would readily observe that nature spirits have their own life to live, tasks to carry out and the need to be left to their tranquility. First hand knowledge is always irrefutable. Then, when you know what *is* true but you say otherwise, as do people pleasers, even the truth you have will retreat from the heart.

The Force of the Mother will tempt, entice and torment you, that you may learn to swim *against* the negative stream and unfold into Godhood. Indulge in her fancy, and she will punish you severely. Those who walk in the Light and deny her worship often encounter great hardships, for she has lost her hold. But the sugar plum of plenty always dangles before the devotee of God. And he may if he wishes return to the open arms of the Mother, to comforts, to material luxuries, and to eternal doom when it suits her fancy.

But there is profound beauty in all that has been said. When after severe testing that can last for many years, the devotee of God proved she can no longer dissuade him, then, and grudgingly at first, the Mother will return to him true bounty and goodness without repercussions. Of course by that time things of earth have lost all fascination and no longer matter, which was the original intent!

To denounce the world and materialism is futile. For the mind will continue to crave, clutch after things and slide along its repetitious track of habit, desire and infernal want. Desire can only be layed to rest by the Greater Love of God.

Through the Mother we become capable of loving, caring and appreciating; capable of reaching every necessary state of detachment, through the hell she allows us! It is through the pain of *becoming* we ultimately find our way back Home to the Father.

THE MYSTERY OF SUFFERING

Since you are told the Holy Spirit will make an end to misery, you might ask: 'then why am I still suffering?' Because it is not until you have gone through the teachings and preparations of the Mother — or *Karma*, that the Spirit of God will redeem you. For this reason some experience delay, while others readily enter the Spiritual Life. But who is to say who is first and who last? And even though you received the Light, you are still under the karmic yoke until all indebtedness has been mitigated.

The Holy Spirit is beyond good and evil and All-Merciful. Though you do not know when it will infill your life, there are lights along the way that will bring you much closer to that Wondrous Event. The Holy Spirit is not found in the pleasures of the world, but the pain of pleasure brings us to *It*. When you look within, with quiet, unrelenting courage, with patience, and tarry there awhile, It will flood your heart and life with Light and Peace — and conquer all.

SATAN, POWER OF GOOD OR EVIL?

Over the ages, the 'Son of the Morning' has received a lot of bad publicity! Nevertheless, this Shining One, clothed with the radiant glow of the Morning Sun and fiery filaments of the Planets, aids the regeneration and ascent of man. There is no devil anywhere as fierce as the raging one of the personality; to which any other devil will gladly retreat.

Catastrophies, world-disease as the plague, you name the traumas — issue out of the energy *man* misqualified. This malignant energy enters the physical, emotional, mental and spiritual ethers and rebounds to haunt him into the remnants of his personal hell. Man's evils reappear on the mirror of his mind through dreams, dark images and whispering voices, that are born of his fears and contents of character. Happiness and despair begin and end with you. For all the pain the human endures no devil other than the human self is responsible. If man tried as hard to find God as he does defending his unwise deeds and persuasions, he would be free of all personal evil, free of fear, and grow quite content and comfortable with himself.

APPROACHING THE GATE OF GOD

The unmastered self is the Dweller on the Threshold in everyone. The character of this entity is of man's own despotic nature and will not let him approach the Gate of God as long as he still carries his baggage of pride, dishonesty, hate, rage and lust. But this Dweller on the Threshold can be transformed into the angel that will establish a strong relationship between soul and God; for it is the Inner Self and Watcher.

Yet, without the confrontation of evil, man cannot attain Soul Awareness or God Realization. Once he enters the Brilliant Light and hears Its Sound, his courage will be tested to the last, for he must face all that lay concealed in Light and *all* that lay in darkness. To gain admittance to the Gate presents a great problem to individuals who see evil in others but refuse to recognize it within themselves.

The Kingdom of God is for humble, self-emptied souls. A true soul is never proud. Haughty, evil thoughts push the dreamer into the abyss of darkness and sometimes over the mental edge.

The Power of Darkness sets up barriers, that by overcoming them man may advance into the Light. Even as God spoke to the Arch Angel Lucifer, He speaks to *every* heart: "When the world rejects thee, I will pardon and again receive thee — but *Not Until Then*." Overcomers can well attest to the rejection of the world, but also to Unspeakable, Heavenly Love.

The Negative Force works through friend, foe, and through your own thoughts. It is the only way it can. The journey from vice to evil and from evil to redemption are but a hairbreadth apart. When thoughts are clean and kind, acts selfless and noble, and the eyes of the soul remain fixed on God, evil flees, never to return. In the *Archetypes of Collective Unconscious,* Dr. Carl Gustav Jung states: "Evil is a necessary opposition of good, without which there would be no good either. It is impossible to think evil out of existence."

NEUTRALIZING EVIL

Evil, as much as illusion is a natural part of lower worlds. Man can turn from it. When you see evil as the energy of sick, erratic minds and know it has no part in you, you take control.

To shift the blame of one's mental state on other persons and to harangue them into a mental brawl to relieve pent up emotions proves lack of self-honesty and absence of God-Awareness. Self-control is the answer. Altered states of consciousnes stem from the individual's attitude and attracts forces of like nature from inner and outer planes that fuel the emotional turmoil. Instead of breaking under the neurotic strain, we need to *break through*!

Evil is a mental condition. In itself evil does not exist. There are no devils with pitchforks, bent horns, golden hoofs and bows in their tails as portrayed, and no ogre that did not rise out of human passions. It is through the abuse of man's innate vitality that energy becomes satanic. Satan is the nature of carnal man. Desecration of power issues out of the ignorance of wicked minds and pollutes the Sacred Energy of God. When the gales of Karma begin to hiss and blow, erring souls find the Guiding Light. Man is of God and must become ruled by the Force.

And what of evil spirits and malicious specters? These wandering, inflecting entities were once human and rose out of the crimes they committed. As do apparitions of those who died an untimely death and are bound to lower magnetic spheres until their natural life term has run its course. And others too, that rise out of the sunless regions of God in search of peace.

Then there are evil souls of another sort, horrid and gross, that emerge out of the foggy mists of the Lands of the Damned. That, when encountered will freeze your tracks, make you shudder and clutch after your reason! But they are only as evil as the humans to whom they are drawn. As with the living, karma continues for the living dead. Individuals who talk about God and Life Beyond with sweeping generality, would be rudely awakened by many unlovely facts.

Another concern of individuals is fear of their deceased enemies, your enemies, real and imagined are your own thoughts. Forgive them all. This will neutralize the energy and set you free. Nothing liberates better than forgiveness and *conscience*. But for the thrill of evil some humans do much harm. Used to it, it becomes their way of life.

ABYSS OF HELL

Earth is a hell plane of sorts, where some live in better quarters than others and all are given ample opportunity to work out their derelictions. Heaven and hell are states of consciousness, both are experienced within. Spiritualists speak of Summerland to be the ultimate heaven, this is not our goal. We want to go back to the Heart of Our Father, to the Supreme Worlds that lay far *beyond* the heaven and hell of man's imagination.

To be in hell means to be out of harmony with Divine Law. As we have learned throughout this book, God punishes no one. Purification is the cause of pain man instituted for himself.

Devils are the product of ignorant minds, that subjugated others to justify their guilts. If ever a devil other than their own appeared to them, or they met up with the sinister spirits of the Abyss, they would turn ashen-faced and faint out of their shoes. Now, since without God nothing was made nor can exist, then the devil or shadow must also be of God. But when the shadow falls on the Light, the Light absorbs it and transforms it to goodness. The devils and demons so demeaned are all on earth. The rest dwells inbetween the veils and in the mental fog of those who delight to bring regret and pain to others.

SORROWS OF THE HELL PLANE

There are no tranquilizers in hell planes Beyond to soothe or numb the senses. No Christ shall save. No God grant Mercy, while the wicked energy of crimes committed against our own nature and against others is being cleansed away. But though obscured, the Light is near and man has a chance to seek his Lord even *there*.

Animal abusers should think long and deep before harassing and tormenting the energy of God vested in these helpless ones! Man reaps what he sows! Now, when children with no place to sleep are hungry, prostituted and used for pornography, that is hell! And a hefty one the offender prepared for himself. There is no such a thing as the instant forgiveness of religions, the *One* Law applies to all people.

In hell planes the force of pain is not equal to the pain man inflicted on others, but intensified a hundred fold, by the pressure and vibrations of Higher Voltage and the woeful vibration of that plane. And felt to the finest atom until purification has met full circle.

Many years ago I knew a man and woman who were unfeeling, insensitive and beastly cruel. After their death, uncommon as it was, I pondered the place, if any—to which they might have departed.

Again many years passed, when I found myself in soul body and entered the hellish slums of sunless Netherlands. The hostile atmosphere was without solace. I found the couple in a simple structure. The interior resembled the place they occupied on earth, but was a bit more dilapidated.Its chalky looking walls did not quite extend to the ceiling. The air was filled with a writhing, foul smelling, seething corruption, breathing from confining walls, that were drenched with stench and permeated by the vibrations of the two inhabitants.

With a strained, painful smile the woman pointed to her mate, (her husband while on earth), who screamed in agonizing pain near oblivion. The purifying Light assailed him in a way that defies description. In undulating wavelike motion it attacked him from every direction. Zigzagging streams of yellow-orange light poured out of its long tentacles, from which there was no escape. Withdrawing and attacking ceaselessly the wailing, shrieking entity, that once was a proud, self-righteous man, who lied to protect himself, and whose diabolic actions destroyed the lives of others without mercy and without a twinge of regret.

There was no reasoning with this merciless, shining force, that held the flogging energy the man and woman forged while still on earth; that none but God could mellow—were He interested! And I thought to myself: strange, how even those in hell will ask your forgiveness. To harm anyone or anything is highly impractical. So long as you bring no injury to others, you have nothing to fear.

Have pity on your enemies, Dear Friend; forgive those who keep you at their mercy. They will have ample time for undoing. You need not wish for the destruction of your nefarious opponents, the Radiant Force takes care of them far better. Justice and Retribution are the same and man reaps the energies of his evils to the last mite.

AGENTS OF DARKNESS

Since the Tempter is appointed to try the spirit of man to the last and to keep him on his toes, he has an alert network of agents that do his bidding. Advertisements seduce you into overindulging, circulating magazines promote lust, lotto-fever inciting greed. Sunday sermons caution that gluttony and greed will send you to the hospital, if not to the pits. While on the other hand, and, in confederacy with the devil, the pious defraud the widow of her mite, pilfer the till, the cradle and the coffin!

The *Divine Tempest* has many channels. Television and video being most instrumental, and scholars who adjust and readjust the scriptures to their own grievances, guilts and woes. Materialism denies Spirit. The *vanity* of materialism obscures the true treasures of the soul. And what you idolize here and now, becomes your reality after death.

AT THE TEMPLE DOOR

Satan is the Impersonal Force that only becomes *personal* when it assails the evil in man. He is the Great Purifier of souls, that in lower worlds manifests as good and evil, light and shadow. He is the Sacrificer and *opponent* of evil deeds; the Fierce Guardian that stand at the Temple Door of Our Most High God, where only he who has been purged of *personal* evils and is *truly* humble can enter. Thus, the only evil we need to fear is our own.

However, to say there is nothing to fear is one statement, to understand *why* there is nothing to fear quite another.

And finally, let us clearly understand, that the Spirit of Darkness is *not* bevexing or evil, but the Great Harbinger of Enlightenment.

And thus spoke the Great Spirit of Trismegistus: "Among the Gods is none like unto him, in whose hands are committed the kingdoms, the power and the glory of the worlds...Satan is the doorkeeper of the Temple of the KIng...he holdest the key to the Sanctuary, that no man can enter therein, save the anointed having the arcanum of Hermes." (see "The Divine Pymander of Hermes", Theosophical University Press, P.O. *Bin* C, Pasadena, Ca., 01109).

HOLY EMISSARY OF GOD

In the Secret Doctrine, Anthropogenesis, Page 235, Madame Helena Petrovna Blavatsky, quotes the Ancient Kabala: "Upon Satan only is the shame of generations. He has lost his virginal estate (so has Kumara by incarnating): uncovering heavenly secrets, he hath entered into bondage...He compasseth with bonds and limits all things......"

Twain are the armies of God; in heaven the hosts of Michael; in the abbys (the manifested world) the legions of Satan. These are the unmanifested and the manifest; the free and the bound (in matter): the virginal and the fallen. And both are Ministers of the Father, fulfilling the Word Divine..." Therefore—"Holy is the Sabbath of God: blessed and sanctified is the Angel of Havas"—Satan.

For, "The glory of satan is the shadow of the Lord": God in the manifested world—"the throne of satan is the footstool of Adonai"—that Footstool being the whole Kosmos....

And she continues: "When the church therefore, curses Satan, it curses the Cosmic Reflection of God; it anathematizes God made manifest in matter or in the objective; it meladicts God, or the ever-incomprehensible *Wisdom*, revealing itself as Light, Shadow, good and evil in nature, in the only way incomprehensible to the limited intellect of *Man*." (Theosophical University Press, P.O. Bin C, Pasadena Ca. 91109)

The Hindus refer to Satan as the "Angel of the Abyss...stand in awe of him and sin not; speak his name with trembling. For Satan is the Magistrate of Justice of God. He beareth the balance and the sword (Retribution). For to him are committed the Weight and Measure and Number".

Satan in Deity called *Jehovah*, is the Omniscient, Ruling Lord of our universe. He is the Lucifer of the bible, the great tempter of souls. Satan is the Reflection of Divine Mind, that illumined man counter-reflects through the seven fold ray. He is the Chief Regent of evolving life, who maintained His Divine Esteem and High Station in Spiritual Government, regardless of what man's scriptures state. Whether he is believed to be good or evil does not diminish his Superior Rank.

Although the Redeeming Light of God is disturbing to profane man, none other can bring him into the calm, peaceful Harbor of God. Even as the river gets lost in the ocean and the raindrop is absorbed by the sea, so the soul may lose itself in the Bliss and Love of God while still on earth.

In his changeableness man must seek the Unchanging. When he does, he will lose his fear of death and darkness and begin to live in the Light of Eternity now. As humanity grows into deeper understanding of God, demons will have outlived their usefulness and the hell of the damned will be no more.

10.

Transcending the Top of the Stairs Without Fear

The buoyancy of life increases, and then slowly ebbs into another cycle within the boundlessness of Eternal Being. Life and death are within our transient nature. The body constantly renews itself, old cells die and new ones come to life. Even as the Spirit of the season withdraws itself and returns to quicken natural forms, so the consciousness of man returns and re-enters a better vehicle that aids his ascent to God.

Fear death, my Friend? *Never!* The death experience is painless, you need not have the slightest fear of death. Man's greatest apprehension is that death will make an end to his ego-existence, and rather than to be no more, he prefers the misery of re-embodiment to nothing at all.

In search of the continuity of life after death some pursue the quest of immortality while others insist life ends at the tomb. Individuals who engage in the nocturnal practice of necromancy to find the essence of life, often end up horrified, when the proof sought is right within them.

To remove all negations, anxieties and fear of death once and for all, you should realize you are more than flesh and bones. *You are the Soul*. The body is your vehicle, the means to an end, which is to attain God-Realization. Wherever you find yourself in any world you are never without a body and do not have to look for one since your other forms are already with you. And, you always maintain your full faculties and identity.

Coma, sleep, dreamstate and death are interrelated. While dreaming you occupy another form and exchange it again for the physical cloak upon awakening. Now does this hurt? Your translation into the Higher Life is no different and no matter what we choose to believe, some things do not change: life is generated from death and death is the Liberator. This knowledge has always been with you, you only need to reawaken it.

TRUTH SETS FREE

After death you are more alive and aware than in this present moment, and since you are forever, why should life when it is worn down be preserved and death be prolonged? To lose the fear of death means to live life fully and in contentment.

Individuals who fear death fear life as much and never realize the happiness that may be theirs presently, mainly because they are wary that something might happen to them if they ventured too far. The death dread is man's greatest obstacle to his physical and spiritual advancement. In example: persons endowed with abundant force, intelligence and good will, may be too apprehensive to press on, because they fear the airplane may lose its tail end or fall apart in midair, or the train might derail or whatever else. Some persons hesitate to go out of doors in rain or snow because they might fall, get injured and die, all of which are phobias that need to be laid to rest.

The old 'what if' is the crippling factor that should be uprooted from the mind as weeds from the garden, then life will become content and fulfilling. Mind is expert in making excuses. When fear rears its head I would wish you to roar back like a lion and show you are the master! And 'what if' your worst fears are realized? Then at least you faced them and will pick yourself up to face them again until the mind gives up to intimidate you. You *are* what you think. If you do not overcome your fear now, you will fear as much when you reach Higher Worlds.

You are what you are wherever you find yourself. Fearful thoughts quickly vanish when you refuse to give them energy to feed on.

And though the world may be set against you, *never give up*. The death dread blocks creative energy and your enterprises! The good life on earth, as the spiritual life are not for the faint and fearful, but for the lion-hearted. Why fear death when it is the beginning of innate happiness? Do not pray to be free from the ills of life but repose in the Calmness of the Lord to know what is truly divine and complete, that after death you may be free of the illusions that solder body and soul to the Wheel of Re-embodiment. But how can a man ignorant of Truth be unafraid of death, so long as the soul is menaced by material anxiety, merrymaking and unbridled passions?

WHY FEAR THE UNKNOWN?

The silent death dread drains life of its wonderful meaning and pirates your vitality. Fear of death is fear of the Unrecognized that exists already within you as life. Since the Unknown constantly sustains you and is the *Known* to your Inner Self, you are closer to *It* than to earth.

Persons who believe the physical world is their only reality, fear death, while others cross its threshold every day. No telling of heavenly experiences can lift man's apprehensions of death and not one single doctrine on earth can provide proof that there is life after death. It remains heresay until your personal experience in God will establish the fact. Then every question is answered.

You must let go of the conscious self to realize you are the soul and the Light. How otherwise can you be born again? When you enter the Worlds of God in total soul-awareness, there will be nothing left to fear. In this transcendent state you find you are not the body, nor the pain or joy, but the immortal self over which death has no power. For you have experienced the deathless Reality of God and Its Truth and Happiness will forever sustain you. Then, at the moment of death you will remain inwardly aware, knowing you are *not* dying — and you just go on.

True believers in life after death will by natural ability and trust part the veil and move into the experience where the Self is revealed and the Unknown only exists as the Known. Many who behold the Vision of the Greater Life still fear death because they lack the courage to take the step Beyond. Only when you yourself are free, can you teach others.

When the Sons of God still walked among the children of earth, before man was endowed with the reasoning power that allowed him to prefer greed and evil to goodness he knew no death. When time arrived, he simply stepped out-of-the-body into the Sunshine of God. Then man knew no dread since he felt no guile, thus feared no retribution.

UNDERSTANDING DEATH

Now, unless persistent evil calls for subtraction, the process of death adds to life. To know the meaning of death sets free and ends bewilderment and consternations. Death does not deprive you of love but permits you to come to know the meaning of love more fully. It is the longing for unrealized love that moves us in-and-out-of higher worlds and back to earth to find It. Your longing for love is your innate need for the Love of God, nothing less can satisfy the soul. The pain of love belongs to the world of sorrow. True Love is within you and nowhere else. But how can you be conscious of what you do not feel inside?

While some may wish for death to find rest, another may long for a better body, for a better life, or to be with a dear one he loved and lost. Whatever the reason, the death wish bears down on you with silent pressure and blocks the way to happiness. If we could realize the Nowness, Hereness and I-ness of the Presence, that we live in eternity *now* and that there is really nowhere to go or to escape to, our attitude about life and death would greatly change and our lives would become uncomplicated and simple.

At death we not merely let go of the physical shell, but also of our finer, inner bodies, until we pick them back up on our higher ascent. These bodies are not severed from us by any means, but by the elasticity of the silver cord are temporarily suspended until purification in the Valley has ended.

The more we are able to adjust to higher vibrations and to our inner worlds while still on earth — through meditation, contemplation and out-of-body consciousness, the more flexible our inner centers and celestial forms become, and the easier it will be to let go of the body at the final hour. For the soul withdraws the energy of the body from the feet upward through these centers, until it departs through the crown of the head. Superimposed death can throw the inner man out ever which way and often the soul hovers near the body in confusion until a Guardian leads it homeward. Where catastrophies and mass-karmic death occur they are always attended by Spirits of Light and Darkness that take charge of the departed and guide each to his merited place.

TO HOLD AND LET GO

Humble, simple human beings never fear death as do those attached to their world. Neither do the lovelorn and friendless cling to life as would the loved and the 'hail fellow' well met, since there is no attachment. At death, the devoted soul follows the Light to the world from which the summon came. Empyreal Brightness becomes its Guide at night and carries it to eternal worlds.

For the materialist the transition is difficult. Body and soul are ready to let go, but he fiercely hangs on to possessions, lust, revenge and passion; and persists in the death-struggle until the electrical energy of the Death Angel severs the connection and takes him into the Courts of God.

Whatever we are attached to or enslaved by in life will assuredly bind us after death. Individuals who worry about what they might leave behind should consider what they willed to themselves in the afterlife. You need more than material possessions to mark your passing. People also fear death because a vague, nudging memory of past purifications in astral hell planes, and that, coupled with the allusion of hell-fire and brimstone can make them quite restless. Now, the world of people is weeping, wailing and gnashing its teeth, it doesn't have to wait for hell, it is already there.

We hear many accounts of after death experiences but the angels or devils facing man are not of another kind, but of his own making. Even as man's perception of heaven and hell are no more than his state of mind, since they belong to the universe of mind and illusion, and are not the True Worlds of the soul. Of late, a man recounted demonic entities were attacking him and tearing his body to pieces. Such happenings hold true in the sunless planes of God, except that those entities were part of himself to which other vicious energies gravitate. When during life man's focus is on charity, compassion and love, these energies will then be the angels that greet him hereafter.

There is need to become re-educated in matters of the Spirit and to break through the walls of fearful indoctrination to find Truth in the Sound Current, that teaches us to die in order to live.

When the soul is thrown out of the sunlight of day into the deep night of Self, only the Inner Light can illumine the way. But how can it guide you through the event of death when you never sought it while living? Moreover, no *living* master whom you believed and worshipped will come to your aid. He will be busy with other things and will have enough to atone for at his own parting. The Holy Light of the Brilliant Sound Current is the *only* Vehicle that can carry you safely across the abyss of death. To It belong your love and allegiance, for It is the Invisible Master, the Holy Spirit of God.

THE INVISIBLE PROCESS OF AGING

Our mortal existence is made up of events and changes that teach us vital lessons and affect us physically, mentally and spiritually. Though we feel the aging process biologically and socially, it bestows much grace on the soul. To graduate from the University of Life one can become quite illumined, since the joy and pain of living build in us a strong character. The lessons of life bring us to feel compassion for the needs of others; to look within, to become obedient to inner laws that direct us to one common goal, and to contemplate the Divine Purpose and whole of life that bring man into Godhood.

Now, individuals think of getting old, but life is not measured by years, but by *energy*. An 80 year old may be as spry as a teen, while a teenager may complain of constant fatigue and feeling old. Energy ebbs off for various reasons. But whether young or old, when weary of the journey the soul longs for rest, the energy of the body begins to run low, recedes into the soul and physical life comes to an end.

Clearly then, when a person *looks* old, it is not because he/she *is* old, but because the soul is slowly drawing the energy of the form unto itself; even as the vegetable loses nutriments, wrinkles and dries up when the essence of life has gone out of it. Life itself is indestructible. You *are* life, because Life *is* God. Therefore not even God will end it. Now, it's human nature to complain about worry wrinkles, but why worry? A little inner serenity goes long way — it can soften the furrow.

THE PASSWORD IS LOVE

Love opens every door, and the Door of Death. The password of death has always been Love. It receives you in Love, but we listen and hear not. In Life and in death, Love surrounds you and none other than Love can carry you inward.

Having gone through the near death experience and passing through its Gate daily, I can attest death is no ogre, but rather alluring and seductive. The unspeakable Love that pours out to you from the Wondrous Light no word can convey. In the death state all you know is Love. I found death was something you *observe* but cannot feel, for *You* cannot die. It takes much more courage to live through life's hassles and port the pain, than to give in to the dreamy, liberating swoon of death. The pale face of death is nothing to fear. After your release into the New World, you will encounter no more than you set forth.

By and by, everyone finds that death is the Doorway to another life, to another world and a new dream more beautiful and noble, that ends when you finally fully awaken to God. You experienced death before you entered this world, This is to say, your separation from God and your Divine Worlds were a sort of death, to which your unknown inner longing of today attests. Now, when you leave this earth you experience a similar separation from those you love, but are reinstated to the Love you sought to find in each, that is the Love of God, and to the Country of your Heritage. Then is death not the continuation of life and rebirth into a more awakened state?

If you truly believe life continues after death, then you must have had a body before you came to earth and you will have a better one hereafter. The Life of God is *Completeness*. To say life is grand and death its destroyer is believing in opposites and invalid. Such an attitude keeps the thinker on edge and haunts him to the end. Life and death intertwine. Separation only exists in the mind until the Light of Love illumines it. Then the heart is at ease and our outlook will be different.

WHAT HAPPENS AT THE FINAL HOUR?

All souls are good. There is something endearing about everyone if we would care enough to see it. Every human being no matter how he lived his life and what his transgressions, has the right to live until his last natural moment. No one has the right to end it for him prematurely. Our prison systems might wish to take this into account. A Greater Law holds *every* individual accountable for his actions. There is no comfort in retaliatory death and no solace in vengeance.

To prolong life by artificial means is equally grievious. We should consider how much pain we unwittingly inflict on loved ones, trying to keep them alive. A braindead body is in irreversible vegetation. The soul has already entered intermediate planes. In some cases it lingers around the corpse, sees spirits of the night, some gawking, some harassing. But bound to the physical mass the soul cannot escape into the dawning Light, nor re-enter waking awareness.

Since man's true nature is the soul, and soul feels more acutely than on conscious levels, the agony is fierce. But goes unnoticed by those attending the body, who acknowledge the patient is *half*-dead, and claim he doesn't feel anything at that point. To the contrary! Each time the machinery exerts artificial pressure, he, the soul, feels violently jerked back into the body and thrown back out of it into intermediate states. Held to the body by artificial means, the *real* man suffers the pain of hell. This should be taken into consideration. Do we think of the loved one? *No*. We selfishly attempt to keep them with us, because we have not learned to let go.

Every person should be able to look to the final hour with peace and the expectancy of all good. Not because it might be a pleasure to get out of the tyranny of others, or misery at large, but because there is something grand and wonderful to be met. Whether the person is conscious of approaching death or not makes no difference. Sensing, thinking and feeling continue on inner levels.

The best way to overcome the limiting fear of death is simply by loving God. Loving Him sincerely, purely, and trusting Him with your whole heart. Then you will anticipate the event with peace and joy, for you will be with Him you love most. This also holds true for those who do *not* know the Reality of God. Thoughts of someone they dearly loved and lost and long to see again, will throw out the bridge to peace.

There are no other infernal agonies to face than those of man's own making. After death the blinds of lying, cheating and innocent pretense drop away and facts are reckoned with. God has no stake in sickness, sorrow or evil. Even during life, evil doers are chased and haunted in their dreams by the demons of their actions. While others enjoy the Love and lively company of those On High.

The human being is an embodied soul or embodied spirit. After death he is then a *dis*embodied soul, and if unredeemed a demonic spirit or devil. Devils are correlated energies of discarded hate, deceit and mortal passions.

GUARDIANS OF THE SOUL

At the final hour you realize you were never alone in all your life nor in death. This realization might have spared you many anxious hours. Whether you enter this world or rise out of it, Holy Guardians overshadow you.

At birth the electromagnetic breath of the Angel breathes life into the soul and the soul into its new form and loosens it from the body at death. I beheld the Angels of Birth and Death many times. They are of noble bearing, of great beauty, power and compassion, some are of enormous stature. Though the Angels of Death are of equal high esteem, some are very radiant and tall, while another group is more corpulent, dark and stern. The Lords of Death look altogether different! Space does not allow to add the many things I would wish to convey; and some I would find hard to describe. The radiant splendor and fabulous heavenly hues of Guiding Angels, as the Unspeakable Love their Presences convey cannot be captured by words.

Still clearly remembering the day *before* my rebirth into

this world, and the very moment of my incarnation, I recall being intensely aware of a shining way that had no beginning and no ending. And remember colossal Beings of Light and absolute sternness, that ushered a great caravan of souls into the world. And then the dark tunnel — I did not want to be born. Much more has been given in my 'Journeys To Worlds Beyond.'

While praying for the dying I beheld Guardians of Light and others that were fierce and dark. The Presence that greets us at death depends on the life we lived. The moment of birth and death, as the memory, is eclipsed by the vision of the new life. The 'end of the journey' is a rest period of the soul to regain its strength, for what good would it do if the soul were too weak to work out its karmic destiny and continue in quest of God?

When you seek the Master's Light while living, He shall meet you at the moment of death and take you home. He is the Conquerer to all who seek Him.

AFTER THE DEATH EXPERIENCE

At death the higher self of man, the soul, ascends to Spiritual Worlds. The elements that composed the body return to matter and reshape to embody the energy of other species.

Suicides and those murdered by the law of man who had no chance to complete their natural life cycles are not fully free after death. Though free of the body they linger around the earth atmosphere until their natural life span has run its course. To suicidal persons the sunny side of life seems draped in shadow, life in general is painful to them. But to rush into new beginnings through quick endings does not solve problems, it creates new ones; since identical conditions must again be faced at another crossroad in another life. There is no escape from lessons we must learn.

When murdered, thus thrown out-of-the-body by force, disembodied individuals relive their experiences of pain, hate and persecution. In this state they avenge themselves on their persecutors or stalk lowlife characters that mirror their likeness. They inject their energy of crime and vengeance into them — that their victims carry out. Which demonstrates itself when an apparently sane individual suddenly goes beserk, kills a mass of people, not knowing why, and ends up facing death.

Those who die in accidents continue in twilight sleep until the natural hour comes to a close. Then they go through the Valley of Cleansing and according to merit enjoy the happiness and bliss of Eternal Worlds. Until time again arrives to take up another form and to continue in search of God.

All that is born must die. All that dies is reborn. The Lord of Judgment is faced by everyone alone, save the Holy Spirit occupied the heart and life of the individual and accompanies him through the Tribunal. Then the Lords of Darkness cannot touch him. God is no respector of persons, religions or cults. The One Law holds true for all, which blots out the lie that if one has a 'living master' he will be spared the Judgment and ushered straightaway into the lands of bliss! Whether this master is met without or within does not matter.

The walls of the world and *conscience*, do echo back to us the energy of our thoughts and actions. Until we are reborn in God's Light, we board one body after another and each new form imprisons us time and again. But can we really call it imprisonment when we are here or There by our own choice and free will? Could it be time to admit our blunders and release ourselves into the Love of God? No other way will amortize our debts. But in paradox we don't have to be perfect, time will make us over and mold us that way! Perfectionism goes on everybody's nerves — but we may be ourself, true as heaven and clean inside. And we don't have to be great, but we may be humble to discover our greatness.

Man's desires, deep cravings, his expressions of virtue, devotion, sexual overdrive and restlessness, as much as his desire for death are his deep subconscious need and unquenchable longing for God; and to reunite with his Source. This is why the human always wants something and after he has it, craves something else. Unfulfilled he remains restless. Only God can satisfy the soul.

DEATH, THE EQUALIZER

Death is no entity of sorts but the transitional state that enfolds you in love and releases you to the Father. Death gently dabs away your tears and removes the veil of sorrow. It clothes you with the seamless robe your thoughts have spun, there is none other it can hand you. It moves you into the brilliant ascension and to the Far Country, where all hurt and bitterness are left behind. The foe of earth is met as friend, for no evil dwells in the Lands of Light where every dream you had of love comes true.

When average man dies he sinks deeper into himself, but the illumined individual steps fully awake into the Light that comes to greet him. Life always moves peaceful towards the last hour, people create their own anxiety and confusion. The dying do not fear death, but the living. And he who found no happiness on earth will not find it after death, unless he discovers it within himself.

The subject of death is surrounded by much heresay, surmising and opinions. It is said the Valley of Death lasts from four days to six weeks. But I can attest I've seen it last for individuals in our terms for as long as two years. Self-acknowledgement and Soul-Realization are vital issues. For if you cannot face the truth about yourself now, the Valley of the Shadows will detain you until you do.

The Angels of Death are agents of the Negative Force. Though death as it were is negative, it is the doorway to spiritual freedom. The end of life's journey is nothing to fear. It will treat you as merciful as you treated your fellows and life. Those who dread death should ask themselves: what harm is there in having a better body for a vehicle to be able to learn nobler lessons? Or in having a vestment more appropriate to carry me to the Heart of my Sacred Father? Is God not the quest and my final destination?

As everyone on earth you are a spiritual being. Therefore your existence has never depended on a physical carriage. Instead of identifying so much with the body and personality you should begin to acknowledge: *I Am The Soul,* and begin to live *from* the soul instead of by the dictates of mind. This will heighten your awareness of God and guide your life into the Way of Light and Peace.

The closer you draw to God the deeper and broader the pit will cleft behind you. Never turn back! When you feel at loss, remember: where the Light is strong, the night is deep, but also the beginning of a Bright New Dawn. God loves *You!* — and all your anxieties, desperations and fears will not change it. In His Spirit all things become powerless and in *It* alone can you transcend the top of the stairs without fear. Where there is God, there is *Omnipotent,* Omnipresent *Love.*

The term immortality implies: life without end. In lower worlds we live through the cycles of evolution. But once Ultimate Reality has been entered, even immortality fades into the I-ness and Everness of God. It is there where the mortal becomes immortal and the immortal becomes Divine.

From the vantage point of the Diamond Soul you behold the purpose of life; see the struggle of every creature high and low. Hear the weeping and wailing, and also behold the upward thrust and ascent of man and species — and the slowly fading strain. The Diamond Self profoundly feels its innate bond with every creature, the downbearing yoke of pain, and also the transcendent joy of their victory and ascent.

From the lowest manifested creature to perfect man, death opens the Door to the Kingdom. Thus, whatever you encounter through life is neither ugly, hurtful, beautiful nor grand, but part of the Unfailing Divine Plan; that leads the soul into enlightenment, permanence and Abiding

Peace. Everything in life has Divine Meaning, so has death. Death is the Grand Illusion; the Imposter that leads man around on the leash of unfounded fear, until the Spirit of God snaps it in two. Then It unveils the Eye of the Soul to see the Truth and scoops it up into Supreme *Reality*. Death has been overcome.

We decorate our bodies with dingles, dangles and are health conscious as we should be. But when after death the body disintegrates, what have aerobics gained the soul?

The lover of God who felt the Blissful Current and entered Inner Worlds, no longer clings to physical life. To him the Presence of God is heaven, and moments when It recedes hell. Whoever stepped through the Door of Salvation can by nature of this experience never again remove his attention from God. For God has become his every thought and very breath. Can a fish live out of water? Or the human without air? Such individuals cannot help being *different*, though the dim-sighted and the lost maintain there must be something wrong! Because they are stuck in the muck of illogical doctrines and in the density of self; while the lover of God exists in the Golden Stream of Life to which earth is but a shadow.

WHY FEAR DEATH?

People cling to physical life and struggle at death because they do not realize the Nature of God is their own. Even those who perform "miracles" still fear death because they never crossed its threshold fully conscious. A famous evangelist who praised Jesus from dawn 'til dusk and healed in His Name, when death approached, stood by the grave of a loved one and cried out: "My God, please don't let me die!" How sorrowful! This is the difference between institutional belief and the realization of those who know God. People profess to love God, but when He takes them up on it, they bulk and quake in their shoes. Out-of-body consciousness dissolves all fear.

Life does not begin at birth and does not end at death.

You cannot escape physical dissolution, but you *can* let go of the fear. When soul gets tired, it simply sleeps into new awakenings. God has no fear and there is no fear when you know God.

Pseudo radicals rise up against the unchanging truth of reincarnation, but live under its strain. While they post their scriptures, that "It is appointed to man to die just once," — their lives give glaring evidence that thus far man has not earned this right!

Soul rolls into this world as a ripple from the Boundless Ocean of Love, Mercy, and *Energy*. At death it merely recedes back into the Sound Wave and Waters of Spirit from which it came.

Death is a sleepy, dreamy feeling in which you grow ever more alert until you fully awaken and the life past has been left behind. As you enter the Worlds of God you realize the difference between the personal I and the Empyreal Ego, for there Spirit dominates and purifies the forces that heretofore dominated the form.

Your physical form is a house with windows where the light of soul shines through. The awakened soul is the lighthouse of the body, and the Light *within* the soul is the Quintessence of God. Blessed Reader, the darkest night shall be a light unto you — when you know God and realize His Presence. Do not seek Him with pressure or out of fear, but with love. Then He will awaken you from the twilight of earth to the Light and divinity that is your own self. *Nothing* is real. Only God is real. And you awaken to God because He wills it. Nothing in life is worse a fear or a tear.

Death is not the Great Initiation metaphysicians declare. There is a vast difference between death and initiation, Death purifies and releases the soul into abundant life. Initiation leads to illumination and means: self-abnegation, dire tasks, rigid tests and full submission to God. Many initiates who revel in their doctrines never experienced the Light nor heard Its Sound. Thus they lack the principle contact with God through which true initiation is received;

since it *is* an Act of *God*. Any other initiation and external rite administered by fallible mortals are no more than bodily exercises and the side-show of the vain.

To some people life is but a dream. But life on earth can only be a dream after death, for then you are embodied in another reality. In whatever conscious state you find yourself, *that* state is your reality for its duration; even though you have the ability to move in and out of other dimensions as well.

We have journeyed far. After each lifetime we had to give strict account, returned to lower worlds to atone for our evils and never earnestly elected to end our coming and going. Soul is much like the youngster who ran away from home. Though the parent always remained in back of his mind, he never bothered to make contact. But the love of the father was so deep and unweavering, the child felt the love and finally decided it was high time to return to the father's house. And so it is. —

Every now and then we might take the time to close our eyes and say: "Father, I'm just stopping in for a moment to say: *I love You!*"

11.

Who Is the Master?

To reach the summit of spirituality is the destiny of every soul, and purpose of man's existence on earth. To realize God means to wake up from dreaming, to become conscious of life in every universe and world and to experience it.

Though the Truly Wise are on the Other Side, they left us a great legacy of ancient wisdom, the heart of which is the Holy Spirit. As we intuitively search out their scriptures we find the masterly guidance that dissolves the veil of ignorance and delivers us to deeper understanding. And every now and then the shining silhouette or full appearance of a High Born Instructor enters our solitude to remind us: no one walks alone.

All souls are good, no matter how evil the personality may appear. Souls are saints in many guise, 'gods dressed in rags', begging the crumbs of the world! But when love is there, when it is great, it brings out the royalty, beauty and goodness in everyone. The heart of Soul is Oneness and Love.

As you follow the Inner Way your life becomes God-directed and free. You will know how to bring the mind to one point and keep it there, and to transcend the senses where you only know what occurs within. And then to let go of the mind completely, to lose yourself in God, where there is nothing more to desire to see and know. Then you will be the very essence of Love and God, no longer theoretically, but your true experience. Then you no longer believe — you *know*. This brings you to realize that in order to be free in soul you must be free in mind and have it under control. The Love of the Invisible Lord makes it possible, and who does not want to be free and throw off the carnal yoke?

THE PERFECT ONE WITHIN

The Invisible Master is the Holy Spirit. During your meditation He appears on the screen of your mind as a softly shining and often brilliant Light. You perceive the Perfect One through inner hearing as the Wondrous Sound that speaks to the heart and slowly manifests His Form. When His Light appears it is not merely a happening, but the Event of events and the beginning of your Great Journey. When you blend with the Melody of the Audible Sound Current you will see only the Light and hear only the Song of Its Love. This then has nothing to do with quality of mind, your patience or wit, but with the Divine Quality of God to which you gradually aspired.

As you continue to seek the Presence with singleness of mind and soul, the Holy Sound will accelerate in volume, pull you into Its Fabric and will take you to worlds within. Then you will know the meaning of: *I Am Soul*.

The *awakened* Word or Sound within you is the Lord of Soul. Thus the Invisible Master is no man on earth, nor the untrue images the mind creates and strange projections it accepts as truth, but the Spirit within. You should rather trust the Winds of Spirit to move you into the Way, than masters whose theorizing is an expression of their own searching views. People will run you around the block — if you allow them and tell you of a thousand different ways to reach God. Mainly, that they are the exclusive conduit by which you may attain ultimate freedom. That the Way is within *you*, cannot be overly emphasized.

Since everyone who reincarnated into lower worlds came here for purification, even the master is *un*perfected. The True Master will take on various forms to fulfill a specific purpose after which He will disappear as quickly as He came. This one will not bamboozle you that he is the *chosen*. No mortal occupies a place so high, nor holds the Grace and Exalted Love of Our Most High God, nor receives His Rod of Power. While the mortal master says: "he will tell you more when he knows more", the Radiant Master is the Spirit of the *Father, All-Knowing!* In His Truth there are no edited editions or deletions, only bare, *Inexorable, Unchanging Facts*. To meet Him Face to Face, you must step through the Door of the Soul and into His Light. There is no *other* Way.

Now, you can't love something you do no know and whoever truly realized God never loved Him halfheartedly. Neither is anyone *required* to worship and love God, since you cannot love Him until you are touched by His Spirit and Will. The experience manifests to man according to his readiness to accept Higher Truth.

To know God you must become receptive to the Power-Current of His Holy Spirit. This requires daily introspection and more than meditating on an imaginary bird in flight. To learn to flow *with* the stream of Spiritual Power takes courage, self-discipline, submission to the Radiant Force and the fortitude to transcend the body, whether by desire or under the induction of God's Will. The Great Teacher Epictetus wrote: "You must know it is not an easy thing for a principle to become man's own, unless each day he maintain it and hear it maintained as well as work it out in life." But who can tell you what the Will of God is to be, but opinion-makers and theologians who read it out of a jungle of printed, transcribed words, that, with a little added threat of doom and horror they claim to be the Holy Will of God.

Now, we should love God for Himself and not for what

He can give us. To look for God anywhere but within is futile. At some point in your destiny He will instill in you a deep yearning to get to know Him and to be with Him, and then He will pull you up from within. When the Invisible Lord becomes visible to you, you will find His Words infilled with Vibrancy, Gentleness and Superstrength and experience an unknown Love you cannot resist; that will carry you into His Worlds. Available teachings can point *to* the way, but *He alone* can take you *into* the Way. All else dwells on the outskirts of God-Reality.

Pseudo masters usually demonstrate some degree of *acquired* power and eloquently present the cataloged comments of their predecessors, since they have nothing else to forge after. Many actually believe they *are* the master and are quite adept in projecting their images to the population. They know how to pose and phrase their words to leave lasting impressions. Their allegorical doctrines reach around the globe and drag seekers to the bottom of dependency. The seeker must prove all things.

The Supreme Spirit is the Peerless Master. Oh, how It loves you! There is none beside It. Anyone claiming Its empowerment is a fraud and imposter. Clearly, the worship of man is the worship of *Moloch*. If the one who staunchly claims to be the Inner Master or 'living master' were the True One, he would have no need to wallow in the adoration of the weak-witted, nor dwell in the strains of physical sickness and degeneration.

As Christ and the saviours before Him, the mortal master would have entered this world all-wise. As they, he would have attained self-mastery in a prior existence, prerequisite to Saviourship. But this only occurs until thousands of years have passed, even a million, when the Divine Spirit takes up a perfected form. None other could endure Its Voltage and would disintegrate. Pseudo masters talk about their illnesses that are clearly their *karma* and do not attest to the physical and spiritual health of a saviour. It gets boring to hear how the *master* is subject to every human limitation, which of course includes every other vice. Such *masters* are driven by a false sense of omnipotence and the ignorant throw themselves hastily into their cults.

Sitting in meditation for a lifetime cannot compensate one moment of *genuinely* loving God and experiencing the fullness of His Presence. A thousand contemplations cannot replace the virtue of man's loving ways and selfless acts. And no matter how often you are baptized and rebaptized, it does no more than rinse your skin. Only the Radiant Lord can baptize the soul. When the season is ripe, the Love of God has a way of superinflecting on the heart. Then the soul is filled with Divine Truth and Great Joy.

SAINTS AND DEVILS

Prophets of old as the saints were limited, since most pleaded for mercy to live and be spared. Thus they never truly knew God nor the meaning of Eternal Life. There *are* true souls to be found on earth, not in the materialistic west, but namely in the clean, honest, humble lives of the Eastern Masters. When you come in contact with a liberated, godly being, his very presence will lift you into the Life of God. For in him the Light resides to much greater measure than in ordinary devotees. Thus he is called Great Master or Mahatma, meaning Great Soul. To meet a true saint is rather the exception than the rule. But as they say: "When the pupil is ready, the Master will appear."

Once I heard a television preacher say: "God is a person!" Sad world. Because man does not know the Form of his Maker and refuses to accept anything he cannot see, dissect or experiment on, he can only identify with shape, rather than with something invisible. Therefore God appears to him in form of angels, celestial beings, as various colored lights and intertwining geometric patterns, to mention a few.

A true saint knows the Real Master resides in every soul and will refer exclusively to Him. The perfect saint never binds by fear-tactics, nor will he exemplify the demise of those who questioned the character and lifestyle of the *master*, for his life is an open book. He earns his own living and uses *no part* of funds for his personal needs. He will certainly never compare his income to his predecessor's!

Since he himself follows the Radiant Lord, he will not claim to *be* the Lord, but point out that not he — but the Inner Being is the link between soul and God. Only where the Light *truly* dwells can you realize peace, progress and Divine Truth.

Now, the poor in heart will promise to hook you up to the Power Line of God. The illumined soul knows its Source, the Holy Ghost, to which Jesus referred to as the *"Whole-I-Spirit"*, or Holy Spirit, that is the Exclusive Conduit through which this wondrous state of Grace is received. When touched by the Master Light there will be an explosive spark, a spiritual ambience you cannot receive from the wrong outlet. Not momentary, but everlasting. Once connected and fused with the Divine Current of direct Power, you will recognize the True Lord and forsaken all others. People who believe mercy, grace and pardon can be received through another human being, forfeit True Grace. Instead of going directly to the Giver, they beg of the bound.

YOUR SOURCE OF ENLIGHTENMENT AND LOVE

Your interconnection with the Radiant Beloved is an event you shall never forget. From then on all you think about, do and contemplate on is under the *Supervision* of the Lord of Light. His Veil of Protection surrounds you permanently now, wherever you go, here and Beyond. And though He has always been with you, now you are distinctly aware of His Presence. You will find, in Him are no vague hopes or shallow promises. What He has to say you will intuitively perceive and find clearly revealed within, you are no longer a stranger.

By and by, when the appointed time draws near, He swaddles His children into His Radiant Cloak and warming

Light, and takes them Home to His Worlds. Within this Radiant One dwells yet a Greater Force — the Primordial Essence of Boundless Love, Light and Mercy, that is the *Absolute* Master of all souls. The Invisible One does not tell you to look within, for He is already there. Thus He gives to every sincere seeker the gift of Inspiration, by which he may search for Him and find Him.

Once awakened to the Lord of Light, you find you carry all you need within yourself and begin to drop the excess baggage. The axiom of the world is: "To have and to hold" — while His Spirit mandates: *release*! In the True Lord you discover your innate relatedness to all beings and you are therefore tied to none. The Master's Work is far greater than our understanding, so is His Mercy and Love. The Celestial Sound and Melody of His Voice is heard throughout all Creation, and all creation is Himself.

In moments of deep reflection His Spirit moves upon the Waters (consciousness). He infills the seeking heart with knowledge, and the listless soul with Light and peace, and ever greater preparedness to move Godward.

Problems only arise when in search of God we get hung upon proliferated doctrines and anyone convincing enough, until we find the *master* has the same human problems as we. Often it is realized too late that the God man worshipped has become his jailer. Individuals who claim exclusive province in matters of the Spirit and impose their non sequitur doctrines on humanity, may not find heaven exactly to their liking.

The Divine Sound, or Word of God gives us what cults and christian liturgy cannot supply. Some organizations vehemently deny affiliation with religions, sects and cults. In their circle the name Christ or Holy Spirit is highly unfashionable — but they will speak of It by any other name.

One gets the distinct impression they are ashamed of Him to Whom they will account! Though self-anointed saviours and nomenclators periodically refer to christian scriptures to boost their credibility, they must have overlooked the following:

> "But the Comforter, *which is the Holy Ghost*, whom the Father shall send *in my name*, he shall teach you all things. . ." He said *Holy Ghost* — not mortal master.

And those of us who worship Jesus more than God the Father, should be more mindful of His Words: . . . "if ye love me, ye would rejoice, because I said, I go to my Father; *for my Father is greater than I.*"

PROTECTION OF THE HOLY SPIRIT

The protection of the Invisible Master (Holy Spirit) is all-redeeming. His Voice speaks to the *inner* man, to one, or to all at once. I heard a man tell his story to the public. A mob was ready to lynch him and he had given up all hope and expectations to be spared, when he heard the Inner Voice speak up: "Release him, he is innocent!" Suddenly his accusers let go of his arm, the jeering crowd silenced and turned to walk away. When the man inquired if they heard the Voice, they had no recollection, And so he asked again: "If you didn't hear it, how come you obeyed it?" (From Tony Brown's Journal.-)

THE MASTER'S HEALING LIGHT

A lady called from out of state, she was quite troubled. While we spoke, a wondrous azure light overlay her forehead and formed a light-blue nimbus around her head and shoulders, which I could still see after the conversation had ended. When I asked if she was aware of the light-blue radiance, it was unfamiliar to her at the time. But I knew with certainty that all in dire need of mending was being taken care of and made perfect.

While administering healing to a far away place, I suddenly beheld a blue band of glistening effulgence correlating around the person's whole body, that remained stationed until the healing was over. My petition was answered. The Love of God, the tremendous joy and bliss of healing! No word can describe it. The wonders I have witnessed over nearly a lifetime would make an interesting menagerie of books.

Divine intervention has been experienced by everyone, when in moments of danger God turned the tide and spared from harm.

My friend told me her story and described: "Rushing home from work I started to dash across the street to get to the bus stop on the other side. I looked to the left, the street was clear, so I looked to the right and hurried forward; when suddenly — and with one foot still up in the air, I was frozen in motion. The whole force of my body wanted to go forward, but no matter how I tried, I couldn't move. Right then a car came from the left with such speed and so close my skirt blew around and almost got caught in the vacuum. It all happened in less than a second. When it was over and my suspended foot went back to the ground, I trembled all over. All I could do was to thank my Guardian Angel, because had I taken one more step I would have been under the car. I shall never forget how my life was spared.

LOVE OF THE MASTER

An incident comes to mind when the Spirit of God entered my dream in guise of a man who wore a long trench coat, collar turned up and a wide brim hat that hung a bit over his eyes. He looked much like an old time detective from Scotland Yard and said to me: "I will send someone to protect you!"

Since in dreamstate you are true to your deepest convictions, I adamantly replied: "No thank you! The Holy Spirit protects me, I do not need nor want any help." But as dreams go, and to reciprocate a kindness, I offered to buy one of his portraits that was sketched in *charcoal,* I saw hanging in another dimension. When I woke up I clearly recalled what was said but was puzzled, since my dreamtime is spent in much sunnier places, where beings looked radiant and smart; and none of them ever wore a trench coat!

Planning to work on my manuscripts before daybreak, I retired early that evening. When a long, drawn out hissing sound and a dull explosion shortly thereafter pierced the evening stillness. The fire truck howling down the hill was nothing unusual, but this time it stopped at our building. People came running out of fear or curiosity and the firemen were busy extinguishing the flames of the car that exploded a few feet from my bedroom wall.

Of course the car was a total loss. My neighbor was quite shaken. When I asked what caused the fire he said: "I was working on my car when it exploded. I cannot understand why I am not hurt, I'm just fine. I cannot understand it!" Not only did the Master save him from terrible injury, perhaps death, but the wind carried off the smoke and fumes as well. Since usually cars were parked side by side, consequences might have been dire. By some miracle most of them were out.

This little story may seem rather insignificant. But in face of burns and painful injuries, perhaps life spared, it is monumental. And I thought to myself: gee, I might have had an extra window blown into the bedroom wall! It is always good to consider: what happens to another may well be happening to us.

THE AIRBORNE INCIDENT

To avoid the hassle of early morning traffic I drove to work quite early that day. The highway was least traveled and I cruised along happy and content, when a long flatbed tractor trailer sped by me. Its left rear axle grabbed my car under the right front fender and sent me airborne across the center divider to the other side of the highway. While I was going south toward the city, I now found myself joining the traffic going north into the opposite direction. There are really no words to describe the shocking event, except that the car and I were carried by an Invisible Force through the air and set back down intact and without a scratch on the other side of the highway. Flying unpropelled about 25 feet through the air is *some* experience, and I felt no impact as the wheels again touched the ground. People were waving and shouting: "Are you alright? You could have been killed!" And someone yelled something about a miracle. Though I now drove into the other direction, I was still too stunned to answer. Who can put into words the Love of the Master?

WHAT MAKES MASTER?

The Spirit of the Radiant Lord manifests to true souls to a greater degree than to average man. And those who attained this Grace earned it to the last mite.

A true master is a man or woman who on the long road to God have overcome their worlds within, on every plane and in every spiritual sphere. Then the mind and form can no longer confine the soul and it is free to enjoy the immensity of Eternal Worlds while still in physical embodiment.

The conquest of the lower mind is the noble goal of every soul. To him who attained self-mastery and thus became the master, nothing remains concealed, whether he turns his attention to it or not. He understands the pain of inward suffering and human want, for he experienced them all.

Ascended or unascended, they are the helpers of humanity and cocreators in every way. While still on earth their work continues in celestial worlds. For such individuals there is nothing left to learn in worlds below. The mirage of death has been dissolved and life on earth is merely a reflection of all that lay within.

The holy self of an individual perfected in the Living Sound dwells *consciously* in God. In lieu of this, and in the allotropy and lofty nature of the soul, he/she can come and go at will, and actively partake of life in any world *equaling* vibrations. But so long as soul dwells in lower worlds the negative force will assail it and attempt to reverse what has been accomplished. Only the strong survive! To regress to old ways would mean to lose ground and no longer to be able to endure the pure and highly charged Altitudes of Eternity; until the soul has again regained its equanimity and impeccable status, which can take lifetimes.

WISDOM OF THE TEACHERS

Unlike modern day prophets, the Sons of God and Ancient Teachers disproved the vanity of show, display of power and necromancy. They challenged every spiritualistic and scientific phenomenon; the conjuring up of spirits and undulating mists, flying guitars, flying trumpets and whatever else sails through the air and falls down from heaven by some strange grace. And they sternly disallowed the use of mentors.

The Ancient Teachers admonished the listening to and entertaining of whispering voices, that rise up from the dark and dismal places of the mind. And they prohibited any other psychic parlor games, and dialogues with disembodied spirits that deceive the human being day and night.

Individuals are often unaware that calling on entities manifests them; and haunted by their own creations, frantically look for someone to exorcise them out of their life. If you call forth anything, may it be the Protection of God! At times people will remark: "Something told me. . .!" When you learn to stay your racing thoughts and to transcend the mind, you will be able to discern between the Still Small Voice and *other* voices, that will no longer trouble you when you have shut them out.

The Ancients taught that every soul is a ray of the One Celestial Sun, and denied the existence of 'other gods'. Since their affections were purely in God, they would accept nothing on faith or belief, but on proven facts they found in the completeness of their direct experience in God.

They had no need for books or scripts, for their Dialogues

were First Editions that issued from the Center of Eternal Truth. Thus they brought sincere seekers into Self-Cognition and Divinity, and into alignment with the Force.

The brilliant luster of the Teacher's Aura would extend through every space, to any distance below as above, and into every cause directed. Never wrathful, always humble, all-enduring, true and kind, the exemplary lives of the Ancient Teachers were a living testament to the Love and Glory of God.

THE WAY IS GOD

Belief in a Supreme Being is fundamental to the well-being of the soul. There is a way, and the Way is God. And those who truly seek *It* shall meet the Radiant Lord. There are many faces you remember and others you forget, but the Master's Wondrous Face and Eyes of Purest Love will always remain before you.

Your spiritual survival does not depend on man, but on Him who breathed the Breath of Life into all Creation and into the soul. All the love and care a human being needs are fully given from within. No systematic teaching can supply us with this bounty. Human needs are *now* and need to be fulfilled *presently*, not at some future time or by some vagrant promise and hopeful prayer! We need to turn to Him Who supplies our needs — in deeper trust.

Though at times you may feel forsaken and forgotten, and walk along a lonely path it seems, you are never alone nor without God. An inward glimpse to the Guiding Light that pours its Love into every heart, and all the trials and pains of life are met with clearer understanding.

Regardless of our spiritual persuasions, we *are* the *Soul* and God is Our Father. And as it must, the day will come when each one of us shall stand as an individuation of the Light — without support, and walk the Golden Inner Way with new resolve and clasp the Hand of God.

Beloved of God, no man on earth can do for you what in this life and time you were destined to establish for yourself. Your spiritual life is far too serious for games, for it concerns your innermost survival. Know, that in the Love of God all lesser states dissolve; and that in Him alone your peace, your strength and health and clarity of mind are totally regranted. And this is what spiritual living is all about: establishing a firm foothold on the Ladder of Ascension, reaching high within — and *never* letting go.

There can be no true perception of God until He is realized in the solitude of soul, beyond the boundaries of ephemeral existence. But you have to go *in* before you can go out.

God is not realized in the twilight zone of psychism, nor through channeled teachings of advising entities no matter how authentic they may appear; for bound to lower worlds they are demonic. No True Master will possess a channel, and no true vehicle of God will allow himself to be possessed. But while some eat the Bread of Heaven, others eat the dust of earth.

An Ascended Master has *earned* his state of Masterhood Consciousness and will not allow himself to be used by lower minds. Spirit communications weaken the mental and physical state of the individual and rob the nervous system of vitality. Moreover, these practices stain and abrade the soul-fabric of inflecting entities, they must again atone for. Thus channel *and* "master" come to justice.

Yes, things have changed, times have changed, but God has not. Nor has His Law. We can deepen our understanding by studying the lives of true holy men, whose purposeful message inspires us to our best efforts, to Goodness and to *God*. Periodically we should align to the True and Wise, who are energies robed in purest Light through which they speak to the seeking heart. Not verbally, but through the Knowingness all souls perceive. The Secret to realizing Divine Truth is to confront your fears of the Unknown.

THE SPIRIT WITHIN

The closer you draw to God the more you become aware

of His Boundlessness, Unspeakable Love, Titanic Force and Supreme Power. Having received uncountable letters from individuals who excitedly talked about their masters, I decided to take up the matter with the Guiding Spirit. No more had I turned inward and posed the question: "Who is the Master?" — a huge book began to correlate out of the translucent ethers and opened up before me. On a bright, shining page these words stood boldly inscribed:

> "God is within. Reach within and touch the Vibration. This is the Presence. The same is Master."

The spirit within will teach you all things. It is the Son, the Only Begotten, the Great Awakener and Unifier. He is the Divine Thoroughfare and only vehicle that can take you to the Father. To reach God is quite simple: close your eyes and you stand at the Door, take a few more steps inward and you are *in* the Presence. . .

At times when you feel a sense of aloneness, God seeks to turn your attention inward, to draw you closer to Him. In such moments you might ponder the story of the old monk who served in a monastery in Spain. When he felt utterly forlorn, emotion-laden and troubled beyond hope, he went to the mountain top to jump off and kill himself.

Standing at the edge of death he threw up his hands and cried out: "My God, why have you forsaken me?" And God answered him: "Lo, I have never left you, I will always be with you!" And the monk came down a changed man.

By and by, you will unfold to the point where you find yourself unable to live without God. Then you will travel after Him unafraid. Now, each time you are happy you relate to God! To love God because He *Is* God, finds profound reciprocation. And when you think of it, we have such a lot to be grateful for!

12.

A Matter of Free Will

I was raised in a world faith, stricter in etiquette than practice. For the most part, everyone followed the path of their own inclinations. Some went to church, others to the synagogue, and I, after my own gnosis would sit by the waters, wander through the woods, visited God's little creatures, and often stayed until the misty veil would lift from the valley. Later on my interests turned to becoming a nun, that pleased everyone, but turned out quite differently.

I doubtlessly felt rather old at times, listening to the family's philosophical edicts, that, though well-meant, were to divert my mystical ways to their belief. Their demanding of my undivided attention made it difficult to slip out the back door. Dear Papa was an upright man of staunch principles and splendid judgment. He was a gentle giant, strong in ways the family couldn't understand, and inflexible when he was right. Though he deeply cared for everyone, it met with vague response, but really, all of them relied on him and couldn't have managed without him. Papa often remarked there was no earthly reason people should heap their belief on others, and maintained that a man's own good conscience would direct him and take care of him. Well, he may as well have talked to the walls.

With due respect, sometimes the ranting of the glory-makers was hard to endure, since all the chatter only stated their own stoic opinions, to which my uncle, a much revered monseigneur, most heartily agreed. But gentle admonishments were more like hissing arrows than anything heaven would demand. By and by, and reflecting some matters carefully, I thought perhaps the elders knew a better way. But couldn't quite let go of my tender little friends that loved me well and knew me better than myself; nor could I curb riding the waves of time, that afforded me a special kind of freedom and the liberty I sought.

RUDIMENTS OF THE WAY

My straitlaced friends were somewhat too victorian for comfort, as was the peculiar company of baneful spirits I saw attached to some of them. At times I would go along to church to keep the peace, and listened to the prayerful implore God's perpetual pardon and to the string of novenas that were to redeem my wayward self. But my visions of inner worlds continued and the Melody of Heaven still played wondrously across the Harp of the soul. My hopes and rainbows were shining brightly!

To live in Other World Reality was as true for me then as it is to me now. At times the Force would lift me high and drop me low, from wondrous states of ecstasy to lonely desolation. It taught me to hold fast to the pinnacle of soul, to soar high at will and — hold stable. It demanded me to stand at the very edge of the Eternal Cliff repeatedly, to free the mind of fear and needless apprehensions.

At times my road as yours was difficult, and there was pain. But for the peace of God I never knew the misery of human discontent. It was easy to survive without the blessings of philologizing man, who saw no God in anything and turned his hapless favors to trickery and usurpation. It could easily be said, my life was equal to the words of George Bernard Shaw: ". . . he had no enemies, but all his friends hated him." And I was grateful for it! Now as in the past, I always say what I think, make no apologies and never explain, for the Truth I know stands for Itself and needs no defense. Knowing God means a whole lot more than shedding a few rueful tears, sipping down a cordial afterwards and maybe extending a few gracious favors.

While just before the 'feast' environments were generously humble and often crowned with the glaring evidences of my blunders and sad choices; I was never more grateful for the Master's Love that saw me through; as He would any seeker, when the anvil of his karmas fell on him. Through every test and trial I saw His hovering, blazing Light, that proved in thousand, all-enduring ways: no one walks alone. But He never interfered when needful lessons had to be encountered.

And then, over the course of time, I carried karmic loads of souls I never met, and of others whose deceitful tears amply wet my feet, who, if they perceived a dire need in others, would shrug their shoulders and walk away. But a seeker well used up learns vital lessons! Along the way we undergo so many transformations. Though the strain of them is trying, it imbues you with serenity and tends to make you humbler, and surely far more gentle and prolific!

WONDERS OF LOVE

And there were blessings all along the way, that would mean nothing to the world at large, but meant everything to me. When I asked the Lord to give me a flower to brighten up the place a bit, He grew it directly out of the concrete floor of the patio. A five-pronged, tall and happy flower, that bore bright yellow, lacy blooms that thrived in sun and snow all year around.

And again I said: "God, give me a bush for shade!" And He grew a six foot bush for me that gradually emerged straight out of the brick wall from beneath the outer windowsill, and branched out high and wide. It covered up the windowpane and more, and kept the moonbeams from shining in my face at night. It's funny now! —

People would walk by and gawk and stare. Until the landlord thought it out of place with the rest of the poor scenery of garbage cans and wasted cars, and came to chop it down. But his axe could go no further than my prayer, for it was God Who gave the bush and mine to keep awhile.

I never ceased to thank for Love, it was my form of prayer. But admittedly remember times when for stifling reasons I envied the living dead, when one more jolt of Fate might have been the last. But it was then when I reached deep within to grasp the Light of the Guiding Force that governed me. But the hand of the heart picked up the pen instead, and the ethereal thread of the Love that infilled me wholly. Like a reindeer running through the snowdrifts and the mountain beast climbing to the top, I mounted up to the High White Peaks of God's Most Holy Mountain; where each soul that conquered can stand proud and free, with outstretched arms and breathe the pure, clean air of all Eternity.

And as any other human might, I more than once sought to abdicate my lofty art and toss out pen and pad with all the rest of earthly rubbish. But unbounded Love resurged. And I again picked up the Golden Thread that unites us soul to soul; jotting down the endless sequence of words and sounds received, to weave the Golden Mesh of God into a text. Some things conceived are far beyond the measure of my keen to reinterpret; that I convey to my beloved Reader, through the silent, golden message of this book, that spells the Love each heart perceives.

The time arrives when Divine Inflections are felt by everyone, when the inner life seeks to gain priority to move us into reawakening to God. While in lower worlds we only know what we are told, we must set sail to find our own truth, and allow the Living Power of God's Holy Spirit to unseal the vaulted mind, to untie our lesser self from all its moorings.

CONNECTING TO THE SOURCE

You can take a thousand routes to God, but at one single

point, at the *Gate of God*, all faiths must meet. And if there is one saint or person anywhere who can say differently, may he speak up at once or hold his peace. There is *One* God for all people, and One Great Way that leads to Him, unfailing and direct: the *Inner Way*.

Too many individuals get sidetracked by sectarians, tractarians and cults, and forget the Lord they came down to earth to find. Untruth shoulders them away, while others storm the Royal Fortress and block out the flooding brightness of the Light. But it is after all: *a matter of free will* — to find or not to find the Light that glistens amidst all human darkness; and to meet the Invisible One that is the steady, stabilizing Central Force that will reconnect you to the *Source*.

It was not by the whip of man's will nor by his tutelage or manifold persuasions that I met God. But by entering the expansive Quietudes of Spirit, in faithful contemplation of the Presence. And then, by deepening introspection I gradually moved into the full Cadence of the Master, that are His Sound Current, Presence, Light and Form. It is a slow, progressive merging into Ultimate Reality, into the Love that swallows up all fear.

MOVING INWARD

I made time, always, to dwell in the Presence of the Unseen Lord. I stilled my senses, withdrew my thoughts from the noise of the world, fixed my attention on the space between the eyebrows and contemplated on the Light. Deepening introspection moved me beyond the Mystic Eye, where the Light appeared and Its Brilliant, oscillating Force steadied and revealed the Form of the Master.

He stood in a Brilliance more resplendent than the sun, that was so bright I could barely endure the glare. His Form was imbued by a shimmering, swirling vortex of outpouring Vitality and Splendor. This is the One each soul must seek and come to. When Jesus said: "No man cometh unto the Father but through me", he did not refer to Himself, but to the One who reigned supremely within Him.

ANOTHER WORLD

Sometimes when you close your eyes and become very still, you behold vivid pictures of places where people dressed in colorful attire go about their merry lives. Then the vision fades; contemplation ebbs off — and suddenly you are transported to worlds far away.

At times, the velocity of Light moves me into Eternal Worlds, and I walk on the ground of another country more beautiful and sublime than the world I know; and share my hopes and views with loving souls I meet and they impart theirs to me. Though I'm clearly aware they are not my people as it were, and feel as a stranger in a breathtaking Beautiful Country, I feel profound kinship with its inhabitants. And after I re-enter my body long to be with them again.

Oddly, when among my own, I feel as a stranger amidst them too, and truly belong nowhere but to the Light, where I feel utterly at home. Thus I belong to all. Experiencing the reality of Inner Worlds proves you must go *in* before you can go *out* into the Blessedness of the Far Country. You must first eat the Bread of Heaven before you can break it with others. Yes, we want to be free, and will be free, when we learn to let go of the conscious self and enter the Spirit and Kingdom of Our Father.

LOVE IS THE KEY

Each individual finds his own way to reach his Maker and creates his own technique to get there. It begins within *You*. I never learned to meditate. Deep longing for God drew me into His Presence. Love taught the way. To inwardly connect was to me as natural as breathing, and had nothing to do with contemplating or concentrating on anything — but God. Within seconds of closing my eyes I would be out-of-body.

Love opened the Way. Because I wanted whatever God

was to me more than food and drink, more than life, and simply — more than anything. Now I enter light-filled worlds as I did in early youth and go beyond them, but with deeper understanding. The Way is the same. The Key is *Love*.

As much as God infilled my heart and life, there were times I felt utterly abandoned. But still I said to Him, that even if He hated me I would love Him still. And other times when I avowed never to believe or listen to one more thing. Yet God did not turn His Light or Face from me, but left me to muddle through. And I conclude, God will love you more for being honest.

Finding does not make perfect. It is rather the arrival at a Major Junction on your Way to God, where 'the old man dies' and a new, wonderful *You* is taking shape.

It is the vital commencement of an exuberant life of great enlightenment; where one mode of living is laid aside and another more fruitful and satisfying is taken up. It is there where the True Voyage to the Heart of the Father begins, and the Great Way.

13.

The Golden Plank

When still a child, my world was filled with Wonders on both sides of the heavenly veil. I beheld Superior Presences, Whose blazing Light would sweep me up to worlds within, where the symphony of Love rolled down from Vast Infinitude over cosmic glades and hilly lands; and snowpacked mountain peaks shone as a thousand brilliant suns into worlds below. As streams of Light poured down on me from God's Most Holy Summit, and the Light grew brighter with each advancing step, I found I could come and go as the wind — and traveled far.

The Spiritual Journey began for me while still in the Old Country. The subtle restlessness God's Love incites, to live, to learn and to find the Sap of Life, often found me wandering through woods and vale; hiking up steep mountain trails, and at play with the fishes of the sparkling brooks that ramble along the Austrian Foothills.

Ah, yes, trees, weeds and brushwood could tell a lively tale, of my dialogues with wondrous nature beings of meadow, forest, stream and air. They were of every sort and shape, of bright celestial colors, that shimmered with an irridescent, oscillating energy of spotless beauty. Their gazing, soulful eyes shone with great tenderness, as glimmers of pure heaven light that sparkled in its fire. Their breath conveyed what only loving hearts could speak.

I understood the thundering voices of dark clouds and listened to the gentle whispers of the wind with great affection. And on a still, clear night I would fix my eyes on midnight's brightest star that poured its Grace of All-Abiding Promise into sleeping hearts. And soon the celestial ladder came into view, that Jacob thus described: ". . . a ladder set up on earth, and the top of it reached to heaven; and beheld the Angels of God ascending and descending on it." And I surely climbed its footless rounds, but fell forgetful of the final rung.

I lived in two worlds for all my life, but what was reality to me then, with all its wonderfilled events, is now but the memory of a beloved past. For my reality became the One, Whose Formless Nature communed with me through all those other forms I held so dear; in which I discerned the Holy Presence of a hidden, Sacred Glory.

And when others couldn't understand my bliss and asked why I choose the quiet life, I just replied: "God turned my head around." I found a different world *within* my world. Reality in unreality. A distinctly different manner of life, profound activity in nonactivity, unity, harmony and unscathed Love fulfilled, all-abiding here and now. And I knew then as I know now, the dominating joy and happiness of inner worlds far outweigh the pain, strife and transient gladness of material existence. In inner worlds, all things rejoice and move in the Dynamism of God's Most Wondrous Love.

Though you presently live in this same energetic atmosphere, it can only become your reality when you reach for the Redeeming Light, that shines out from the center of every heart and lights the path of every man.

LONE TRAVELER

Though sheltered in youth, I seemed to belong everywhere and nowhere, but aloneness granted me a rare sense of pleasure and freedom. Most of my summers were spent in the sleepy, affluent resort of my beloved Grand-Mama's estate. Raggedy by choice and loving to go barefooted, I was considered a sheer disgrace to all prestige. But I deemed it much too soon to become the lady etiquette required, since this would make an end to my adventurous excursions.

Because of my peculiarities, that have not changed to date — opinions would mildly flare. But for all of goodness sake I could not extend such loyalty as to exchange my cherished time for the Kaffee-Klatsch and gossip of the upper crust, who withered on the "old maid's vine". Since I knew some of them had neither servants, butler nor a footman, and didn't qualify, I chuckled at the travesty. But it wasn't mine to mention. If they suffererd me — I scarcely noticed, too many dreamy, happy thoughts captured my attention. I just wanted to be like other ordinary people. Many joyful hours shared with needy, loving friends, who allowed me to be myself, found me utterly at home.

I also frequented the other kind, who seemed endowed with loving depth, but embarrassed of my apparel would quickly usher me out of doors when some friend or relative arrived. And well it was, for they were stranger to my world than I to theirs, their ways were a departure from everything I believed. Content, I wandered on alone and thought to myself: people look at the many poor with disdain, because they dread it to happen to them. But did not humanity and society create them? When glitz and shekels turn to mockery and rust, and the sleeper awakens to count his losses — what has he gained?

HEAVENLY SECRETS

It was always exhilarating to find a hidden place or some big mossy rock for a perch to dream on, where I could lift my thoughts and watch my secret wishes disappear into the sailing clouds. Or to slip away to the watchtower in my uncle's forest, to see what my friends the creatures had to say. Often I sat quietly and listened to the whistles of the gasping wind ruffle the treetops and saw through the jungle of branches.

At times ribbonlike streams of bluish-white and golden light would fill my sight, and a rapturous melody would fall on my ears. But for all the beauty 'round about, nothing could compare to the worm-eaten plank down by the lake. Since every sunday like a ritual I had to sit in the stuffy church and afterwards march off to the graveyard to visit the dead, hours spent alone were most cherished.

I loved the fog and misty steam that rose up from the lake; loved running through the drenching rain and let the wind dishevel my hair and kiss my face. Sitting by the seaside, flashes of other worlds came unexpected and there were times I thought I would die with loneliness for God. Some days I would trail after the help down to the white, sandy shore adjoining Grand-Mama's estate to steal away to the secluded spot beyond the towering pines. I'd carefully make my way to the far end of the old, gently swaying plank extending over the treacherous deep. Every now and then a few villagers could be seen rinsing their bushels of laundry in the crystal-clear waters off shore, of the gigantic lake that felt cool and misty even in the heat of day.

After a prickly barefoot run through the narrow footpaths of the dense pine forest — and pine needles, I would kick up the waves to soothe my feet, felt free as the breeze and oh, so rich inside! Since my impetuousness was at times considered appalling I was rarely missed except at the vesper hour. Mostly arriving fashionably late, sand and mud dripping from my shoes when I wore them, it met with an occasional stern glance. How I dreaded formalities — but acknowledged my shortcomings. Usually in a hurry, I slurped my soup to run the race with 'Mitzi' (my cat), and scoured up my plate to provoke a little more disdain; which would point my way back out-of-doors. Ah, freedom! But beneath all that crude pretense was a restless spirit that needed to find God at all cost. Though now and then a bit remorseful, I cherished the extra hours I could sit by the waters undisturbed, lost in a reverie of thoughts and ponder what the God I so ardently sought might be like.

Often my eyes traveled over the hills and scanned the distant horizon, watching the rosy glow of sunrise and gleaned the snowy mountain slopes flaming in the fire of the evening sun. But later on the rising evening mists, singing of crickets and whispering Melodies of Worlds far away meant so much more.

At early evening, the sweeping view of mountain ranges and snowy peaks obscured by webs of clouds softly came aglow with rose and purple shades, as the touch of the Angelic Wand threw out its sparks to ignite the light of peace and hung the evening star. The pastoral beauty of the scenery was stunning. Towering mountains stood as a wall of vigilant, gigantic watchers around the small alpine resort that nestled peaceful and secure below. But the Mountains of Eternal Worlds are much more beautiful and grand. The alpine resort was the only place on earth I then knew about, where people could swim in the blue expanse of mountain lakes and climb the misty mountain heights to ski all summer long.

Gazing and musing into space I heard the symphonic sounds within the moving air and dreamy melodies from inner worlds. Living shades of golden rosy light played across the quiet water. The downstreaming light of the evening sun cast its effulgence over the whole spectacle of nature and turned into a labyrinth of rainbow colors as it touched the waters. Trees and mountains robed in mystical attire stood in dark contrast against the rosy evening sky. Every corner and pattern of nature's incredible sophistication bore the Signature of God.

INVIOLABLE TREASURE

Entranced by the mystic air and nature's peaceful setting and lost in its tranquility, I barely noticed the wooden slivers of the dear old plank poking me at every turn. Until a canoe pulled up to drop off the old villager, who, shouldered with his big saw, would carry off the decrepit slab of wood that was attached to the abandoned warf.

After I threatened to fling myself after him, float into the lake and leave it to his conscience, he sniffed a few frostbitten words into his beard and ranting all the way crawled back into his canoe. Small exchange, I thought, for being able to keep my magic carpet! And as far as it went, at least for that time, the old warped board was the center of my world. For that is where the Light flowed in, and the Heavenly Love I began to rely on.

BEYOND THIS WORLD

Yes, the old plank was golden indeed and could tell many secrets of the heart. I felt its wormy wood and the fishes below shared in my adventures.

All was still, save jumping fishes rippling dimples into the still waters. An orchestration of croaking frogs hovered in the dewy grass near the warf, and the baying of a lone dog could be heard at the distance. Of course, the hooting of 'Gretchen', my befriended owl, joined the chorus. She always hovered near the topmost limb on the same old pine nearest the lake, just so nothing would escape her. Yet she seemed indifferent, almost too wise to care what went on in the world. And I thought to myself: smart Gretchen!

Every now and then when a yacht laid anchor, waves would clash against the rocks and shore and ripple back into silence. Now vivid lightning played across the sky. Restless fire-spirits danced by the declining light of the evening sun and disappeared. Even the swarm of pesky mosquitos ceased singing and vanished into the reeds — touched by the strange Mystic Power that began to transfuse the atmosphere.

Still trying to see the sandy bottom of the clear deep, my eyes followed the little fishes shooting back and forth like arrows in the wind, playing hide-and-seek underneath the drying sea stalks. As though in a heavenly trance, profound stillness and the glow of love now blanketed the whole scenery. Or perhaps myself had entered the Great Silence.

At which point it was I cannot tell, but it seemed right then that the suddenly darkening waters dissolved into a blue-white mist that formed into a swirling vortex of dazzling Bright Light — that spun my head around like a top. A velocity swifter than light swept me straightaway into the Radiant Energy of the Master's Presence, and I stood on the solid ground of a strangely beautiful country.

The air was pure and clear. The polygonal Mountains of Creation stood as Gigantic Fortresses, towering high into Cosmic Mists. Their diamond peaks and radiant slopes of crystal-white Light cast ice-blue shimmers over endless fields bursting with lace-petaled flowers, colorful ferns, snow-blooms resembling Edelweiss and multiflorous atomic life. At a distance, blue-white cliffs shone like crystal palaces in the Radiance of the Cosmic Morning. Nearby nature terraces, silver-blue ramparts and bowers were adorned with profusions of irridescent foliage that graced the sunny land stretching to immeasurable distance.

Heavenly murmurs of quiet streams and wind song mingled with the deep celestial drone and Eternal Humming Sound of the Majestic River of Light that ran broad and wide through this Supercelestial World. An exhilarating, fresh fragrance of blooms and foliage swished through the air, touching the Mist of Love that hung outstretched and suspended over the Great Valley.

IN THE PRESENCE

Wide, scintillating streams of Cosmic Effulgence flowed down from Above into the Auric Radiance of the Master, Who stood before me in Blazing Light. The golden effluvia of His High Esteem beamed forth in Eternal Power and illumined our pathway ahead. Moved by the Force of the Master's Light we now descended to the regions of the Universal Lord.

All around reigned boundless Love. Much greater than my words can express, nor any heart could find in the selfish maze of human love. A Love it was so pure and bright it ran icy heat and shivers of effervescent joy through every fiber of the soul, that nearly feigned my senses as the Master turned to me to speak.

In the radiance of His dark, dreamy eyes shone the triumphant Love and Sacred Shimmers of Eternity, that reflected from the amber-brown of His Masterly Features and beamed forth rays of blinding light into all directions.

His stately Countenance and noble bearing stood to enormous heights, and though I clearly saw the Master, and felt the mighty pull when His Energy bore me up; for all the energy and brightness I barely saw at all and trembled like a limp and tender reed, that finally steadied by the Master's calming Gaze.

The dark waves of His well-groomed hair at times turned fair, by the Eminence of His fantastic Light. His flowing raiment ran loosely to the ground, His tender feet were caressed by sandal straps of yore.

The Master's Love and Tenderness were everywhere! And so was I. My heart leaped high. Ah, to remain with Him forevermore! 'God, make these moments last!' whispered the heart. And so they did — for all my humble life. How could there be any other Love before or after Him? It was He, they call the One in all, and by so many other names, that took up a cloak of human likeness to commune with me; Whose Grace is all sufficient for each single day, for all the world and all of life.

And when He called me by my name, I knew He was no apparition, for the fleeting steps of those who bore no light as clear and bright as He, and came in by any other way, departed swiftly as they came; while He forever stayed. His wordless Gaze imbued the listening soul with deep serenity and peace. Thus He imparted many secrets to the heart, the soul quite well absorbed and filed away in gladness; to use and share some other day.

THE MASTER SPEAKS

Ah, yes, He spoke to me of holy, righteous things and pointed out: ". . . you here perceive your breath is of the One same Breath that is the breath of every soul. The light you see by is the selfsame Light by which all others see. The sky of earth and ground beneath are the very roof and resting place where all others live and dwell; and every element, and plant and every creature high and low share your roof. And all who share and breathe the Breath of Life are born of One Great God, of One Great Source, the One in all."

And within the Force and Sound of His Most Holy Voice, He took my heart to yet another Sphere, where all that laid concealed in thought and word and deed was well uncovered and laid bare. And He spoke to me of One Almighty Ear, that Ear, said He, is everywhere! And hears the faintest whisper of Its every creature, even the smallest prayer — and every silent sloth.

And of the Truth spoke He to me, that does not fall on vulgar ears, nor does it flow from tongues that lie, nor does it lay Itself into the hands of thieves. And He imparted furthermore:

> "Mark well, Beloved of the Light, and adhere your feeble mind and ear to better understanding; that your withered bough of love shoots not the poison dart of hate into another's heart, nor evil thoughts to other minds. For verily, I say, as death follows each birth, they shall find your heart again a thousand strength; and as birds of prey devour up your bread of life and sponge away the sap, and suffer you to die.
>
> "The demon gods man worships and calls saints, are but reflections of his own and lesser grace, deceits and impure states of mind that may be pure some day; that lead the soul astray from

> its purported way to God. Beloved scribe, turn away thine adulations now from Me — and look to Him alone Who gives Himself through Me and all as Light and Life; and not to him who steals away the Light of Soul.
>
> "Relinquish then", spoke He to me, "your wish for life and death and even for your God, that then He must be realized *at once* — in the quiet center of your seeking heart."

And every now and then the Master-Light would blaze — and fan itself to such a glare, the Master too would disappear from sight and left me sitting all alone with God.

Until forgetfulness again befell the senses of the seeking soul and I reawakened to the muffled sounds and lofty rhythm of the breaking surf; and to the waves that lapped against the Golden Plank, and kissed the rocks and hugged the shore. . .

And He Who spoke to me of long ago, still speaks to me this day, through His Wondrous Sound and All-Abiding Light. He walks with me across the many narrow planks of earth, and lifts the soul to sunlit Inner Worlds that are its Home.

When soul forgets its earthly wants — and life, its heart begins to beat with the Living Sound of its Eternal, Sacred Source; that loved each soul through every age. Its Voice intoned and droned throughout antiquity of time, from the depth of Creation, to the heart of every humble soul:

"Lo, *I Am With You* — always!"

14.

From Soul to Soul

To many persons the subject of God is like an old story, something they are used to hearing about but could more comfortably lay aside, while others may become inspired and aglow by merely feeling the vibration hearing the Name of God incites.

On our long pilgrimage through many lifetimes we move from stage to stage. From God-seeking to illumination, through many dire tests and tasks to initiation and finally into God-Awareness. Assuredly, we will reach the point in destiny when Our Most Sovereign Lord is no longer a myth or belief, but our full realization. The immeasurable blessings of Spiritual Liberty belong to *every* soul.

THE SOUL IN LOVE

There is nothing as wonderful and romantic as souls in love with life and God, for such souls put an extraordinary effort into all they do. Each day is entwined with wonder, each night enveiled with Love. So much to do, time seems all too short to fill the Orders Love set forth. But patience, laughter, earnestness and all-pervading trust in God prevail, for they are hallmarks of the soul that sees things through.

A soul in love with God knows a grand and boundless joy, and a steadfast inner peace no sloth can mar nor any storm unseat. For when the tempest rips and roars through the quiet life of soul, an inward glimpse to the Guiding Light and blessed calm pervades its life and every inner space.

When day is done, soul turns its face to Love with joyousness and greatest expectations and realigns to the Beloved's Shining Brightness; where it finds its quiet rest in outstretched, waiting Arms, that clip the wings of every wayward thought and snatch the soul away from the gripping talons of illusions, that it may slumber deep into the Music of Eternal Spheres. There heaven worlds stretch far into Infinitude and shimmering beams of moons and the effulgence of a thousand golden suns abound; which light the Way to Royal Lands.

And soon all else dissolves below and soul's keen eyes awaken to the scenery of bright celestial worlds. To widespanned vistas that lay in fragrant Upper Heights, where sparkling waterfalls and crystal cliffs and reefs and islands of tranquility repose within the calm and shoreless Cosmic Ocean. Soul meets the Noble Company of those who once were men on earth, who sought and found the Countenance of God; and meets the Wayshower of High Esteem, Who guides it deeper into the Heart of God.

A GREAT NEW DAY

Refreshed and bright the loving soul returns, to face each single day with fortitude and newborn strength; 'er the winds may blow or the tempest roar, it matters not. And with a vision clear that sees into all eternity, and sees the slide-of-hand of wicked man — and Fate, it beholds man and beast and every living thing as shining lights of God; and every pain and joy within the heartbeat of all things as one. And of the One, the All in all, were none is less and none is more than that which dwells in him.

Soul's every labor and each task well done, its piety and

indolence, its suffering and useless strife as well, it lays at the Beloved's Feet, in ardent hope its life would be a testament of merit. Each wound bound up and healed is but a fervent praise and grateful song to God, and all its works a gift to the Beloved.

Soul's vital gait and heart attained to lofty things, it never gleans another's thoughts, nor reiterates what others say. It has its own to give. It pays no heed to lack or outward poverty, nor does it feel deprived by mortal lovelessness. For poverty became its fortune — the Self in Light unveiled. Its tears for God became the pearls of comfort and deep joy. And rich it is beyond the measure of all things and wiser in the ways of God than its hapless, fearful mockers; whose lot is marked by grief at every turn, that stalks their days and restless nights.

The True Soul is richer yet by far and freer than Old Poverty Herself, that burdens souls with binding gifts to disprove the beggary of patronizing men, all shorn of love and self-esteem, to prove to man the fallacy of gifts and gold that are iron shackles to the budding soul.

THE WAY OF THE SOUL

A soul in love with God walks the grounds and hills of earth as any other man, but knows to fling itself to footless heights on thrice-winged feet, where those yet bound by hate and greed cannot endure. It knows what it tears down today, it must again repay and leaves no debt. And knows the nature of the Self — that as it thinks so must it also be.

The true Soul asks no more than its own heart can give. It takes from earth no more than what it needs and gives of what it has beyond all measure. And while it shuns the gold of Mammon, it eats the Bread of God.

Whilst it is so that living things must die, soul knows its deathlessness and immortality. Its Guiding Light is neither friend nor foe of death and death cannot delay the forward thrust and upward climb of soul.

The illumined soul moves along the path of life unrecognized, wherever it goes it leaves behind the thread of Golden Love it spun. Soul is the silent wanderer to which windows, walls and mountains, aye, the star worlds step aside. Its call is heard throughout Eternal Mists and penetrates the longing, weeping heart with comfort. It pulls the sufferer into its love and healing peace, that he too may hear the whispers of the Guiding Light, that ah, is just one breath away!

A soul in love with God shall never flee the tedium of irksome tasks, but sees them through with the grit and gladness of a thankful heart. Its lips give the Beloved praise, Who returns the Holy Breath to nestle in its heart. And such a soul speaks not of binding ways to those yet anchored to the Shadow, but shows the Way all pilgrims walked and found the Light and Life of God.

Of long ago, the Inner Teacher spoke these words to me:

> "The soul in man is the very seat of God. A heart within the Mighty Heart that gladly bears the strain of pain of His beloved. And it is there were all the singleness of mind and thought and will of soul become the Will of God, that neither a heaven, nor a hell, nor any man of earth can break.
>
> "For a heart imbued with Love and Holy Will has Holy Understanding; that renders the duality of mind to naught, by which alone the heavens manifest to hearts on earth. For then the soul breaks loose its moorings from the world of lust and greed, and learns at last to die to live. For unless the soul contends to yield its hungry heart to eat the bitter golden Fruit of God and drinks of God's Immortal Cysterns, and bathed in the River of True Light, thus drank the Blood and Wine of Life and ate the Bread of God — it can in no wise come to know the glory of its Second Birth, nor can it be Thrice-Born. And must continue in the dead weight fetters of the planets —

to live and die.

THE LIBERATED SOUL

A free soul is a happy soul, it does not seek dominion over other lives, but rules itself. It has no need to covet any earthly nor etheric thing, nor fortune's fame, for its renown is found in humble, selfless deeds that stand illumined brightly and exalted *beyond* the Mists of Time.

To the soul in love with God whose ship has crossed the troubled sea of life and weathered every storm, each breath it takes is infilled with Light, each breath expelled infilled with power.

The True Soul lives to please no man, but every fiber of its strength it offers the Beloved. And it fashions of Love a wedding band and crowns it with the Diamond Self, and lays it naked at the Beloved's Feet.

And then, over the course of time, and with growing introspection, soul ardently looks to the day when by the Beloved's Gentle Touch its mortal eyelids close and lull it into slumber. And then the Breath of God shall touch the fingertips of soul and bid it to arise. And so it will; all garmented in beauty — in the bridal vesture of Celestial Light it spun while yet on earth; to enter the Beloved's Shrine and Worlds of Love, that stay the grief and agony of seeming separation.

This is the tried, true way of every soul in love with God. But the Touch of God must first occur and its Vitalness *remain* before man can come to know the Power and intensity of All-Abiding Love. Man must step forward, towards God and earnestly desire to know his Maker, before His Spirit opens the floodgates of the heart to let the Light pour in. Soul's inner life and outer world are ablaze with Love and Light, it's in the heart of soul that Love assembles, and from the heart its joys deploy.

ENDLESS LOVE

Since time immemorial the message remains the same:

One Supreme Creator, Who is Sovereign Lord, Eminent, All-Pervading — Absolute, the Father of all people. His Emanation is the Indivisible, Invincible Spirit to which belong your fondest love and every worship. Its emanating essence and Presence reside within *You* as Sound and Light, that pour down from the Heart of God into all Creation; from the *One* Eternal Power from which you came and to which you shall return.

Geometry ruled: "The shortest distance between two points is a straight line" — and so is the direct Way to God: one on One! The Path so called is but a metaphor. There is no path, but the *Way* — and the Way is within *You* —and always in the direction you seek God.

The Door of the Soul is where your inner and outer world meet. Sometimes God seems far away, and often overwhelmingly close. Words cannot convey the Fantastic Reality of His Presence, thought cannot grasp it — yet you know.

Beloved of God, allow the Light of Love to beam forth from you. Let it shine far and wide for seeking hearts to find enlightenment and comfort. May Empyreal Brightness surround you always and continue to illumine your way; and the Force carry you onward until you reach the Royal Pavilion of the Beloved.

Be ever so mindful of the All-Wise Presence that overshadows every detail of your life with Love, Power and Protection. Until the day your earthly ties dissolve in God, by your own *free will, conscious* choice, and Holy Passion for the Beloved.

On the marker of the heroic expedition to the Antarctic these words stand boldly inscribed: *"To strive, to find, and not to yield"*; which is the essence of this book.

My sincere gratitude to all who shared in the teachings of *"Milestones To God"*. In all you do — I wish you Godspeed! The Blessings of Light, Love and Peace rest upon one and all.-